WILD THOUGHTS
SEARCHING FOR A THINKER

WILD THOUGHTS SEARCHING FOR A THINKER

A Clinical Application of W. R. Bion's Theories

Rafael E. López-Corvo

First published in 2006 by
Karnac Books Ltd.
118 Finchley Road, London NW3 5HT

British Library Cataloguing in Publication Data

A C.I.P. for this book is available from the British Library

ISBN-10: 1 85575 400 2
ISBN-13: 978 1 85575 400 3

Edited, designed and produced by The Studio Publishing Services Ltd,
www.publishingservicesuk.co.uk
e-mail: studio@publishingservices.co.uk

Printed in Great Britain

10 9 8 7 6 5 4 3 2 1

www.karnacbooks.com

CONTENTS

ACKNOWLEDGEMENTS

I am extremely grateful to Anamilagros, my wife, for her substantial and continuous support; also to Lucía Morabito Gómez for her dedication in examining the manuscript, and to Susan Glouberman for being kind enough to discuss some of the chapters with me. I am also indebted to the members of the Toronto Study Group on Bion: Dr Ian Graham, Anamilagros Pérez, Dr Cynthia Saruk, Dena Tenehouse, and, especially, Dr Mary Morris for her kind dedication. Finally, I wish to express my gratitude to Leena Hakkinen, my editor at Karnac, who is always so patient and efficient.

To my grandson, Evan D. López-Bryce

ABOUT THE AUTHOR

Rafael E. López-Corvo is a training and supervising psychoanalyst, Venezuelan and Canadian Psychoanalytic Societies. He is former associate professor of McGill University and Program Director of the Child and Adolescent Unit at the Douglas Hospital, McGill University, Montreal, Canada. He is also a former member of the editorial board of the *International Journal of Psycho-Analysis*. He maintains a private practice of psychoanalysis in Toronto, Canada.

Introduction

"Of all things the measure is Man, of the things that are, for what they are, and of the things that are not, for what they are not"

(Protagoras, Plato, Teaetetus. London: Penguin, 1987)

"And this slow spider, which crawls in the moonlight, and this moonlight itself and I and you in the gateway ... must all of us have been there before? And return ... must we not eternally return?"

(Nietzsche, 1892, Thus Spoke Zarathustra.
New York: Penguin, 1966, pp. 157–158)

"Be not too hasty, skimming over the book
Of Heraclitus; 'tis a difficult road, for mist is there,
and darkness hard to pierce, but if you have the truth
as a guide, then everything is clearer than the sun"

(Diogenes Laertius, Lives of Eminent Philosophers:
Heraclitus, Vol. IX, Part XII. London: Henry G. Bohn, 1853)

As I read Bion I experienced the challenge of attempting to find a clinical continuity between Classical Psychoanalysis and new conceptions introduced by him; after all, truth would be available to any mind willing to access it. Different conclusions could often represent dissimilar perspectives or vertexes used in order to approach the same truth. Let us take two different issues very much present in human beings, apparently unrelated to each other, to which not great significance has yet been adjudged, notwithstanding the extraordinary importance both appear to represent when they seem to disclose a powerful presence of nature. I am referring to the existence of the hymen in women and the unconscious's *universal illiteracy* with which we are born.

The "culture of pain" associated with virginity and sexual penetration at the age of eleven or twelve years—at a time when pregnancy is already possible—induces a girl to postpone sexual intercourse to an older age, five or more years ahead, granting herself an opportunity to manage better the unprecedented "violence" brought by maternity as well as the opportunity to provide the baby with a mother better endowed.

We are born unable to understand the complex and puzzling language of the unconscious, as observed in dreams for instance, and will require the need of a translator such as the psychoanalyst in order to unravel its cryptic meaning. I believe this illiteracy represents a protection from the "violence" implicit in truth, which is continuously revealed by the unconscious and only grasped by consciousness once there is a willingness to deal properly with such revelations. Bion suggested that Oedipus's insistence on obtaining the truth from Tiresias at any cost, at a time when he was not prepared to deal with it, represented the existence in his character of a combination of "curiosity, arrogance, and stupidity". The Oedipus myth is a narrative dealing with lies and concealed truth; the Sphinx for instance, presented people with a riddle, and they were instantly killed by the monster if they failed to provide the right answer. Oedipus however, after killing the king at the crossroads without knowing he was his father, provided the right answer to the Sphinx, who, not withstanding the power of truth, committed suicide. Grateful for this accomplishment, the city presented Oedipus with the tragedy's true substance: the "recently-vacated" crown of Thebes that had belonged to the King, his father, and the "recently-widowed" Queen Jocasta, his mother.

Psychoanalysis trains the conscious to receive and *contain* the truth continuously released by the unconscious in a manner that will induce growth instead of tragedy. Bion presents three possibilities in the interaction between *contained* and *container*: (i) the three benefit from each other, meaning the unconscious as a revealer of truth, the preconscious as a receptor of the unconscious, and the truth itself; (ii) one destroys the other, as dreams that do not have a mind to read them become stray thoughts or disappear; (iii) the terror of truth is so great that consciousness closes itself completely to the unconscious revelations, forcing the unconscious to overflow the conscious like a dam unable to contain the water, thereby producing a psychotic condition.

"Truth is to the mind what food is to the body", expressed Bion, and he used the digestive system as a model to understand the mechanisms of the mind. Food, similar to "reality facts", follows one of three paths: (i) it is assimilated and transformed into energy and physical growth; (ii) it is stored as fat which might be used later on in case of famine, like provisions for an emergency; (c) it is expelled as "undigested food" through the emunctories (urine, sweat, faeces). Following Bion, "reality facts" such as food, conceived as raw material or beta elements, are perceived through the sense organs and will also follow one of three routes: (i) they are digested by alpha function and transformed into mental growth; (b) they are stored (like fat) in the memory as indigested thoughts, beta elements, or wild thoughts waiting for a mind to digest them; (iii) they are expelled through "mental emunctories" (sense organs) with the use of dreams, myths, hallucinations, or projective identifications. Alternatives (ii) and (iii) result from lack of alpha function, capable of containing the always menacing violence of truth. In this condition, consciousness (or, more precisely, the psychotic part of the personality), being influenced by the pain–pleasure principle, experiences reality as a threat. Such threat induces the need for the use of defence mechanisms that act as lies to cover up awareness of a presumed menace from reality. Undigested facts are then stored in the memory, some of them representing wild thoughts waiting for a mind (alpha function), like a psychoanalyst, capable of making proper use of them.

Just imagine a thirsty dinosaur, possibly a tyrannosaurus, walking slowly one early summer morning to the edge of what might be now a vanished lake or sea. One hundred and eighty million years later, a group of geologists, for instance, while examining some interesting sandstones in a ditch freshly washed out by heavy showers, discover footprints engraved in the limestone revealing the route of that thirsty dinosaur's long-ago walk. It might have been a regular uneventful act repeated regularly, although this time, on that particular morning, the presence of a series of variables conjoined at once to preserve the footsteps for ever. The massive weight of the animal, plus the quality of the sand or mud, together with weather conditions such as temperature, humidity, and so on, managed to safeguard the tracks. It meant, in summary, that now, when there is no longer a lake and the dinosaur has been erased from the face of the earth, its footprints, produced in just one instant, can be seen, preserved for posterity. In other words, what should otherwise have been a temporary event became a permanent fact; an overwhelming absence became a significant presence.

Similar to a wheel running on a track, *reality* touches only one point, rests on one instant, the present, while incessantly flowing from the past to the future, at the pace of Heraclitus's river. If reality represents a temporary event circumscribed by one instant, we could then ask what penumbra of circumstances, similar to those that granted preservation to the dinosaur's footprints, would implement sufficient weight in order to change what otherwise would have been a person's transient moment into something permanent. What would make a temporary absence a permanent presence? There are conditions that, by their very nature, would break through Freud's "protective shield", would not be contained by the mother's reverie, and eventually could inflame the self forever, like fossilized "footprints". They will be changed into the substance of dreams, phantasies, or transference and countertransference dimensions, "wild thoughts" eternally seeking for a mind that, by containing them, would provide a history and a *truthful* meaning that eventually will allow them to be forgotten. The "alive" mind, different from a dinosaur's "inanimate" footprints, provides "life" or emotions to the prints, similar to the mind that invents a ghost to compensate for a lost limb. In other words, "undigested truth keeps returning searching for a thinker". Such "aliveness" I consider analogous to Freud's "instinct of mastery", an implacable search for truth that Grotstein (2004)—considering the intensity with which wild thoughts search for a thinker—has very recently posited as representing a veritable "truth instinctual drive". In the same line, Bion (1967) has suggested that,

> Freud's analogy of an archaeological investigation with psychoanalysis was helpful if it were considered that we were exposing evidence not so much of a primitive civilization as of a primitive disaster. The value of the analogy is lessened because in the analysis we are confronted not so much with a static situation that permits leisurely study, *but with a catastrophe that remains at one and the same moment actively vital and yet incapable of resolution into quiescence.*[1] [p. 101]

Let us look at a session from Elena, a thirty-four-year-old schoolteacher, single, and in her second year of analysis. She has lately been dealing with the mental pain induced by her parents' divorce when she was only three years of age. In the transference it was obvious that her apprehension of trust, as well as her need to control, was possibly a defence against her fear of being rejected, forgotten, or ignored, which is how she felt her father treated her. She always takes off her shoes before she lies down on the couch. This time she is wearing boots and does not take them off, something I noticed but said nothing about. She mentioned an argument with her father, and realized she harbours a great deal of resentment against him. She had a dream: *there was a huge cockroach and she killed it but then, out of the dead insect came like a thousand of smaller ones.* She refers to a classmate who is rather contradictory; she will say terrible things and then says the opposite. The other day this friend told her that Elena's feet smelled, and then, when Elena stood up to put a book on a shelf; she said that Elena had a "tight ass", and that she could "crack all the books with her ass". I said that I was wondering if her fear of being dirty made her not want to take off her boots. She denied it and said that she didn't do it because it was too much trouble; however, I did not believe what she said, but said nothing. Then I said, that feet, if dirty, could be washed, it is something temporary, but if the dirt is related to her feeling that her father left her because she had a dirty "tight ass" that attacked and destroyed any "knowledge" of him, it was then a permanent issue, like the cockroach that, if multiplied into a thousand, became permanent and impossible to get rid of.

Because external reality is incessantly becoming, it will present a temporary state that is continuously changing. We could avoid external reality, but internal reality, such as "unthought thoughts in search of a thinker", stands for an inner and permanent threat. It is the continuous pressure from these wild thoughts that, according to Bion (1967), will manufacture an apparatus for thinking. While the non-psychotic part of the personality deals with reality and transient issues, the psychotic part is contained by the permanency of "wild print-thoughts". While splitting of space changes a fact from private to universal (as in projective identification), splitting of time changes a fact from temporary to permanent (as in transference). Dinosaur's footprints have been there for many years, meaning nothing to the neophyte's eye, until becoming significant to the geologist's gaze, similar to the way in which penicillin was recognised by Fleming or the unconscious by Freud.

* * *

"*It being the case that thou, Galileo, son of the late Vincenzio Galilei, a Florentine, now aged 70, wast denounced in this Holy Office in 1615: 'That thou heldest as true the false doctrine taught by many, that the Sun was the centre of the universe and immoveable, and that the Earth moved, and had also a diurnal motion: That on this same matter thou didst hold a correspondence with certain German mathematicians . . .'*", read the Sentence of the Tribunal of the Supreme Inquisition against Galileo Galilei, given the 22nd day of June of the year 1633.

Over 2000 years before, in 399 BC, the State claimed Socrates' life for the same reason, although in his indictment the accusers stated that the motive was otherwise, that "Socrates the son of Sophroniscus of Alopece is guilty of refusing to acknowledge the gods recognized by the State and of introducing new and different gods. He is also guilty of corrupting the youth. The penalty demanded is death". However, according to Diogenes of Laerte,[2] the motives were different:

These were his words and the deeds of his life, to which the Pythian Priestess was referring when she gave her famous answer to Chaerophon, "Of all men living, Socrates is the wisest." This was the cause of the envy in which he was held, above all because he would challenge those who thought highly of themselves, making them out to be fools, as he treated Anytus, according to Plato in the

Meno. Anytus could not endure being ridiculed by Socrates, so he stirred up Aristophanes and his friends against him. [1972, p. 171]

The purpose was not to destroy a "perverse agnostic", but to "murder a mind" that compulsively and continuously fed on truth.

Such documents, like many similar acts in history, represented a sustained attack on creative minds, a capricious domination of lies and magic over empirical and candid observation of reality. The Renaissance was not a re-birth of creative truth that had remained dormant until that particular moment but rather the opposite, it was the result of the pressing need of a few courageous men to discover facts at any cost,[3] which continuously eroded and finally broke through the power imposed by other men, who attacked and destroyed the thinking of those who fed from the "tree of knowledge". This incessant struggle could explain the presence of what now might appear as an absolute incongruence, that science and religion sat side by side in the minds of some innovative men such as Descartes. It was not until Nietzsche declared "God is dead" that men felt less restricted and were able to express their minds freely, ushering in what some have considered as the "narcissistic age", meaning the capacity of men to experience enough freedom to exercise their own rights and to satisfy their own needs, instead of a hypocritical sacrifice in the name of God. Another indulgence like that of Descartes's would now be absolutely redundant.

Jung remembered a conversation he had with Freud:

Once he said to me: we have to turn the theory of the unconscious into a dogma, to make it immovable. Why a dogma, I replied, since sooner or later truth will have to win out? Freud explained: *We need a dam against the black tide of mud of occultism"*. [McGuire & Hull, 1978, my italics]

It is quite possible that Freud was then implicitly referring to infantile sexuality, the main disagreement that eventually separated the course of these two great thinkers. It required immense courage for Freud to struggle against the "black tide of occultism", when he publicly declared in the midst of Victorian ascendancy, that otherwise innocent and angelical children were the site of a kind of "polymorphous perversion". From then on, Freud's name, and words such as "libido", became, in the eyes of neophytes, synonymous with "dissolute" and "licentious". It was easier to misrepresent the true sense of new discoveries on child sexuality than to comprehend the revolutionary depth of their meaning.

For Melanie Klein, "the black tide of mud" came from psycho-analysis itself, possibly from "hesitating to forget its founders", to quote Whitehead (Kuhn, 1962, p. 138), and her contributions are unfortunately still alien to many important schools of psycho-analysis. Although Bion is perhaps too fresh yet to be considered, there are already important sources of misunderstanding of his thinking on the horizon. Let us take, for instance, what he has described as "O", a concept that has such relevance that I think it could perhaps be compared with Freud's conception of transference or Klein's metapsychology of affects as stated in her notion of "positions". I will not go into details now about the meaning of O, but will refer the reader to Chapter Twelve, which is devoted to the comprehension of its particular phenomenology. I would like to say, however, that a pertinent source of confusion has already been set off when O is conceived of as the expression of Bion's allegedly reli-gious wondering: "O, then, has a metaphysical and religious mean-ing . . . Bion introduced O, which is essentially a religious and metaphysical concept", said Symington and Symington (1996). Not to argue this statement carries the danger that later on, an "immov-able dam" of misunderstanding will induce a "black tide of mud of occultism" that will make O synonymous with *religion*, just as *libidi-nous* is synonymous with *lascivious*. Indeed, O cannot be so easily categorized and tied down, it is the unknowable, the unthinkable, the ineffable, the truth itself or ultimate reality that could be grasped only intuitively and is always changing, continuously becoming, like Heraclitus's *universal flux*.

For years I struggled to comprehend the meaning of Zen Buddhism, but it was only after reading Bion's book *Transformation* and investigating O, that I recognized I was already using Zen in my every day psychoanalytic practice, without even realizing it. Oriental civilization, different from Occidental, attempts to disre-gard the weight of conscious reasoning in order to allow intuition to make itself present. Zen Buddhism, as Watts (1950) stated, is not a religion, it is

> . . . a way and a view of life which does not belong to any of the formal categories of modern Western thought. It is not a religion or

a philosophy; it is not a psychology or a type of science. It is . . . a "way of liberation" [p. 3]

Suzuki (1960) attempts to explain the differences between West and East with the use of two poems, one from Tennyson and the other from a *haiku* written by Basho, a Japanese poet from the seventeenth century. Basho wrote:

> When I look carefully
> I see the nazuna blooming
> by the hedge!

while Tennyson said:

> Flower in the crannied wall,
> I pluck you out of the crannies:
> Hold you here, root and all, in my hand,
> Little flower—but if I could understand
> What you are, root and all, and all in all,
> I should know what God and man is.

Suzuki explains:

> . . . Tennyson's plucking the flower and holding it in his hand, "root and all", and looking at it, perhaps intently. It is very likely he had a feeling somewhat akin to that of Basho who discovered the nazuna flower by the roadside hedge. But the difference between the two poets is: Basho does not pluck the flower. He just looks at it. He is absorbed in thought. He lets an exclamation mark [!] say everything he wishes to say. For he has no words to utter; his feeling is too full, too deep, and he has no desire to conceptualize it. As to Tennyson, he is active and analytical. He first plucks the flower from the place where it grows. He separates it from the ground where it belongs. Quite differently from the Oriental poet, he does not leave the flower alone. He must tear it away from the crannied wall, "root and all", which means that the plant must die . . . As some medical scientists do, he would vivisect the flower. Basho does not even touch the nazuna, he just looks at it, he "carefully" looks at it—that is all he does. He is altogether inactive, a good contrast to Tennyson's dynamism. [pp. 11–12]

I think that Bion attempts to point to these differences when he refers to the concept of "Transformations in O", as a sympathetic unity with the Other, with the analysand's unconscious, that will allow communication with the patient's unconscious, awareness of the unconscious phantasy as an illumination, similar to what Saint John of the Cross experienced at "The Ascent of Mount Carmel". I gather the notion of O came to Bion as a possible way out from the imperceptible abysm of incommunication with the patient, to know if what the analyst is thinking when listening is in at-one-ment with what the patient is saying.

O represents a sign that might be finally fulfilled with an "act of faith", a reverence for the ineffable, or amazement at the *obscure illumination* of intuition. "O", said Grotstein (1996) with great exactness:

> is like Marlowe's description of Tamburlaine's Samarkand, always on the horizon, ever distant, always receding. Bion introduced us to a cosmic domain that spatially, temporally, philosophically, and existentially existed beyond our sensual capacity to comprehend, although psychotics and mystics have always known of its existence. [p. 147]

* * *

In this book I will be referring to inner and unconscious consolidated attacks against the mind, made in different forms. Some will follow patterns related to defence mechanisms, similar to those found in the somatic dimension, like autoimmune diseases. Others will relate to early and significant *traumas* that haunt and enslave individuals for the rest of their lives with the impetus of a frantic prowler. The mind is also targeted by issues related to social pressures and complicities, such as ignorance and fear of the unknown (like the unconscious), fixation on concreteness, fascination about appearances or exterior looks, terror of truth, or violence due to confusion between animate and inanimate. The first chapter attempts an overview of these social matters.

I very much agree with Meltzer (1983, p. 51), when he distinguished three important limitations to Freud's metapsychology: the first was determined by his training in neurophysiology, which created, at the beginning of his career, difficulties in discriminating between mind and body; the second was the influence of the physics of Freud's time, resulting in the assimilation of properties of the steam engine into the dynamics of the mind; the third was the impact provided by Darwin's significant understanding of animal drives and instincts, a concept that induced Fairbairn (1952) to refer to classical analysis as an "impulse psychology".

The first limitation was amended by Freud himself, who, in latter years, fought fiercely to protect psychoanalysis from being overpowered by somatic medicine. This issue is still very relevant as currently both truth and psychoanalysis are subdued by millions of dollars acquired from selling the same medicine to treat the same old psychiatric symptoms, which are being continuously rebaptized. The second limitation related to the steam engine model, which was changed by Klein (1946) and Fairbairn (1952) when they introduced the phenomenology of an internal world structured by memories of early experience representations, conceived as part objects that incessantly interact. Dealing with "objects" instead of "steam", allowed for "repression" to give way to "splitting" and for "sublimation" to change into "reparation". Klein also established, through the elaboration of the paranoid–schizoid and depressive positions, the presence of a metapsychology of affects, adding to Freud's *cognitive* notion of "things representations" changing into "words representations", in order to become conscious.

The third limitation, related to instinct theory, was worked on by Bion, who introduced the architecture of the mind based on the existence of a function (alpha) that could continuously transform thinking to higher degrees of sophistication, ranging from raw sense impressions to mathematical calculus. These transformations are "contained" by the mind that can use them in various ways: (i) to elaborate hypotheses; (ii) to fend off the possible violence of truth brought on by thinking; (iii) to remember them and, by paying attention, investigate, and finally change them, or not, into action. Bion did not refer to "drives" or "instincts", and although he did not explicitly associate it with the notion of "preconcept", the relation is obvious, implying with this idea that the "drive" is contained by a mind, different from animals that lack an apparatus for thinking. In this sense Bion follows Protagoras, because men cannot free themselves from being men and, at the end, the finitude of the mind will be fatalistically "the measure of all things", "for what they are and for what they are not".

Establishing the physiology of the mind, Bion introduced the *corpus delictum*, meaning a mind to have or a mind to lose, a mind to enhance or a mind to murder. What Lacan described as the "place of the supposed knowledge", or the belief by the patient that the analyst "knows it all", for Bion represented the sign that the patient is "mindless", because he has split his mind and projected it—with the use of projective identifications—and then needs to borrow the analyst's mind in order not to think for himself.

Bion's first clinical papers carry this impressive insight: the terror induced by the "psychotic part of the personality" towards the inflexible weight of reality results in a need to attack and feverishly destroy the apparatus that conceives it. Bion (1967) states:

> . . . the differentiation of the psychotic from the non-psychotic personalities depends on a minute splitting of all that part of the personality that is concerned with awareness of internal and external reality, and the expulsion of these fragments so that they enter into or engulf their objects. [p. 43]

A crucial matter elaborated by Bion refers to the difference between the "psychotic" and the "non-psychotic" part of the personality. Bion clarified the long-standing confusion between normality, neurosis, and psychosis, with which we were familiar but chose to ignore. As far as I understand it, the discrimination between the "psychotic" and "non-psychotic" part of the personality is based on the contained–container theory, in the sense of which part contains which, meaning that there is a quantitative gradient between both parts of the personality. For instance, in a psychotic individual, the psychotic part "contains" or overrules the non-psychotic, whereas in the person free from psychosis, the dynamic is completely the opposite because the psychotic part is now "contained" by the non-psychotic. But the dynamic within the psychotic part, regardless of the diagnosis of the person, is always the same. In other words, what takes place in the psychotic part, within the psychotic individual, as well as in the non-psychotic person, has absolutely the same dynamics. What changes is the relation between the container and the contained. It would be something similar to the comparison between a small piece and the total picture in a hologram. (See Lopez-Corvo, 2003.)

The psychotic part is controlled by undigested beta elements that interact internally with each other. They may be used as projectiles to induce action in the person contained by them, or projected into other persons or into inanimate objects producing bizarre objects. They remain completely refractory to metamorphosis into alpha elements manufactured by the "alpha function" and conjoin to create "narcissistic conglomerates" or narcissistic organizations that behave, according to Rosenfeld, as internal "Mafiosi gangs" that pervert and destroy the mind. This aspect is discussed in full in Chapter Six. But the most important characteristic of the psychotic part is the hatred of reality that induces a need to split the mind that is capable of perceiving this reality and to project it outside the self. Bion (1967) states:

> I wish to emphasize that in this phase the psychotic splits his objects, and contemporaneously all that part of his personality, which would make him aware of the reality he hates, into exceedingly minute fragments, for it is this that contributes materially to the psychotic's feelings that he cannot restore his objects or his ego. As a result of these splitting attacks, all those features of the personality which should one day provide the foundation for intuitive understanding of himself and others are jeopardized at the outset. [p. 47]

Chapter Three offers a clinical evaluation of this mechanism as observed in early preconceptual traumas.

Patients are always dissociated between: (a) the non-psychotic part of the personality, that might desire a change from the suffering induced by a narcissistic structure, where the patient feels trapped by compulsively repeating it; and (b) the psychotic part of the personality ruled by lies and the need to preserve the status quo, in spite of the suffering implicit. For this latter part, changes induced by the interpretation would represent a threat that would be robustly opposed by the narcissistic structure. In other words, what is desired by the non-psychotic part is at the same time rejected by the psychotic part, representing the core of the ambivalence within the pathological paranoid–schizoid position, present with more or less intensity, in all psychoanalytic therapy. This issue is investigated in Chapter Eight.

Another important intention of this book is to use some of Bion's contributions to evaluate, from a clinical perspective, "classical" psychoanalytic concepts such as narcissism, transference and countertransference, interpretation, the false self, the unconscious and its relation to consciousness, and so on. In addition, a clinical evaluation of some of Bion's models such as "O", animate–inanimate, container–contained, caesura, nameless terror, and the Grid, among others will be attempted. I must also confess to being responsible for adding, here and there, some interpretations of my own related to notions like self-envy, preconceptual trauma, Zen Buddhism, and Structuralism.

Different from other scientific fields of knowledge, but similar to religious believers who search for a Messiah to follow, psychoanalysts often entrench themselves behind cultural and geographical accidental differences, instead of pursuing more aggressively a more enlightening and progressive scientific quest. See, for instance, Hartmann and Rapaport in relation to "ego-psychology", as well as Kohut in relation to "self-psychology" in North America; or Lacan in France and Klein and Bion in England. This represents a predicament that induced Wallerstein (1988) to wonder if we were dealing with "One psychoanalysis or many". Bion (1970) approached this issue from the point of view of the contained–container model, stating that a psychoanalyst could face a similar dilemma to a Messiah, who could either contain an idea or be contained by it; if contained, he might change it into fanaticism, but if capable of containing the idea, he could grow and transcend it.

An essential side effect of inner splitting and dissociation is the considerable energy used by the ego to maintain the structure of a paranoid–schizoid position. This involves maintaining the separation between different inner self parts, the selection of what is to be projected and what is to be introjected, the continuous protection of good objects from bad ones, and so on. It would be logical to conclude that there might be little free ego left to invest in the structure and maintenance of a true self, which, for these reasons, will remain left out and "forgotten". Winnicott's "false self" theory, if used to understand the nature of such a "forgotten" true self, faces the limitation of not taking into account the negativistic side of the false self that, when considered, bears a resemblance to Bion's notion of negative links (–H, –L, –K). These complex matters are carefully and clearly evaluated in Chapter Two.

"Communication" represents another central issue in Bion's psychology, such as the danger of two individuals not being able to communicate with each other; or the need to preserve a distance between different parts of the mind in the same individual, or consciousness not being able to grasp messages forwarded by the unconscious. The risk of a "reversal of perspective", of parallel views that never touch in both analyst and patient, is always a significant menace. True distance and separation, says Bion (1992), is not represented by the space that separates us from the galaxies, but in what separates comprehension from incomprehension. Finding the right word to carry the precise message and to avoid the danger of choosing signs that time and erosion have moved sideways, is a task of which any practising psychoanalyst must be continuously cognizant. Take, for instance, the word "alter", synonymous with "to modify" or "to change", a meaning different from its original Latin denotation synonymous with "other" and equivalent to the expression "othered". Chapters Nine to Fifteen refer not only to communication between the unconscious and the conscious, but also evaluate these communications from a completely different perspective, such as considering the classical concept of *repression* as the expression of a complication from a "reversal of perspective" between those two entities.

Words are often pregnant with ancient meanings that might need to be broken down in order to find the piece of history trapped inside. The word "suspect", for instance, is composed of the Latin suffix *sus* meaning "under", and prefix *spectare* "to look"; or in other words to "look under". Rupturing the words in this manner, could allow us to see inside like a kaleidoscope and to imagine for instance, someone arriving in ancient times at a hostel and being considered an "under-looker" or "sus-spicious" by the owner, because of insistently "looking under his bed". Bion suggests that we practise this form of "archaeology of semantics" and look at words just as we might look at some of Henry Moore's sculptures, completely ignoring the material that frames the internal empty space, and concentrating on this space until the light that is trapped in it becomes meaningful. For instance, one could look at a right-angle triangle forgetting completely about the mathematical meaning of Pythagoras's Theorem, and focus on a different perspective—also stated by the Greeks—that the sides of the right angle could symbolize both parents in coitus (the vertical representing the father and the horizontal the mother) while the hypotenuse could represent the child. Or in other words, captured behind the mathematical representation of a right-angle triangle, there is also the light that illuminates the Oedipus complex.

Besides communication, Bion (1963) also gave special relevance to mental growth and the capacity to learn from experience. He represented "growth" with the letter Y and described it as a "preconception in search of a realization". This tendency could be either negative (−Y) if directed towards narcissism or positive (+Y) if aimed toward "social-ism". Mental growth could be conceived from other vertices, such as progressive shift from dissociated states of the mind, as observed in the paranoid–schizoid position (−Y), to more integrated states of mind in agreement with the depressive position (+Y). Mental growth could also be conceived as the continuous tendency of the psychotic part of the personality (−Y) to be contained by the non-psychotic part of the personality (+Y).

There are circumstances that interfere with this normal process of evolution, usually conditions capable of inducing high levels of anxiety at a very early age. Bion refers to them as the "nameless terror" of dying; resulting from a lack of mother's reverie or her incapacity to contain a significant threat, like for instance, important preconceptual traumas. One important unfortunate consequence in dealing with "nameless terrors" could be the splitting of the mind and the body and the projection of them outside of the self, together with the traumatic object, using projective identifications to do so. The attack is not so much an attack on the mind and the body itself, but against what links to the self, such as love (L), hate (H) or knowledge (K). Unsuccessful attempts to recover the misplaced body can be observed in acts of piercing, cutting and tattooing, so common these days. Splitting and projection of the mind translates into an incapacity to contain the terror, and this will require borrowing somebody else's mind in order to deal with the anxiety. This condition is very much present in the transference that acts as an important defence against reaching autonomy and mental growth.

Notes

1. *Lives of the Philosophers*, "Socrates".
2. Grotstein (2004) has referred to the possibility of a "truth instinct" (personal communication).

CHAPTER ONE

Murdering the mind

From the perspective of Bion's container–contained theory

"Science . . . commits suicide when it adopts a creed"

(Huxley, 1907)

The need to diminish feelings of persecution contributes to the drive to abstraction in the formulation of scientific communications.

(Bion, 1967, p. 118)

Humpty Dumpty sat on the wall,
Humpty Dumpty had a great fall.
All the king's horses
And all the king's men
Couldn't put Humpty
Together again.

(Nursery rhyme)

Introduction

There are "mental confusions" that interfere with and destroy the faculty to think rationally, that hinder the positive growth of the mind, and that obstruct the capacity to discriminate between reality and phantasy. Bion (1963) described Growth (represented as Y) as a "preconception in search of a realization". For Bion the tendency of such realizations could be either negative (−Y) if directed towards narcissism, or positive (+Y) if aimed toward "social-ism". For instance, a nice-looking, intelligent young woman who, as a child, had a surgical intervention to correct a genetic defect around her genital area, was very resentful towards both parents and herself, found her body ugly, and had difficulties in establishing lasting relationships with men. After a year of psychotherapy, she managed to resolve an important confusion between her early traumatic experience and her present situation as an accomplished young woman. As a consequence she now sustains a relationship with a man and feels very fond of him. At a critical moment she had a dream where she was playing Monopoly with her boyfriend's relatives and was trying very hard to be attentive to the game. She concluded that perhaps she was trying to fit into her friend's life, and I add that she seems to be seriously taking a chance. She was starting to shift from the vertex of a narcissistic involvement with herself to a more social form of linkage.

Growth could also be conceived from other vertices, such as progressive shift from dissociated states of the mind, as observed in the paranoid–schizoid position (−Y), to a more integrated state of mind in agreement with the depressive position (+Y). Another example is the continuous tendency of the psychotic part of the personality (−Y) to be contained by the non-psychotic part of the personality (+Y). However, there are circumstances that interfere with this normal process of evolution; usually such conditions are capable of inducing high levels of anxiety at a very early age.

However, I wish to discuss here more universal forms of confusions that impede growth in broader systems. Some are culturally related, such as confusions between medicine and psychoanalysis; some are the product of unresolved early fixations, like those confusions connecting animate and inanimate objects; some are circumstances imposed by a particular system or establishment, as for example a lack of discrimination between container and contained; and, finally, some confusions are related to a lack of methodological differentiation or discrimination between diachronic and synchronic dimensions. In a manner similar to the patient I have just mentioned and analogous to experiences most psychoanalysts are familiar with, resolution of such confusions will result in an enhancement of communication between psychoanalysts from different cultures, as well as in an increment in growth of psychoanalysis as an essential instrument to investigate the abstract side of the mind.

Confusion between inanimate (not-alive) and animated (alive) objects

Very frequently we are confronted with patients who present difficulties in discriminating between human beings and inanimate objects. These patients demonstrate a kind of projective identification and resistance with the purpose of denying important ties of dependency and feelings of persecutory anxiety. These patients believe they are going to be mended by the therapist, following the specifications of some kind of private and idealized model. The patient takes a rather passive role, acting as an inanimate object that will be repaired by the analyst, who will in turn be responsible for any kind of "wrongdoing". If the analyst acts out (counteracts) due to his/her own narcissistic needs, and identifies with the patient's idealized phantasy, he/she could then face the possible complication of a negative therapeutic reaction or of a self-envy mechanism (López-Corvo, 1995). In such situations the analyst could become the target of sadistic superego demands, similar to the reaction displayed by unsatisfied clients who take their car (inanimate object) to a mechanic. The patient feels the analyst should perform "the treatment" on them, while they remain as observers, as if it were a medical consultation. Patients can also feel they are coming to "see" the analyst, as in a social visit, something often reflected in the difficulty to free associate, and in the refusal to use the couch. They prefer to talk face to face instead. Such patients may also feel that the pursuit of the analysis is a matter of concern to somebody else, including the analyst, but not to themselves. Such attitudes, I believe, are often reflected in the preference of attending not more than once a week, as if the enthusiasm for an analytical setting, for a serious investigation of their mind, is mostly a concern of the analyst and not of the patients themselves. If the analyst's mind lacks the serious conviction of an analytical culture and goal, psychotherapy will be the modality of preference, even if indication for psychoanalytic therapy is the best choice.

Bion (1962) established that an overvaluation of the inanimate over the animate could be the consequence of enforced splitting associated with a disturbed relationship with the breast. He stated that when envy obstructs the relationship with the good breast, provider of love, understanding, solace, knowledge (Klein, 1946) during the schizoid–paranoid position, the persecutory anxiety present could obstruct the physical need for sucking and thereby jeopardize the infant's life. "Fear of death through starvation of essentials", said Bion, "compels resumption of sucking. A split between material and psychical satisfaction develops" (1962, p. 10). This situation leads to an enforced splitting between the physical need for survival on the one hand, and psychic satisfactions on the other. Such a condition, according to Bion, will be achieved by destruction of alpha functions:

> This makes breast and infant appear inanimate with consequent guiltiness, fear of suicide and fear of murder [it is easier to destroy something inanimate than something alive!] . . . The need for love, understanding and mental development is now deflected, since it cannot be satisfied, into the search for material comforts. [1962, p. 11]

Confusion between the animate and the inanimate is the consequence of the child's long term and natural dependency upon parents, who experience their baby as an object "belonging" to them. However, autonomy of the self and consciousness of aliveness is something to be achieved by the individual, a potential that is dependent for its development on the parent's capacity for reverie.

Another important vertex on this issue is given by Bion in his book, *Cogitations* (1992), where he refers to those attacks made by the baby against objects linked to displeasure, something that will induce persecutory anxiety and, as a consequence, there will be a need to placate these objects by mechanisms of idealization. This process of idealization is reached by providing them in the future—usually after they are dead—with superhuman qualities and changing them into objects of adoration and worship. Bion states that,

> Contrary to common observation, the essential feature of the adored or worshipped object is that it should be dead so that crime may be expiated by the patient's dutiful adherence to animation of what is known to be inanimate and impossible to animate. This attitude contributes to the complex of feelings associated with fetishism. [1992, p. 134]

In other words, the punishment for attacking bad objects is produced when the dependency upon an inanimate (dead) object—now animated and idealized—is assured to provide nothing, like the believer who expects a miracle from a wooden statue. It seems as if the unconscious incapacity to differentiate the animate from the inanimate works both ways: dead objects acquire life, and living objects become inanimate. The main issue in this conflict seems to be a strong narcissistic need to attack the process of separation and individuation. Alive objects that are made inanimate, or the opposite, inanimate objects made alive, represents a schizoid–paranoid interaction that attempts to exercise possessiveness and complete control of the object. The conflict is usually related to anal sadistic forms of object control, meant to deny the fact that, different from faeces, alive objects are autonomous and have lives of their own. This conflict or condition obstructs the possibility of a mourning process and the establishment of the depressive position. Such conflict works either way, not only in relation to the outside object, but also with the self. There will be present a feeling of deadness and of "non-existence", a dynamic I consider of great importance in the understanding of any form of pathological depression. Bion states:

> The patient feels the pain of an absence of fulfillment of his desires. The absent fulfillment is experienced as a "no-thing". The emotion aroused by the "no-thing" is felt as indistinguishable from the "no-thing". The emotion is replaced by a "no emotion" . . . "Non-existence" immediately becomes an object that is immensely hostile and filled with murderous envy towards the quality or function of existence wherever it is to be found. [1970, pp. 19–20]

Confusing the mind with the brain,
or psychoanalysis with medicine

The incapacity to differentiate animate from inanimate can expand to confusion between body and mind or between psychoanalysis and medicine, a confusion that was present in Freud at the beginning of his discoveries when, in 1913, for instance, he states that psychoanalysis is a medical procedure that attempts to cure certain forms of nervous illness with the use of a psychological technique (1913j, p. 165). There is extensive psychoanalytical literature, both critical and seeking to justify the fact that psychoanalysis does or does not meet several characteristics found in scientific methodology; moreover, that it is not capable of empirical verification or validation, nor of operational definitions that satisfy the same logical criteria observed in other natural sciences. Paul Ricoeur (1970) concluded:

> The scientific status of psychoanalysis has been subjected to severe criticism, especially in countries of British and American culture. Epistemologists, logicians, semanticists, philosophers of language have closely examined its concepts, propositions, argumentation, and structure as a theory and have generally come to the conclusion that psychoanalysis does not satisfy most elementary requirements of a scientific theory. . . [p. 345]

The problem, I think, of great relevance here, is on the one hand the confusion between the phenomena of the mind itself, and on the other hand the psychoanalytical methodology used to explore and change the mind. To accuse psychoanalysis of not being an exact science is, in summary, a barbarism, a pleonasm. To be more specific, it is equivalent to stating that surgery is too bloody, car mechanics too greasy, or swimming too wet. In other words, is vagueness the problem in psychoanalytic methodology, or is such vagueness a characteristic of the organ to be explored?

Psychoanalysis, similar to structuralism, can be considered a methodology that has the specific purpose of investigating and understanding how the mind functions, and in order to properly achieve this purpose, psychoanalysis needs to follow closely and to model itself upon the specific patterns of the phenomena under investigation. It is just those characteristics of the mind, its loose openness and imprecise structure, that have allowed humanity to evolve and progress. It is different for the body, which remains the same from prehistory to the present time. It is precisely in the mind, and not in the body, where many differences between primitive and modern men are to be found. If the mind had been as rigid and structured as the body is, humanity might have been unable to move forward. Accusing psychoanalysis of being an imprecise doctrine that lacks the accuracy of a scientific body epitomizes the incapacity to discriminate between the methodology used as an instrument with which to investigate and the phenomenon under investigation. In a dialogue, Bion states:

Roland: I thought psychoanalysts take religion seriously.
P.A. [Psychoanalyst]: How could I take people seriously if I do not take seriously one of their most important inclinations . . . We should be aware of the distinction between "talking about some-thing" and the "something" itself . . . [1975, p. 303]

In other words, one thing is the noumenon or the "thing-in-itself"—to use a Kantian approach—and another is psychoanalysis as an instrument acting upon the phenomenon in order to reveal the true nature of the noumenon.

Freud never made any attempt to defend psychoanalysis as an exact science. On the contrary, as we shall see, he was more interested in the opposite. Through most of his writings he feared the precise-ness of the medical profession and chose instead the vagueness of psychology, sociology, and even the clergy. However, on the other hand, if we were to be methodologically more meticulous, we might be able to infer that in the basic outline of psychoanalysis, not withstanding Freud's important attempts, he remained attached to some of the neuro-physiological theories present in the Project, such as, for instance, his instinct theory, the mechanisms of repression and of narcissism. Perhaps a few articles published near the end of his life, such as "Splitting of the ego in the service of defence" (1940e), hinted at a possible shift from his basic biological orientation.

From the defence of Theodore Reik, a prominent non-medical member of the psychoanalytical association, concerning quackery, at Vienna's court in 1926, Freud produced the well-known pamph-let of "The question of lay analysis". Having the possibility to choose between the exactness of biology and the approximation of psychology, sociology and related fields, Freud favoured the latter, and openly proclaimed his resistance to restricting the practice of psychoanalysis to the hands of medical practitioners alone. He said:

> What is known as medical education appears to me to be an arduous and circuitous way of approaching the profession of analysis. No doubt it offers an analyst much that is indispensable to him. But it burdens him with too much else of which he can never make use, and there is a danger of its diverting his interest and his whole mode of thought from the understanding of psychical phenomena . . . Psycho-analysis is a part of psychology; not of medical psychology in the old sense, not of the psychology of morbid processes, but simply of psychology. It is certainly not the whole of psychology, but its substructure and perhaps even its entire foundation. [1926d, p. 252]

I do not think that the emphasis placed by Freud on the defence of lay analysis was solely the consequence of Reik's accusation. The intensity and almost personal passion Freud invested in the whole issue speaks of a different and perhaps even deeper predicament. Peter Gay (1988) quotes Freud saying, in a letter to Ferdern written in 1926: "The struggle for lay analysis must be fought through sometime or other. Better now than later. As long as I live, I shall balk at having psychoanalysis swallowed by medicine" (p. 491). And one year later, he stated: "The physicians among the analysts have been only too inclined to engage in research closer to the organic, rather than in psychological research" (p. 497).

This attitude was by no means anything new in Freud. Thirteen years earlier, in his introduction to Oskar Pfister's book *The Psychoanalytic Method*, he stated:

> The practice of psychoanalysis calls much less for medical training than for psychological instruction and a free human outlook. The majority of doctors are not equipped to practice psychoanalysis and have completely failed to grasp the value of that therapeutic procedure. Educators and the pastoral workers are bound by the standards of their profession to exercise the same consideration, care and restraint, in much the same way usually practised by doctors . . . [1913b, pp. 330–331]

How did Freud develop such an animosity towards doctors, when the great majority of his followers were physicians? Furthermore, in 1895, at the time of his well-known dream of Irma's injection, he had encouraged it otherwise, by saying that a proper evaluation of physical ailments should be disregarded previous to any psychoanalytical proceeding. But perhaps Freud's greatest critical differences were with the North American Association, who, until only a few years ago, had limited psychoanalysis to medical personnel only, as a form of dealing with several cases of charlatanism and of non-medical persons who were involved in "improper conducts" while practising some kind of psychotherapy. On this account, in 1927, Eitingon and Jones organized an international symposium on the subject of lay analysis, where opinions were completely discordant, and where the Americans, directed by A. A. Brill, held a more radical view in support of physicians being the only persons certified to practise psychoanalysis, a proposition that created almost enough friction to cause Freud to break from the International Psychoanalytical Association.

> By early 1929, as the controversy did not die down, Freud wondered whether it might not make sense to separate from the American analysts peacefully and remain firm on the matter of lay analysis. Brill's uneasy feeling that Freud might want to force out the Americans was not just a fantasy without foundation. [Gay, 1988, p. 500]

Freud even went as far as to doubt Jones' integrity, and in a letter to his daughter Anna, he stated that she should be glad that she did not marry Jones. Was this passion and personal commitment to the defence of lay analysis an expression of Freud's protection towards his friends and followers such as Pfister, Rank, Reik, and his own daughter? Or, perhaps, his pledge was also the expression of his shrewd intuition and awareness that mental processes represented something completely different from the physical world, and that even if psychoanalysis faced the danger of being ostracized from any possibility of claiming itself as an exact science, Freud considered it wiser to support its openness towards other less precise fields of knowledge. Then, perhaps by stubbornly doing so, the material difference between the unconscious act and that of physical reality would be firmly established. We learn from Jones (1953, p. 253), that Freud saw medicine as a handicap for anybody attempting a psychoanalytic training. Referring to a meeting with Freud, Clarence Oberndorf (1953) remembers Freud asking with a "tone of annoyance and impatience", what did he have against lay analysis.

> I tried to explain to him that the laws of New York State forbade it, that the members in America thought a knowledge of the physical manifestations of organic illness necessary so that the physician might compare them with those due to psychological disturbance, that especially in America quacks and impostors, extremely ignorant of the elements of psychoanalysis, presumed to hold themselves out as analysts. Freud waved aside my replies with an abrupt "I know all that", turned and walked very slowly towards the house. [p. 182]

Peter Gay (1988, 310n), quotes a letter from Freud to Hendrik de Man, dated December 13, 1925, where he asserts that "extra medical applications of psychoanalysis are as significant as the medical ones, indeed that the former might perhaps have a greater influence on the mental orientation of humanity". If Freud was not defending a legal, ethical, or political issue, what position was his concern?

In ancient times medicine, in order to differentiate itself from the spiritual arts, was considered *muta art*, or mute art. In *The Aeneid*, Virgil, through the mouth of Iapyx, who is trying to cure his wounded father, says: "He prefers to learn the powers of herbs, a healer's ways and practice without glory silent arts" (1992, pp. 542–543). The body, or corporal self, will always be rather unknown, unless the patient is a medical doctor. This means that such natural ignorance and alienation about our body's physiology will make a visit to the doctor something very similar to a consultation with the car mechanic. The mind, on the other hand, represents the proper site of the self and the locus of our understanding about what we really are. It is where nobody else could ever be, even if, due to repression, we have decided not to know about something and prefer, through projection, for others to do so, as some kind of "epistemophobic" disposition. Lacan has already referred to this mechanism as the "place of the supposed knowledge", meaning that the patient will come for consultation with the transference conviction—as he might do with a general practitioner—that the analyst ought to know about his own mind, more than he himself could ever know. For the psychoanalyst, unless there is a significant pathology that interferes and makes the psychoanalytic process impossible, medicine, as in Virgil, is a *silent art*, of absolutely no concern during the psychoanalytic process.

Such confusion between body and mind[1] is present in many ways during an analytic therapy and it represents the patient's lack of awareness of their uniqueness as human beings, something also often reflected in their concern with statistics and their need to compare themselves to others. They seem to lack the awareness of being human, of being unique and capable of experiencing an unconditional, non-negotiable quality and, therefore, the right to be different from a thing and not to feel valued instead like a material object for some specific and idealized feature. A newly wed and pregnant young woman complained bitterly that she felt like a parasite to her husband, because she did not contribute economically to her household, as if her presence, her love, company, friendship, etc., meant nothing in comparison to the money. Psychoanalysis will eventually help to discriminate between the quality of "being inanimate" and the capacity to feel human, to be loved for what we are and not for what we do or have, different from "things" that are liked for how they look or provide.

Self-envy is another vertex from which the mind–body controversy can be investigated. One of Scott's (1975) descriptions of self-envy refers to the envy experienced by consciousness towards the unconscious, as he states that, ". . . the waking ego might envy the dreaming ego and break the link, spoil the connection and have none of it—or, at the most, only the memory of a token dream" (p. 336).

The envy of consciousness towards the unconscious might perhaps help us to understand the debate related to some ailments being exclusively considered to be of genetic origin without evaluating the possibility of an emotional etiology; such as for instance, drug addiction, homosexuality, Alzheimer's disease, endometriosis, rheumatoid arthritis, lupus, and so on. There is also a strong resistance in many psychoanalysts to consider understanding the complex abstraction of the internal world. Instead, they are being driven towards a more *concrete* appreciation of the mind, seeking an immediate and tangible causation, instead of a complicated and abstract one; and prefer to make use of tranquil-lizers or antidepressant medication rather than develop a dynamic understanding of the psyche. Basically, this practice could be explained as the expression of envious attacks from the conscious mind against the creativity and marvellous power of the uncon-scious mind.

Confusion between diachronic and synchronic dimensions[2]

If astronomers were asked to choose between an Aristotelian geocentric representation of the universe or a Copernican heliocen-tric one, they would for sure and without hesitation choose the latter; signifying that the determining force of diachronic and progressive discoveries is imposed. In psychoanalysis, however, perhaps because of the abstract and insubstantial constructs of the mind, synchrony overpowers diachrony, allowing psychoanalysts to consider the existence of "different models" either historical or geographical, denying the weight of a progressive diachronism. Even though Freud's, Klein's, and Bion's contributions, just to mention the most extensive discoveries made in psychoanalysis, follow an historical order with many years of difference between them, they are continuously considered side by side as if they were contemporary, denying the possibility of a progressive achievement of new discoveries. Such difficulty in integrating knowledge according to diachronic evolution is often complicated by the need to defend one form (or "model") of psychoanalysis over another, as if some kind of narcissistic identity confusion were involved, or as if the object were not distinguished from its background, or the "observer" from that which is observed. To understand the differ-ent forms of link interaction between these two entities—observer and object of observation, or psychoanalyst and the mind—we could use Bion's "container–contained" model.

Bion discriminates between three different forms of links between container and contained: "commensal", "symbiotic" and "parasitic". In the "commensal" form of link, both the container and the contained benefit from each other; for instance, Freud's model of id, ego, and superego, or Bion's use of preconcepts. The analyst forms commensal links at the moment of producing an insightful interpretation, which benefits himself by demonstrating that he can be a creative thinker, benefits the patient who is being thought of, and benefits psychoanalysis as an instrument of investigation. In this form of link there is a certain independence between the thinker and the object of investigation, because there is a recognition that "truth does not need a thinker", since it pre-exists by itself like the notion of Platonic forms. If the rationale is that Freud, Bion, or any other analyst had not made such a discovery, anyone else would have been able to do so.

In the "symbiotic" form of link, one element, container or contained, will destroy the other. For instance, if the observer—or psychoanalyst in our case—is "contained" by an idea, depending on its "passion", such an observer could lose neutrality and become a "believer", sometimes a fanatic believer. He/she might defend his/her credence just as a political activist or a football team fan would, inducing an artificial struggle to prove he or she possesses the best form of psychoanalysis. Religious fanaticism is present in most wars existing today, the opposing forces trying to establish, by killing each other, whose God is better. Religion is also a good example of how synchronicity dominates over diachronic views, when books written thousands of years ago are still used to make the future become "present" or even "past". The fact that religious people refer to themselves as Jews, Muslims, Christians, Catholics, or Christian Protestants seems rather similar to psychoanalysts calling themselves Freudians, Kohutians, Kleinians, or Bionians. This is something that does not take place in other fields of knowledge, such as astronomy, where one would never hear anybody calling himself Aristotelian, Galilean, or Einsteinian. When, in 1972, during an invitation made by the Los Angeles Psychoanalytic Society, British psychoanalyst Donald Meltzer stated that Klein's psychoanalysis represented contemporary analysis, while classical psychoanalysis might be considered psychoanalysis from the beginning of the twentieth century, such a statement was felt by many American psychoanalysts to be an expression of "inflammatory arrogance and superiority" (Kirsner, 2000, pp. 174–175).

In the "parasitic" form of links, both container and contained destroy each other; as, for instance, in the use of medication as the therapy of preference in the treatment of neurotic pathology, or when an insurance system excludes exchange of money as payment for the service provided. During the psychoanalytic process, money represents the indispensable difference between reality and transference, ensuring that the analyst is not a parental figure. The analyst can only provide a "conditioned" assistance to payment. It is exactly this absence of unconditional concern—provided only by parents-that is one of the important issues psychoanalysis needs to deal with. The analytic process should induce separation and object loss mourning in order to allow the ego to move from the schizoid–paranoid to the depressive position. Mourning for the lost object will allow symbol formation, which will in turn induce mental "growth". If money is absent from the analytical transaction and separation mourning is not properly achieved, termination of analysis could become an impossible task, as it would necessarily be introduced as an artificial imposition instead of as a natural process (comparable to the ripe fruit falling from the tree); in a way, similar to how Freud imposed termination on the Wolfman. Under these circumstances, the modality of payment for missed sessions might create the phantasy of money as a kind of punishment or a form of "acting in", instead of being the expression of a "conditioned" reality. However, when some analysts, in order to avoid the difficulties introduced in to the analytical process by the absence of payment, choose to charge above the covered fee, they will then face the risk of a discrepancy with the system legally. Also, there is the danger of "murdering" the process by either losing the patient or creating collusion or a "perverse pact" for a blind spot in the analysis of perverse pathologies; in either case, investigation of truth as a purpose to know about the unconscious content becomes an impossible task.

Confusion between presence and absence of the patient

During the treatment of Emmy von N. (Baroness Fanny Moser), Freud learned that hypnosis was useless because it left the patient "out of treatment" and therefore it represented an inadequate procedure. Freud observed how contradictory it was to confront Emmy with significant historical material previously obtained during hypnosis, because when afterwards he insistently questioned her, "she grew annoyed, pretty surly, and demanded that he stop" (Gay, 1988, p. 70).

Although history-taking, diagnostic classifications, and developmental theories have a determinant importance in psychiatric and psychological research, from a practical perspective they have little value in psychoanalytical technique. From the point of view of patients' psychological awareness and capacity to learn how to read their unconscious messages, there is little value in such practice. "Trusting what he saw," says Gay, referring to Charcot's emphasis on clinical observation, "he defended practice over theory, an observation he once threw out burned itself into Freud's mind: *La théorie, c'est bon, mais ça n'empêche pas d'exister*" (*ibid*, p. 51). However, I am not attacking issues such as diagnostic classification, clinical history, or developmental theories. Instead, I would like to emphasize the danger of ignoring the patient's mind as the "main character" to be present during the psychoanalytical process. There is a better chance of implementing a meaningful therapy when the material in the session is examined through the light of *transference* and of *intrapsychic* mechanisms (Lopez-Corvo, 1999). Transference is important because, as a window from the past, it closely portrays the individual's historical truth of how early events really took place for the patient. But transference also represents a mirage, a displacement of internal object relations being projected on the analyst. The real drama, after all, is intrapsychic and, therefore, takes place within the patient's mind. To disregard the transference and to investigate from other sources (parents, hospital records, etc.) how early traumas might have "really" taken place carries the danger of excluding the patient's effort to find his/her own truth during the analytical setting. It is important to be aware that we do not analyse people but minds, just as heart surgeons operate on hearts.

Humpty Dumpty: "iatrogenic splitting" and multiple personality

At birth the mind is always fragmented in bits and pieces, but as we grow (+Y), it will progressively integrate, emotionally as well as cognitively. Growth represents, in other words, the immediate consequence of mental integration.

Following Klein, the shifting from paranoid–schizoid[3] to depressive position will require, among other things, a successive integration from split object representations (part-objects) to whole objects. Whatever interferes with such a natural process of emotional assimilation, such as early traumas, for instance, will result in the generation of powerful and reiterative narcissistic structures that will control the mind and perpetuate fragmentation by resisting mental integration. Psychoanalysis is, overall, an instrument that cultivates positive growth and integration, as ontogenetic truth is systematically being revealed. Obviously, promotion of any kind of mind fragmentation, as observed in the uncanny folklore of "multiple personality", would represent an attack on the *authentic intention of psychoanalytic theory and praxis*.

In this disagreement I am not denying the existence of a multiple personality syndrome. I am only arguing about its meaning within the dynamics of transference–countertransference interaction. It will be similar to a patient arriving at the emergency room with a broken leg. Obviously, the doctor will place the pieces together and fix the fracture in a manner that will restore the leg's previous functionality. The doctor will not attempt to preserve the fracture indefinitely or, even more, will not attempt to break the leg in more pieces in order to recommend that the patient join a circus to show his newly acquired "flexibility". I have previously referred to this issue (López-Corvo, 1995):

> Since the publication of *The Three Faces of Eve* (Thigpen & Cleckley, 1958), it has been common to see therapists introducing patients who display, not just three faces but as many as twenty or more—a kind of competition for a greater number of "personalities" with different names, dissimilar postures and all. I have often thought that such conditions represent a perverse relationship between these therapists and their borderline patients, who, via projective identification of exhibitionistic tendencies, induce in the therapist a need to act out, countertransferentially, their voyeuristic counterpart, generating a sort of vicious cycle or perverse collusion: the greater the interest of the therapist in the patients dissociation, the greater the number of "personalities" the patient will happily provide for the therapist, the greater the interest of the therapist, and so forth. [pp. 58–59]

Understanding confusions

Confusions such as the kind stated above can be understood with the use of Bion's "theory of thinking". For example, these confusions could be a consequence of the difficulty in not using the proper "apparatus for thinking" thoughts, the proper "machinery". In Bion's own words, the conflict hinges on the use given to the thinking apparatus, which might be used for ridding the "psyche of accumulations of bad internal objects" instead of thinking thoughts. "The crux lies", Bion concludes, "in the decision between modification (thinking) or evasion of frustration" (1967, p. 112).

When the mind is dominated by intolerance towards frustration in the absence of the object, "steps are taken", says Bion, "to evade perception of the [negative] realization by destructive attacks" (*ibid.*, p. 113). Space and time are equated with a bad object and destroyed, "the realization that should be mated with the preconception is not available to complete the conditions necessary for the formation of a conception" (*ibid.*). In this condition, confusion takes over and space becomes a space for projection and time a time of transference,[4] resulting in the impossibility of outlining a conception of the surrounding reality.

There is also the possibility of creating an intermediary phase between the extremes of frustration tolerance and frustration intolerance. Bion has referred to a stage where omnipotence is used to deal with the negative realization of the object's absence. Under this condition, instead of "thinking" or "evasion" there is the assumption that *omniscience could be a substitute for learning*, where the difference between true and false would be established in a dogmatic or dictatorial fashion, the individual taking the attitude: "this is like that because I say so, and anybody who says differently is against me".

A final word about growth and splitting: We are born in pieces and progressively, as we grow, we change into a more integrated self. Our primitive self is by nature inchoately divided, like pieces in search of a mind that could constructively integrate them as an expression of mental growth; similar to that which can be observed in the narrative of a dream, where all the characters portrayed represent inner part objects of the dreamer. If such a state of managerial and creative direction is not achieved, splitting will become a tendency, or perhaps it will even become the main defence exercised by the ego as a way to deal with anxiety. However, to conceive the mind as puzzle pieces, which are kept together by the ego's continuous tendency towards a managerial capacity, could be experienced as rather threatening, even by individuals in the field of psychoanalysis. A consequence could be to deny the natural splitting of the mind and attempt to deal with "total objects" instead of partial ones. For instance, in relation to the Oedipus complex, the characters presented in unconscious oedipal relations would be conceived of as interacting as total parents and total children, instead of as part-objects. Once the Oedipus complex is truly conceived by the mind as made of total persons, the conflictive aspect of the drama can be already solved. However, it is the narcissistic object relation between part objects that constitutes the true core of the unresolved Oedipus phantasy, not the relationship established between total individuals. Pathological Oedipus relations are always narcissistic in nature, and are always the expression of part-object interactions.

Notes

1. *"Rex Extensa"* and *"Rex Cogintans"* or *"Noumenon"* and *"Phenomenon"*, from a Cartesian and Kantian point of view, respectively.
2. Diachrony refers to changes extending in time, while synchrony relates to events taking place in a limited space–time.
3. *"Schizo"* (σιψημιζο) meaning split.
4. In relation to time confusion, Bion uses as paradigmatic the Mad Hatter's tea-party in *Alice in Wonderland*, where it is always four o'clock, demonstrating how temporary becomes permanent.

CHAPTER TWO

The forgotten self

With the use of Bion's theory of negative links*

What is that which always is and has no becoming; and what is that which is always becoming and never is?

(Plato)

If you bring forth what is within you, what you have will save you. If you do not have that within you, what you do not have within you [will] kill you.

(The Gospel of Thomas: 53)

The false sub-selves

Winnicott polarized between false and true selves. However, in a previous paper (López-Corvo 1996a), I presented the hypothesis that Winnicott's false self could be considered as containing two false sub-selves, one complying or pleasing, to which I referred as the "complying false-self",

---

* This chapter also published in *The Psychoanalytic Review*, *93*(3): 363–377, June 2006.

and the other aggressive, which I called the "negativistic false-self". The latter is often confused with a true self.[1]

Polarization of the false selves

In summary we have: (a) a "complying false self" that attempts to deceive an imaginary castrator projected into the object by providing the object with what he believes the Other wants. This false subself is related to early oral fixations; (b) the other "negativistic false self" is hidden, revengeful, and related to anal-sadistic early object relations (Meltzer, 1966), usually determining certain forms of acting out. This negativistic false self is the complete opposite of the complying false self. Between the two false selves a paranoid–schizoid sort of circularity takes place, in which a great need to comply and deceive induces castration anxiety and fear of "fusing" with the Other, of just becoming the Other's wish and changing into a lie. This fear increases the need for a negativistic false self as a way of attacking the castrator and providing an identity, even if it is a negative and false one.

The complying false self

This represents a universal form of defence, present to a greater or lesser degree in most patients, although more obvious in borderline pathologies. It characterizes a pleasing behaviour with the purpose of deceiving, pacifying, and controlling a possible castrator, and determines the direction of the transference as well as that of interpretations. It could be described as an inversion of the natural order of desires, where the Other's wish is privileged over the wish of the self. Let us now examine some clinical material.

Joseph is a rather difficult patient who is always late or missing sessions and regularly resorts to delinquent acting out behaviour. During the sessions there is a regular and repetitious pattern: he is always apologizing for being late and complaining about all the "bad" things he feels he has acted out, and the "good" things he has not performed. I have the impression that he responds, in the transference, to an internal castrating object projected into the analyst that forces him to continuously show an already punished child, who has failed in his attempt to stand up to the demands expected from such a castrating object.

Elizabeth is an attractive, married, professional young woman, who presented a history of early emotional deprivation. Her parents were divorced when she was only three years old and she was raised mostly by maids and a chronically depressed alcoholic mother. During the sessions her behaviour resembled that of a clown. She would crack jokes and talk with exaggerated gestures. It appeared as if her main concern was to entertain in order to pacify a castrator, identifying herself with an internal element representing the depressed, distant and often absent mother.

Isabel, a young married woman, consulted because of phobic anxiety. She grew up in an upper middle-class family with a very religious background and with a mother whose history resembled that of Cinderella. She described her mother as very envious, critical, and demeaning of her when she was a little girl. Her father, on the other hand, considered to be rather frightened of her mother, was privately often sympathetic with Isabel. Her attitude at the beginning of her analysis could have been compatible with a "nun–prostitute" condensation, for she was always attempting—as a reaction formation—to appear as a "model" of asexual asceticism, with the purpose of hiding her sexual as well as aggressive Oedipal phantasies. She attempted to give the impression of a "good girl": always being on time, well behaved, following the rules and never complaining, attending church every Sunday, and so on. She had the phantasy that the castrator, who was projected in her transference, was always expecting this kind of demeanour from her. Therefore, she was determined to make sure that no one, but mostly herself, would ever suspect her concealed Oedipal phantasies. Whenever these defences failed, she would faint in church, for instance, for she felt threatened because God was "spying" on her thoughts from on high.

The negativistic false self

Behind the façade of the "deceiving false self" there is not a true self, as Winnicott (1960) originally stated. Instead there is a negative, destructive, and anal-sadistic structure that remains hidden inside. This is usually difficult to recognize because it falsifies the image of a more significantly true self: it has the intention of being a true self, but is actually only a negative identity, the exact opposite of what could be considered as the Other's wish. Repression in relation to the negative aspects of a false self is usually related to anxiety about the retaliation for aggression, sensed as an all or nothing kind of attitude. This may be observed in the fear of destroying the "goodness of the object", such as the need to protect the continuity of the analysis. The "deceiving" and the "negativistic" false selves represent two faces of the same coin, for after all, to always do what the Other wishes, or to do the opposite, will obviously add up to the same thing, that is, they will both mean to remain "othered". The deceiving false self attempts to deceive, guided by the hope of complying, while the negativistic false self attempts to destroy, guided by a hope for revenge.

Joseph, a patient I referred to above, had the omnipotent phantasy of becoming a powerful person, a fearless sort of "Superman", for which he consumed cocaine in order, as he said, to hide his "Clark Kent". Under the effect of this drug he participated in armed robbery, gunfights with rival gangs, physical aggression, etc.; behaviours that contrasted with the "punished child" attitude he continuously portrayed in the transference with the purpose of deceiving a possible castrator. If the analyst was satisfied with the "punishment" he had exercised upon himself, he did not need to further investigate his destructive and revengeful behaviour. The intention of his acting out, on the other hand, was to attack the castrator by giving him/her the opposite of what he thought the castrator wanted: a good patient to his analyst, a good husband to his wife, or a good son to his parents. Not only did he never achieve this, but also he always ended up punishing himself instead.

There are other reasons, for acting out. In the case of Elizabeth, she experienced major anxiety outbursts followed by alcoholic binges lasting several days to the point of severe confusion that demanded hospitalization. During those crises she completely neglected her children, husband, work, and treatment, feeling afterwards very fearful and guilty, apologizing for all the damage and concern she felt she had caused to others; at the same time her husband and close relatives bitterly complained about her irresponsible behaviour. Therefore, under the influence of such a negativistic false self, the only thing Elizabeth seemed concerned about was others, and thus she kept forgetting totally about herself. She attacked within herself what she felt others expected from her, not giving them the exact thing she felt others wanted; that is, the "good" daughter, wife, mother, etc. By doing so, not only did she punish herself, but she did not consider herself, as if she felt unworthy of any good things, as if she did not exist at all.

In the case of Isabel, the negativistic false self appeared in the form of clandestine, omnipotent masturbatory phantasies, which took place at the same time that she provided the castrator with the impression of a nice, obedient, and well-behaved girl. In her sexual phantasy she was rescued by an extraordinary man with whom she then established a relationship that caused tremendous envy in her mother and sisters. In the transference she believed she was the perfect patient, and that at the end of the analysis, as a reward, I would participate in her sexual phantasy.

Bion's theory of links

Bion referred to the phenomenology of three type of links: +L (love), +H (hate) and +K (knowledge), as well as negative ones: −L, −H and −K. According to him, "negative" links do not represent opposite emotions; for instance, −L is not equivalent to +H. About −L and −H, as far as I know, Bion said very little, whereas about −K he was much more explicit.

Positive links are related to truth, while negative ones would be associated to lies, falsehood, and evacuation processes. The former would be the product of a "maternal reverie", which could be observed during normal growth, when a mother–child relationship is established as a container–contained interaction dominated by a "commensal" link, that is, when the three variables involved: ego, object, and the relationship between them, all benefit from each other. Under this condition, the baby projects his feelings inside the mother, for instance, feeling that he is dying, and then reintrojects them after the mother has changed them into something more bearable to the baby's mind. This condition represents a basic model where the apparatus for thinking thoughts will be structured as well as the growth of K (knowledge). However, if the situation were dominated by envy—baby and mother's—the baby would split and project his feelings inside the breast together with envy and hatred, which will hinder the possibility of establishing a container–

contained relationship of a "commensal" type. Under such circumstances, the breast is felt enviously to denude all good and valuable
elements capable of metabolizing the baby's fear of death, and
instead it will force back denigrated residues that will determine the
manifestation of a high level of anxiety or, in Bion's terms, a "nameless terror", or a container–contained interaction between the baby
and the breast, represented by Bion as $-K$. Such a condition is serious indeed, because not only does the breast not mitigate the fear of
death, but it also takes away the desire to live (1962, pp. 97–99).

Because complying is not real love and revenge is not true hate,
I believe both false selves are related to negative links: where the
"complying false self" corresponds to $-L$, and the "negativistic"
one to $-H$. Though we might promptly agree with complying being
equal to $-L$, there might be some disagreement as to why $-H$
should not be considered true aggression. It is possible that Bion's
use of the term "hate" was not as accurate as Freud's use of the term
"aggression", but Bion might have preferred to use hate because he
was referring to an emotion and not to a drive. In any case, what
seems to be important is to discriminate between what we might
have called a true or a false feeling of hate. Why should the aggression present in the revengeful behaviour of a negativistic false self
be considered false? I believe the difference depends not so much
on the nature of the feeling itself, but on the nature of the object
towards which the emotion is being expressed. For instance,
aggression expressed in transference towards a "father like" internal object projected into the analyst is not true aggression against
the analyst; instead it represents false hate or $-H$, aimed at a narcissistic object placed outside the self by means of projective identification mechanisms. Such aggression can also be directed towards
an internal object, in ways I have previously described as mechanisms of self-envy (López-Corvo, 1995).

Both the compliant and the negativistic aspects of the false self
are related to mechanisms of projective identification present in the
schizoid–paranoid position. They are a defence against the awareness of the process of mourning towards separateness of the object
and one's dependence upon it, proper of the depressive position
and of a true self.

In summary, I am now considering the hypothesis of a direct
relationship between Bion's concept of negative links $-L$ and $-H$,

on the one hand, and the complying and negativistic false selves on the other. I am also adding that a significant amount of false self, such as the one observed in borderline pathologies, induces a state of −K, or a kind of "scientific deductive system" that could be considered an empty self. Winnicott (1960) declared that the false self hides the true self; I would like to add that not only does it hide it, but it also hinders, alienates, proscribes, and forgets it, making it impossible for the true self to evolve. Expressed in terms of the theory of links, it could be stated in the following way: −L and −H induce a condition of −K, of "without-ness", which I propose to call an empty or "forgotten self".

The forgotten self

What I referred to as the forgotten self is also not a true self. The true self is just possibly parallel to Bion's O, similar to the becoming of time, something that takes place and then vanishes, because it only exists while it is becoming, bearing a resemblance to Plato's expression presented at the beginning of this chapter. The forgotten self, on the other hand, is a negative presence that stays still until it is changed with the help of insight. It is a "minus self" directly linked to minus knowledge or −K.

We shall now examine some clinical material. Martin is a young patient who consulted because he wanted to give up a chronic consumption of marijuana. From the very beginning I was suspicious that he was caught within a dissociation between two opposite aspects: (i) "the consumer" part, which represented his true reality, and (ii) "the non consumer", a fantasized and idealized aspect, which stood for what he wished to be but was unable to achieve. Both these parts made up the false self, that is, the complying or non-consumer and the negativistic or consumer. I also suspected his intentions were to attempt—and in his mind he had already done this—to project the "non-consumer" element into the analyst while at the same time he would continue to act out the "consumer" aspect; all in an endless circularity. Within the transference–countertransference dimension, he repeated the same dynamic of his relationship with his parents.

He conscientiously worked every day, but equally every day, as soon as he arrived at his house, he compulsively drugged himself with marijuana and masturbated while watching a pornographic film; at the weekends he often garnished the sordid ritual by adding the presence of a prostitute. When invited to a party he drugged himself and got drunk, giving such a terrible impression that "decent girls" always avoided him. Because, during sessions, he continuously accused himself for what he was doing, it introduced the possibility of a latent danger that I could respond with advice, recriminations, or watching his behaviour as he felt his parents had done in the past. It was as if I had only two options, either to comply as an accomplice or to recriminate. This situation represented the risk of a tautological collusion where we could both become trapped in an endless repetition, draining off any possibility of analysis. This condition, however, characterizes one of the limitations that take place during institutional treatment of drug addicts, as well as limitations with many psychotherapeutic procedures that fail in that they become themselves defenders of projective identifications of idealized images of the "son free of drugs".

Stated from the point of view of false self pathologies, this collusion represents a continuous interaction between the "complying false self" or "non-consumer", projected into the analyst and determining the countertransference, on the one hand, and the "negativistic" or "consumer" aspect preserved inside the patient and determining the transference, on the other. Such an endless interaction hinders any possibility of achieving a true self because the ego is locked in between pleasing and attacking the other. In such interactions the patient is unable to understand that, in the end, the conflict is taking place only within himself, that it regards only him and nobody else, forgetting that he is a free man capable of choosing how to manage his life. His decision whether or not to use drugs is of no relevance for the analysis, for, after all, it is his sole decision. What is really important and, therefore, must be analysed, is the dissociation to which he is subject; that is, between a part that continuously needs to use drugs and another part that continuously needs to feel guilty about it and repent. Furthermore, what is most important of all is that such incongruence hinders all possibility of finding or developing his own true self; that is, what he really wishes to be regardless of the Other's desire. In this way, the possibility of struggling to acquire a true self is left out, it is forgotten and his own wish is ignored.

The danger of this kind of perverse collusion is the possibility of a sort of "minus container–contained" interaction, where the analyst can act out projective identifications and insist on the conflict between both false selves, instead of investigating the forgotten aspect of the self that obstructed the possibility of finding the true self. Such a situation corresponds to a kind of "parasitic" interaction where all components are destroyed, a condition of minus container–contained ($-\female\male$) where the analysis is contained by the projective identification of the patient, instead of the other way around, by the analyst. Seen from another vertex, this condition can also be understood as an envious attack perpetrated between different parts of the self; more precisely, against the link towards a true self.

Some time later, when these dynamics became more obvious, I had the impression that Martin was somehow "dead–alive", unable to structure and determine a sensible project to carry throughout his existence; he seemed to remain tautologically trapped between guilt and shame for what he did, and the wish to do the opposite. The real conflict was not due to idealization of what he was not, nor to the attack of that idealization. Instead, the real conflict was the very fact of having an ignored being, a forgotten self. Martin was a young, good-looking guy, intelligent, pleasant, and with financial prospects; yet he conducted his life in such an empty and sad manner, without any hope or ambition, or any sensible future prospect.

Further investigation introduced the situation of his mother's death, something he referred to at the beginning of his treatment but on which he did not elaborate. His relationship with his mother was rather turbulent and ambivalent, since he felt suspicious from very early on that she had been unfaithful to his father with several men. She was shot and killed in her car, and Martin never knew whether she had been murdered by his father or by one of her lovers. He also experienced great impotence, repressed incestuous feelings as he identified with her lovers, as well as emotional emptiness about her loss and intense anger. He remembered the day after the fatality, when he and an older brother celebrated her departure. In a desperate effort to deny her death, Martin split his mother's memory in such tiny bits that they infected every action and every place that surrounded his life. In the transference he attempted to reproduce his relationship with his mother while she was alive, presenting a masochistic need to be punished for his continuous acting out behaviour. Furthermore, an intense and senseless rivalry with other partners coloured his situation at work, similar to the condition at home, where sibling rivalry for his mother's attention was an important issue. The sordid ritual that surrounded his drug consumption was related to the omnipotent delusion of preserving a narcissistic fusion with his dead mother.

A few months later the analysis took a different twist, as he started to feel that the conflict was more between different inner parts of him rather than a difficulty with others; that is, he was finally able to grasp that he was trapped more within an internal affair rather than within a transference matter.

Another case

In most cases the "complying false self" acts as the manifest part, while the "negativistic false self" remains hidden and distant, acting as a possible internal saboteur of the analytic process. There are situations (Joseph, 1975) when the "complying false self" might present itself as a "collaborator" of the analyst, procuring scenarios or examples that would corroborate interpretations but at the same time always giving the impression that interpretations are solely based on the analyst's own theories, that the patient would never have thought of such a thing by him/herself, and that he/she complies because that is what the analyst wishes. It seems as if objects or facts exist only because the analyst says so, and not because the object or the fact exists on its own and can be observed or thought by either of them—analyst or patient. The patient seems to provide the analyst's words with an omnipotent power that his words do not have. The patient appears always ready to cooperate and to accept any interpretation, regardless of how peculiar it might appear. The patient seems always ready, always there, but in reality he is not.

Let us examine yet another case: Louise is a woman in her early fifties, the second of four sisters, divorced, the mother of two sons, and has been in analysis five times a week for the past three years, at the moment of this presentation. Her son's psychiatrist originally referred her to me because she was considered to be a "co-dependent" in her son's abuse of illegal drugs. She did not have genuine insight into her own conflicts and suffering, and she felt that she was attending therapy exclusively to help her son's recovery. For a while we had been investigating an envious and terribly self-destructive element related to a rivalry against her sisters that filled her with remorse and persecutory anxiety. In one session she arrived and lay down, remaining silent for at least ten minutes. Finally, she said that she had absolutely nothing to say, that she did not have time to prepare anything for the session and that she was only thinking about getting ready to travel that afternoon to her native town in the interior of the country. Usually she speaks continuously as soon as she lies on the couch, and I often felt suspicious that she had previously prepared the material as some kind of "make-up" in order to hide other elements. "My mind", she states, "is occupied with other things that have nothing to do with this treatment." I clarify that everything in her mind has to do with her analysis and, on the contrary, there exists the danger that important aspects of her would remain excluded if she tried to please me by telling me only what she thinks I am interested in and leaving out important aspects like, for instance, the preparation for her trip. She continues explaining that she had thought about, but decided against, calling her younger sister to tell her she was leaving. She had cleaned her apartment thoroughly before her departure, washed the sheets, and taken all the rubbish out. She continued, "As you can see these are just unimportant issues. I did not want to leave the keys with anybody, and the concierge told me someone else had left his keys, and when he came back found that several long-distance calls were made from his phone." She cleaned the refrigerator meticulously and threw away leftovers that were getting spoiled. She was planning to leave that afternoon around two o'clock, and preferred to drive herself instead of being taken by her driver, because "he continuously spoke about X", a well-known politician being accused of corruption and murder.

I then stated that perhaps she did not want both of us to know (she does not inform her sister and thoroughly cleans the apartment of any "trace") about the existence of an unconscious "child element" who wishes to murder her sisters by poisoning mother's milk with faeces (she cleans the refrigerator by throwing away spoiled food). Also, she wants to have complete control and not to have any surprises (she does not want to give the key to anybody or to receive surprise phone calls) She wishes to be her own "driver" because if I were to do it, like her driver, she fears I might continuously denounce in her, the existence of a corrupted and murderous "Louise X". She then remembered, and spoke with obvious difficulty, that during the previous session, when she interrupted to go to the bathroom, not only had she urinated but she also had defecated. I then stated, using material previously interpreted, that it seemed as if there was some kind of connection between her brain and her anus and, parodying Freud, I added that perhaps we should invite her ass to join the conversation. She laughed, and after a short pause talked about her younger sister, how she is demanding and mistreats her, envies everything she might be doing, makes remarks about her son's drug addiction, etc. She agrees with everything I say but does not seem to have a sincere insight: "You are right; I think I want to kill my sister but I don't want to know anything about it."

I think the interpretation might have been correct, perhaps because it was about material that she was not going to share spontaneously, and only referred to it after resistance was interpreted. However, I also felt at that moment that this was not a main issue because, after the interpretation, an important splitting took place, which allowed her to comply again with everything I said in order to render the interpretation completely useless. The interpretation was the analyst's own theory and she could go along with it but without any true insight. The possibility of any insight would be changed into faeces by the power of a very significant envy, and then defecated right on the spot.

At that moment I recalled X's fascist form of demeanour, of how he would use the same shibboleth against the opposition that they might have used against him. For example, if they said he was "corrupt" or "criminal", he would say the same about them. I felt Louise could conform to whatever I said: she could, like a chameleon, accommodate to any interpretation, while always keeping hidden away an envious and destructive part of herself. Next Monday, I thought, she will remember nothing of what I said, as if nothing had taken place, and she will easily conform to whatever I might then say. I felt she was trapped between the terrible need to comply while being fed through her ears with my interpretations, and the need to control a primitive and powerful envious element that changed whatever she might have received into faeces. It was as if there were not a thinking apparatus in her mind, but a primitive digestive system. Bion represented this state as $-(\female\male)$, qualified it as a "without-ness", and has alerted us to the seriousness of such a condition, describing it as:

> ... an internal object without an exterior. It is an alimentary canal without a body. It is a super-ego that has hardly any of the characteristics of super-ego as understood in psycho-analysis: it is "super" ego. It is an envious assertion of moral superiority without any morals ... The process of denudation continues till-$\female\male$ represents hardly more than an empty superiority–inferiority that in turn degenerates to nullity. [1965, p. 97]

The true self

Though we have learned about the difficulties that interfere with the realization of a true self from psychoanalysis and other therapies, it is important to keep in mind that other sciences, such as philosophy, are also concerned with this issue. There are always important resistances that impede the search for a sense of a true self, perhaps a tendency to avoid the painful attainment of individuation, loneliness, or the fatalism of becoming, of inexorably shifting towards nothingness. Ironically there is not a true self, for it becomes as it is made; there is not a path towards attaining it, for it takes place as we walk along. Winnicott (1960), states:

> The concept of a False Self needs to be balanced by a formulation of that which could properly be called the True Self ... [that] comes from the aliveness of the body tissues and the working of body-functions, including the heart's action and breathing ... There is but little point to understand the True Self, because it does no more than collect together the details of the experience of aliveness. [p. 148]

An intelligent adolescent, who was attempting to find a true expression of himself in comparison to his need to continuously please others, stated that the only situations in which he felt clear about not being an extension of others, were all related to his physical needs, such as thirst, hunger, or going to the toilet. "There," he said, "I am certain that it is me, I might agree with someone else that I want to urinate, but the urge is always mine." Likewise Freud discriminated between a central part of the self in direct contact with the instincts, and another part related to the outside world. Similarly, a patient who could not perceive that attacks to the setting were attacks she made on herself, produced the following dream almost at the end of her analysis. Her mother was stabbing her father because he had been unfaithful, but there was no blood. Then the mother was lying down on the floor, very pale as if she were dying, and was telling the father to call an ambulance. In the dream the patient could not understand why it was that the mother was dying if she was the one who had stabbed her husband, and why she was telling him to call an ambulance. There was no blood because it was as if the wounds were inside. "It was as if what my mother had done to my father she had really done to herself. Whatever happened to my father also happened to her. If I murder the analysis I murder myself."

True self is an attitude, a complete openness towards truth or towards the capacity to "contain"—as in container–contained— internal truth and deter internal lies, regardless of possible consequences. Bion said that truth is to the mind as food is to the body. The true self is the product of a process of reparation achieved by means of schizoid–paranoid and depressive (Ps $\Longleftarrow\Longrightarrow$ D) mechanisms, not as a purpose but as a corollary, as the product of a process of growth. The true self is not something to be achieved, but the consequence of a process summarized by a poet's expression: "Walker! there is no path, the path is made as you walk"; or by the Chinese word *shodoka*, used by the Zen master, meaning: *sho* = "the evident", *do* = "path", and *ka* = "song"; in other words, "the celebration of the evident path", or by the apothegm quoted from Plato at the beginning of this paper: what is that which is always becoming and never is?

Note

1. "This was the moment at which the first encounter with Mrs B's fiercely *guarded real self* appeared in the analysis. Her compliance, both in the analysis and at home, vanished. Now she expressed fury with me at the least sign of my not having understood her . . ." (Pines, 1982). "Her 'false self' came to the sessions, sat in the chair and talked for 50 minutes, while her 'true self' only appeared at the exit line" (Gabbard, 1982).

CHAPTER THREE

Preconceptual traumas and the "internal traumatic object"[1]

From the point of view of Bion's concept of "caesura"

"DOCTOR; You see her eyes are open
GENTLEWOMAN: Aye, but their sense are shut"

(Shakespeare: *Macbeth*, Act 5, Scene 1)

"God is a circle whose circumference is everywhere and whose centre is nowhere"

(Nicholas of Cusa)

I n this chapter I will be referring to clinical issues that obstruct the normal process of "mental growth" by hindering the mind's capacity to reason. Bion (1963) described mental growth (represented by Y) as a "preconception in search of a realization", where the tendency of such realization could sway like a pendulum, being either negative ($-Y$) if directed towards narcissism or positive ($+Y$) if aimed towards "social-ism". There are certain mechanisms that will result in enhancing while others will deter the process of mental growth. I will now consider those aspects that obstruct growth and which result in *murdering of the mind*, such as the

49

psychotic part of the personality *containing* the non-psychotic part, abhorrence of reality, identification with inanimate, self-envy mechanisms, and, most of all, splitting and projection of the mind and body as a defence against realization of traumatic events. This last aspect is the central theme of this chapter.

The caesura of time

The word *mystes* (μυστησ) from which words such as "mystery" or "mysterious" derived, was used by ancient Greeks during the practice of the "Eleusinian Mysteries," and meant "initiated", "adept", or those "whose lips were silent". The ritual consisted of a single night's experience that reunited about three thousand *mystes* and took place every year at the beginning of winter. Celebrated for more than fourteen hundred years, it was related to the myth of the goddess Persephone's return from the surface of the earth, as she reunited with her husband Hades, master of the underworld. What exactly took place during this experience, attended over the years by well-known Greeks and Romans such as Aristotle, Demosthenes, Plato, Marcus Aurelius, and so on, was completely unknown until recently, when in the mid 1960s, Karl Kerenyi (1997), a specialist in myths, discovered that the *kykeon* (κψκεον), a mixture of oats and mint, drunk by all the initiates during that night, was also contaminated with ergot (LSD). The toxic and hallucinatory reaction we often see now with hallucinogens is so private that it would have been impossible for the Greeks from those years to share the experience even among themselves, mostly because they did not possess the knowledge of its phenomenology and significance as we do today.

I have previously referred (Lopez-Corvo, 1995) to the "schizoid secret" to describe a similar kind of experience, sometimes observed in patients who were unable to remember facts that took place at preconceptual (or preverbal) stages in their lives and that were at the same time extremely significant. These could not be named or made conscious spontaneously because there was not yet in existence a language or an apparatus capable of thinking about them and understanding them. Instead, they were split off and projected, translated into feelings, sensations, somatic language, or incomprehensible actions similar to "ideographs" (Bion, 1967, p. 57). They might be found as material that structures dreams, as substance for transference and countertransference dimensions, motor discharges, tics, and so on, and are very often detected only by these means (Frank, 1969; Pines, 1980).

In "Inhibitions, symptoms and anxiety" Freud (1926d) states that "that there is much more continuity between intra-uterine life and earliest infancy than the impressive caesura of the act of birth would have us believe" (p. 138). Bion, on the other hand, has extended the metaphor of caesura to include the presence of a threshold that unites/separates different dimensions, like intra and extra-uterine life, night and day, or preconceptual and verbal thoughts. The caesura could be penetrated from either side or dimension, such as the way that occidental and oriental cultures had influenced each other. Picasso, said Bion, "once painted a picture on a glass that could be seen from either side, and women are penetrated from inside during childbirth and from outside during intercourse". He states: "Investigate the caesura; not the analyst: not the analysand; not the unconscious; not sanity; not insanity, but caesura, the link, the synapse, the (counter-trans)-ference, the transitive–intransitive mood. [1987, p. 56]

The "deaf-mute object" represents a preconceptual or pre-symbolic object impossible to name or seize, because it signifies the phenomenology of a distressing occurrence or trauma, which took place at such an early stage that processes of symbolization were not yet present and "naming" the absent object was unfeasible. The spoken word represents both a separation from and a link with the original object, requiring a process of mourning to occur in order to be able to move from the paranoid–schizoid to the depressive position, which represents the capacity to symbolize, to link the absence of the original thing with its representation. Projective identification, on the other hand, the mechanism used by the mind to rid itself of the continuous pain induced by trauma, stands for a language of action, an absence of mourning over the separation with the object, that which Segal (1957) refers to as the "symbolic equation".

Unable to become symbolized, the traumatic experience penetrates the caesura of time between the primitive preconceptual dimension and the present verbal one, representing an anachronism that declines to be named, like someone who could not understand the planetary movements because the differential calculus was not yet created. "After all", says Bion,

> if anatomists can say that they detect a vestigial tail, if surgeons likewise can say that they detect tumours which derive from the branchial cleft, then why should there not be what we would call mental vestiges, or archaic elements, which are operative in a way that is alarming and disturbing because it breaks through the beautiful, calm surface we ordinarily think of as rational, sane behaviour? [1987, p. 308]

However, this "deaf-mute" object is now in control of the "verbal mind" of these patients and is responsible for their incapacity to learn from experience and be able to find a way out of their mental pain. The problem of the analysis, on the other hand, is to penetrate the caesura from the other side, from the verbal to the preconceptual as a way to help the patient finally to name and seize the "spectre" in order to contain it instead of being contained by it. Bion also suggested the existence of certain conditions that could appear at a given moment so ephemeral, so imperceptible that we might not even be aware of them, but that could later on become so real that they might even destroy us without our even being conscious of such a happening (Lopez-Corvo, 2003, p. 152).

Phenomenology of the "traumatic object"

Deaf-muteness

I have observed a kind of resistance common to patients who share the history of significant traumas, genetic or induced, which originated during the preconceptual stage of development. The frequent concern that brought these patients for consultation was a high level of chronic anxiety, phobic preoccupations or symptoms, behaviour inhibition, or paralysis and depression. It was possible for the analyst to relate their symptomatology to the phenomenology of their specific trauma. The most important feature during the analytical process, common to all the cases, was a discrepancy between an apparent pressure and willingness to engage in analytical investigation as well as a fair understanding of the interpretation provided, while at the same time, there was an assiduous stubbornness to maintain the status quo. It was as if the patient were continuously dealing with a perpetual "absence" impossible to mourn or to contain. I had the phantasy of a surgeon unable to close a wound because there was not sufficient skin.

There was also an obsessive dissociation between an intellectual attitude and disposition about the understanding and handling of the interpretation, on one hand, and the splitting of emotions related to the circumstances of the trauma that were placed outside the self via projective identification. On the other hand, these emotions were experienced in the countertransference as a passive resignation, a sense of hopelessness and despair, of being trapped, as if there was "no way out", an angry need to be assisted, to be cured, and looked after or of having to do something.

Although the mental pain felt by the patients and the countertransference feelings experienced by the analyst were recognized as related to the trauma in the patients' discourse and intellectually understood by them, these patients presented a persistent incapacity to establish a true emotional link with those feelings that might have been elicited during the traumatic experience. For a significant part of the process the analysis presented the characteristics of a negative therapeutic reaction.

The patients understood what was interpreted, and often, as a willingness to help, added something of their own to the hypothesis presented by the analyst; however, at the next session the discourse was adamantly similar to the discourse of the preceding session. I had the feeling that the patient listened but did not hear what was introduced by the interpretation, as if we were dealing with a "deaf object". At the same time, the material discussed during the session, was not used by the patients afterwards, as if it vanished between sessions, or as if the patients were not able to talk to themselves about what was discussed during the analytical hour. I had the suspicion that the patients were not capable of talking to themselves either, because we were dealing not only with an internal "deaf object" but also with a "mute" one.[2] An important outcome was the discrepancy between the model the analyst progressively elaborated in his own mind following the understanding of the transference (in relation to how the traumatic event might have taken place, as well as the emotional implications it had on the patient), on the one hand, and the rigid pattern of defence continuously repeated by the patient in the analytical discourse, alien to the analyst's representation, on the other. These two models existed parallel to each other without ever touching, depicting Bion's concept of "reversal of perspective". The patient will always refer to the analyst's attempts of reconstruction as the "analyst's theories or models".

Splitting and projection of the mind

This condition seems to represent the consequence of a *minute splitting* of the early traumatic experience and the projection into the outside world, in such a way that it fills up and controls most of the livelihood of the person, although at the same time, the source or origin of the trauma was obstinately ignored or repressed, like the presence of an absence, or as something that very much *is*, but at the same time, *is not*. According to Bion, a crucial complication in dealing with the mental pain induced by early trauma is that, tangled with the projected split parts, there is also the mind lost in the projection, which is also absolutely necessary in order to revert the issue, meaning to contain and digest the mental pain involved. The attempt to recover the mind that has been split and projected together with the traumatic object, during the analytic treatment, could often result in the "catastrophic change" as a side effect observed when the analysis is relatively successful.

Another important aspect refers to the difficulty these patients seem to have about reversing the direction of projective identification, because as Bion stated,

> . . . these objects which are felt to have been expelled by projective identification become infinitely worse after expulsion than they were when originally expelled, the patient feels intruded upon, assaulted, and tortured by this re-entry even if willed by himself. [1967, pp. 62–63]

One of the patients I will refer to below once presented a dream where she was speaking nicely to her husband and there was also a man present, whom she did not recognize and who was there quietly listening. Then this man left but came back shortly after looking very disturbed, dirty, uncombed, with his fingers dappled with nicotine and signs of having used drugs, being very noisy and interfering with the conversation. I told her that the man represented the state of her projected terrors that she feared were trying to make their way back into her mind through my interpretations. Very often, projected part-objects are changed into faecal destructive elements coming back to attack and destroy internal good introjects.

Besides splitting and projection of the mind there is also a splitting and projection of the body, more significant in those cases where early traumas are related to the body's dysfunction, like genetic pathology. Splitting and projection of both mind and body could translate into a feeling of non-existence, something we will be dealing with in the case of Irene presented later.

Anal-sadism

One very important characteristic of the "traumatic object" refers to significant anal-sadistic traits, experienced as feelings of shame and persecution. A dream presented by Irene—a patient whose early trauma included an operation on her back—depicted the following:

> she was running because bad and mean men, who look like beggars, dirty and smelly, were persecuting her. She was running through her house, although it was not her house either, because it was like a maze. She was running with a little girl who was an orphan or something like that. She manages to get out of the house and is hiding behind some bushes. The little girl is making noises and she fears the men might hear and discover her. Then she found herself in her own bathroom but the floor was completely covered with excrement, and there was someone there, perhaps the mother of the little girl, and she felt very ashamed and was apologizing.

She said that she felt very disgusted and ashamed to talk about these things. I asked if she had soiled her underwear before she was operated on and she said she did not remember.

Envy against other siblings, experienced always as strong feelings of rivalry, is later on extended to anybody else who is felt free from the conflict implicit in the traumatic situation. The traumatic object presents itself as a cruel and persecutory superego element that induces a sense of shameful imperfection, which contrasts with split idealized parts projected into the outside object, that are enviously attacked in an attempt to invert the situation. This condition seems to be the consequence of an unconscious belief that feelings of "well being", if experienced, will induce the fury of the traumatic object and all the threat and anxiety attached to the traumatic experience will be re-experienced again. Suffering then becomes a protection that will neutralize the cruelty of the traumatic object and will induce a significant splitting of the personality. This splitting, always present in traumatic conditions, has an impact on the outcome of the analysis, because at the same time the patient's motivation for treatment hinges on the need to become free of mental pain. However, achieving such a desire automatically induces sadistic threats from the traumatic object about the traumatic condition being implemented again. Or, in other words, the ego is trapped between a desire to feel well and the terror to do so. This condition then explains the dynamic of the deaf-mute characteristic of the transference.

The cases

Now I will refer to three patients who shared in common serious preconceptual traumatic experiences, and who also presented a series of characteristics in their analysis related to their incapacity to distinguish and verbalize the emotional impact of these traumas. There was the consequence of dealing with the "nameless terror" induced by an *extreme* absence which at the same time determined an *extreme* presence. For instance, I had the feeling that one of the patients became a medical doctor in order to make sure that he was not going to know what he so much feared to know. Other factors in common were the existence of other siblings who were not exposed to any trauma and who became a source of intense envy and rivalry, as if an important aspect of the traumatic experience pivots on the relativity of the contrast, when they compared themselves with trauma-free siblings. There is also, at the same time, a great amount of envy from trauma-free children towards the traumatized sibling, as a consequence of misinterpretation of the care and concern provided to these children.

A very important matter I have previously stated, and would like to repeat, is the need to split the mind and to project it outside as an essential defence to avoid repetition of the painful impact of reality as it was experienced at the time when the early traumatic incident took place. The problem, however, with this kind of defence is the fabrication of a trap where the continuous projection of the mind, or "apparatus for thinking", as a way to get rid of the trauma deprives the patient of what is now required to solve the problem.

Case 1

Irene is a twenty-five-year-old fraternal twin to another girl, single, intelligent, physically attractive, who has just finished school and is looking for a job. She was diagnosed as having a spina bifida occulta and had to experience, when she was five or six years of age, a series of medical examinations and, finally, a surgical intervention. At the beginning of high school she was diagnosed with learning disabilities and limited intelligence, having to change school from the "nice one" she was attending with her sister, to another far away from where she lived, filled with "dropouts and losers". She started to use drugs and changed into a "rebellious punk" until her parents denounced her to the police and threatened to commit her.

She complained of chronic *phobic anxiety and crises of panic*, lives with her parents, has no friends and seldom goes out even at weekends. She was previously treated for two years with psychotherapy and medication without any result. As happens often with patients experiencing early traumatic experiences, Irene attached little importance to the event of the operation and this only became obvious as the analysis progressed. It was a difficult and painful process just to talk about this experience, which she has fragmented and projected into the external world because she experienced such discussion as a possible reintrojection of the spina bifida and its operation. For over a year she refused to come more than once a week, strongly entrenched behind the resistance of not making her anxiety her own affair, refusing to make use of her mind to think, but projecting her conflict into the analyst instead, in order to borrow his mind while remaining mindless. As the analysis continued, she was able to accept interpretations pointing out the importance of memories of images and emotions such as terror, uncertainty, distrust, anger, frustration, and so on, related to the event: "like being repeatedly manipulated and tortured, around the genital area by masked men, with her mother's consent"; about the extension of the scars, how ugly they looked, and about her body being deformed, not clean, damaged and imperfect. She feared to "reveal" her body, always wearing trousers, well-buttoned dark-coloured clothes, even in summer, as a shield of protection to placate her fear of feeling exposed, as if the scars were everywhere; a condition also present in the transference. By the beginning of the second year of treatment she accepted coming twice weekly.

Envy towards others considered "healthy" was an important issue; to her sister more than anybody else, to the point that they had little to do with each other and frequently got involved in bitter quarrels. Not being able to understand the true nature of her disease and suffering, her sister also reacted with envy because she felt excluded from the "special attention" she thought Irene was receiving. She always initiates her sessions with strong criticisms of boyfriends, classmates, family, and so on, as if she was enviously attacking them as a protection against the pain of exclusion, because she felt absolutely certain everybody, including the analyst, has already robbed her of being healthy.

As the analysis progressed, certain changes started to take place. There was a switch from a narcissistic kind of object relations to a more social one. She finished her studies as a designer and initiated a love relationship with B, a former classmate. Reference to the spina bifida operation became a common issue, without eliciting the anxiety previously experienced. On one occasion she said that her parents were away and she was sleeping with her boyfriend. Her sister came in late and came up to her room to let her know she was also with her boyfriend, and for her not to "freak out" if she were to meet him. She explains that she is always afraid someone will come when she is alone and do something bad to her. This is why she asked her boyfriend to stay. "I fear to see someone when I look at myself in the mirror, somebody from behind that could attack me." I said she wished for me to reintroduce the projected "spina bifida" part in a way that it will not be frightening for her, and will not make her freak out, as she usually feels when she experiences panic attacks or feels that the spina bifida part will attack her from behind (her scars from the operation are on her lower back).

She then remembers a dream in which she met a boyfriend she used to go out with, who was very crazy. He was very nice but became very aggressive when she rejected him, "I was afraid of him". I say that ignoring the spina bifida will make it dangerous and could make her crazy, but to remember and to contain the pain related to these memories, might render it friendly. She says she fears that if she talks freely about what the little girl in her went through, it will be as if she will forget the terrible things she experienced, meaning the anger, the frustration, and the feeling of revenge. (I think this fear, of the return of the projected trauma, might be responsible for the passivity often observed in traumatic situations.) She feels "marked", like broken merchandise nobody wants, and as a consequence, feels she has no rights to anything, like asking her parents for money to pay for her treatment or to find a good job. She has no place of her own, feels guilty even for being alive, occupying a place, even for breathing and existing. Then I said, "As if you would have to become your trauma in order to find your place."

At the next session she says that she wants to understand what I say about remembering her operation, that she tries but does not seem to be able to do it, to remember it. There is a long silence. "I remember once going to a fair when I was around six or seven, it was about the time of the operation. I was in one of those games and I won and could choose any of the stuffed animals they had there, I wanted to choose a big black cat, but my mother and my sister, who were there also, said that it was too ugly, that how could I choose something like that, and in the end I gave up, although I didn't want to choose anything else because I only wanted that cat." I said that an internal "mother–sister object" also convinced her that her operation is like the stuffed cat, too ugly to be remembered. "Yeah," she answered, "it was like that because my mother is that type who doesn't want you to think about something that is unpleasant, and she did not want me to think about the operation because it was horrible and it was over." "But the conflict seems to continue," I said, "so that not to think about it because an internal mother is forbidding you to do so, is not helping you to get rid of its terrible consequences either."

She then said she had two cats, one very friendly that goes out and she fears it could be stolen and another one, frightened, that usually remains inside the closet. She says she feels the same in relation to her sister, who goes away anytime without ever being afraid; she just came back from holiday and said she had a good time with her new boyfriend in the Caribbean. "She travels and changes boyfriends without any difficulty, very different from me." I said: "Similar to your two cats." "Yes," she answered, "I once went to the Bahamas and I couldn't move from the airport because I had a panic attack." Then she narrates a dream:

She is in a party at a big house and there are many known celebrities, all actors that she recognizes. They go upstairs and one of them strikes her back and smacks her buttocks, something she finds disrespectful but she turns away and says nothing. She likes the environment of the dream, but she feels it is similar to what she sees at some places where she has been looking for work, a bunch of "bull-shitters".

The actors are from a television police programme she watches often, and she feels attracted to the main character. She provided no further associations and I say that the dream seems to present dissociation between the "spina bifida part" and another idealized or "celebrity part". She dreams about what she wants but fears she cannot have, like a position she feels is accessible to her sister and other privileged people such as celebrities, who are free from the horrible mark of the spina bifida. Not to complain when she gets smacked by the actor in the dream represents her desire, that someone like that man could desire her, meaning that she would be free of the mark; but at the same time there is the ambivalence, the spuriousness of her own idealization, because she fears they could be a bunch of "bull-shitters". After I make a comment about this issue, she remarks: "I have to find the real me."[3]

Some time later she says laughingly that she asked her boyfriend to change the sheets that had been on his bed for over a year. After a pause she says that she was eating with her parents, and her father was chewing and making funny noises with his mouth and her mother was also making noises when she breathed because she is a heavy smoker. After a while she left the room. Next Friday she will be going to the beach with her boyfriend for four days. She feels angry at him and feels like kicking him, because he is not strong and lacks initiative, "I know what you are going to say"—she responds rapidly, perhaps parodying my interpretation and trying to placate me—"that he is the kind of man that a part of me likes, although another part of me does not, but that I need him as someone to be angry at because he is like a lazy part of me." I said that perhaps she feels entitled to something better, like a cleaner sheet, and is also tired of living inside her parents' ass listening to their bowels' "noises", and that she might want to have someone to rescue her. She remembers a dream:

She is shopping using a cart to buy healthy food, not like her boyfriend and his family who like junk food. After she finishes buying, she leaves the carriage unattended and someone takes it away and she has to find another cart to do more shopping, something she finds upsetting. Then she wants to buy some corn on the cob but when she tries to put the cobs into the carriage she feels they are mushy, but decides to take them.

She speaks of that being strange, because corn is always hard and cannot get all soft like that. I said that she came to shop at the analysis for something "healthy" she could take with her during her trip, but that the "spina bifida" part of her, out of envy, robs her of her "healthy" shopping, but she is learning to struggle against that and even if it is unpleasant, she buys the healthy items again to avoid being like her boyfriend, feeding on unhealthy faeces like food. However, she also feels that her boyfriend's penis,[4] and perhaps her father's and my own, are mushy and do not protect or rescue her from being lost inside her parents' ass. "After all," I said, recalling something she has previously said, "you only remember your mother being present, but never your father, during the time of the operations."

A few days later she presented an interesting dream:

She was with her boyfriend trying to rescue a little girl who was snatched by bad men; however, not only were they unable to set her free, but every time they tried, the little girl became even younger and Irene was afraid that at the end she was going to disappear without them being able to save her. There was also the fact that every time they met the little girl in the process of liberating her, she was never able to recognize them.

Irene identifies in this dream her own struggle with the "spina bifida issue". I add that her boyfriend in the dream may be related to me, and also that the cruelty of the spina bifida aspect in her is represented by the snatchers, the bad men. She is striving to think differently, to be less deaf to what we talk about and more aware of those associations that relate to her fears, her traumatic experience, and her work connected with rescuing the frightened and elusive good-child part in her. Resistances about such recognition is also present in the tendency of the child continuously to become younger, as well as in the incapacity to recognize her rescuers, perhaps as an expression of her own difficulty to grasp and name the preconceptual elusiveness of the early trauma. This is often translated into the transference as a "deaf-mute" element that hinders her capacity to grasp, to recognize, and to make use of the interpretation afterwards.

A week later she brought a dream that portrayed two important issues: (i) defences pointing towards a possible "catastrophic change", or the tendency to accuse the analysis for being responsible for disagreeable side effects, and (ii) the cruel and envious menace from the "traumatic object" that demands that she suffer or be "dead", instead of feeling well or being alive.

> She is walking on a road by herself near the border of a cliff when suddenly a silver car appears and stops right in front of her. It is a four-wheel-drive, modern-looking car. Then a little girl comes out and starts to attack her, trying to stab her and she falls down the precipice and lies there and pretends to be dead to prevent the little girl from killing her, but she is uncomfortable and then moves and the little girl attacks her again, but she manages to get hold of a stick that then changes into a pencil, and she stabs and kills the little girl. Then she climbs up the precipice and the silver truck is still there and they open the door and invite her in. The people in the car seemed like a family, and there were other little girls inside that were ready to find other people and then, if killed, were going to be exchanged like they did with her.

The truck she associates with me: "the silver hair", she says, although she wonders about the car being modern. I said that I have "actualized" the "spina bifida issue", and made her aware of its relevance. This envious internal element would attack her only if she is alive, but not if she is "dead". It is an inner part envious of her own aliveness; she would have to be dead, meaning to suffer continuously and to be so frightened that she could not go out but be confined inside her parent's house–anus.

She said that today, when coming to my office, she suddenly felt different from other times, she felt unaware of people around her as she usually feels, and that she felt fine. She is always aware of other people and senses them as if they were different, from a different planet, usually threatening, and she feels frightened. This feeling of been unaware of people around lasted only a few minutes and then she went back to her usual self. I said that all will depend upon whether she manages to deal with the threat from the "spina bifida part" in her, that then she might feel she has the right to be alive and feel well like the others around her. If she gets rid of the spina bifida, she will be part of my family and will go in my silver car helping others to do the same with their own spina bifida. I also said that she might fear those other people different from her because they do not have spina bifida, the people who were attacked by her due to envy and who might retaliate, something that keeps her from venturing outside without being very frightened.

Some time after, she arrived very late and stated that her father had asked her to accompany him while moving her sister's belongings to a nearby city, where she is going to attend university, that they did not care about her appointment, although she clearly told them she had to be back at a certain hour. "My sister doesn't care about anything. When she was leaving, she handed me a pair of pants I thought were hers, but she said that they were mine and that I have to unstitch them because she fixed them to fit her." I said she is trying to unstitch her twin in order to find her own skin. She then remembers a dream:

> She was in a raft with somebody else. There were many sharks in the water and somebody threw a dog that was in the raft into the water where it was attacked by the sharks.

She said that she does not like dogs because they are too unpredictable, vicious, and dangerous. I said that the dog is an angry and vicious part of herself and the sharks are the spina bifida that eat her aggression and feeling of righteousness, which she needs to fight for herself. She came late because she is struggling to try to find for herself a way out, to unstitch herself from her twin sister, because she feels trapped between two extremes, either remaining forever stitched or unleashing anger that could become vicious and unpredictable.

She remembers another dream:

> She is walking with an actor from the 1980s at night in a large city she does not recognize. She can see the lights of a "wow" city. There is only one road that goes up and down. Then she realizes she has a hole in her left arm that starts to get worse; now she can see through it and her arm becomes hollow inside and she goes to see a doctor, who says that it is a cyst, but she will be fine if the cords don't get pinched.

She did not associate it with the spina bifida but when I ask, she recognizes that her operation might have been in the 1980s. She did not know what a cyst meant but "should be something similar to what you get in your breast". I said her spina bifida occulta could have been like a cyst, and also suggested that the image of the hollow arm in the dream could represent what the spina bifida was for her in her mind at the time of the operation, as she was unable to look at it because it was on her back. By this time we were over the hour and while leaving, she added something very important; she associated the street that goes up and down in the dream, with her spine: "it was only one street and it was very long".

She came on time to the next session, and said she had had an interview for a job that went very well; lately she has been doing some research about where to call to find work, and found these people; she feels very enthusiastic, although a bit scared. She talked to an old friend she had not seen for some time because she thought he was angry at her because of something she said, but it was all right, he was very warm and she feels it was all in her imagination: "I am always throwing the dog to the sharks", she said referring to her last dream. She talked about her two cats. She is helping the frightened one to get out of the house, bringing him out and then stroking him nicely in an attempt to keep him outside. She feels she has been very successful so far, because she managed to keep him outside for as long as an hour. She gives him treats when he manages to stay longer. Pause. She remembered the dream from the other day, about the "hollow arm": "I have been thinking about it, and the city that I see with the road going up and down. I think I told you that the road is my spine and the city is what we have talked about, that my spine and the spina bifida I find them everywhere in the whole city. The doctor in the dream said that the 'cords' should not be pinched, and I don't know why she said 'cords' and not veins, because I saw only veins in the hollow arm, but my parents had always said that the doctor who did my operation 'cut some cords that were holding me down" and that I grew about an inch and a half immediately after the operation."

I think there were, at this time, important changes in Irene. This dream represents an attempt to remember exactly what took place during the spina bifida operation. It is also a beautiful condensation and displacement, representing something we have talked about often, the projection of her trauma "everywhere in the city", portrayed by the city's only street going up and down, representing the spine. Other changes are portrayed by her serious search for work; her attempt to find out about her friend and the conclusion that it was the product of her own projection that induced the feelings she held for so long towards him; also, her spontaneous involvement to change the fearful behaviour of her cat. However, the most important achievement was a new attitude about being able to talk to herself regarding what took place during the previous session, of thinking regarding the dream and bringing fresh hypotheses, as if she was resolving her "inner muteness" and, for the first time, was indeed attempting to talk to herself. Another issue of great relevance was the act of "throwing the dog to the sharks", present in the dream of the raft. I think this element portrays the part of herself she needs in order to contain her fears and to struggle for sanity. Bion (1967) has stated that "As a result of these splitting attacks, all those features of the personality which should one day provide the foundation for *intuitive understanding of himself and others* are jeopardized at the outset. (p. 47, my italics).

In summary, traumatic events provoke "terror of reality" that also induces the need to get rid of the mind, as the organ that perceives it, by means of minute splitting and projection outside; however, an important complication of this mechanism is that the mind projected, like the dog in my patient's dream, is also required *for the intuitive understanding of herself.*

A year after the session I have just referred to above, Irene has managed to find a steady job, is driving a car alone for the first time, and has improved, to a large extent from her phobic anxiety. At one session, she begins by saying that she has lowered her status in her new employment, in comparison with the previous job: "On my new business cards I am a designer while on the previous one I was an art director". However, she feels better in her new position because "people are nicer". I said that she seems to have doubts about her true "selfness" and needs a card to certify her status. After a pause she states: "There is something very important I want to tell you. My mother insists that I am bulimic, that she heard me vomiting in the bathroom, and this is absolutely false, and I denied it, but she insisted and then told my father who believed her, although I insistently told him that it wasn't true. I am concerned because she will make me do something." She looks worried. I ask: "What does it mean, to do something?" "Well, to see someone, I guess", she answered. "Like whom?" "A doctor, I guess." I then said that she seemed to be dealing with many confusions at once, that she is convinced, and is trying also to convince me, that she will be unable to produce a sensible argument with her mother about the vomiting and, even worse, she will not be able to convince the doctor either, who will be, like her father, an extension of her powerful and dangerous mother. I also said that I am wondering if she might not be dealing with something else, similar to the card that "decides" her status, as she does not seem to know if she is dealing with an internal or with an external mother. "Well", she answered, "my mother could kick me out of the house like she did with my brother." She remained silent for a while and then said that she remembered a scene where she was at the hospital, in a tall bathtub, or maybe she was little, perhaps five or six years old, and her mother is washing her hair, or giving her a bath: "I have a feeling, then and now, that I was touching bottom, a feeling of emptiness and hopelessness. I think it might have been before or after the operation." I then said: "I wonder if it could have been before the operation, that your mother was bathing you for the operation, and you felt caressed and loved by her at that moment and then asked if she was taking you home with her and she said no, that you have to stay for the operation next day. Then perhaps you felt hopeless, that you had touched bottom, like someone condemned to capital punishment, who has extinguished all possibilities and is waiting to die; and also, you might like me to protect you by preventing these feelings of emptiness and hopelessness from continuously assaulting you."

It seemed as if the main issue she was dealing with at this particular moment was the considerable power that she felt came from a cruel "internal maternal object", often induced by an envious, hidden, "bulimic" attack against parental harmony, also present in the transference. This dynamic induced early experiences—like the bath that took place nineteen years before—to change from a temporary into a permanent event, like an everlasting print that did not become, but trapped her instead, as if she still were a helpless little girl, paralysed and useless, who lacked the freedom to decide and stand up by herself.

Case 2

Beatrice is a twenty-seven-year-old, single graduate of Italian descent, who worked at a hospital as a research fellow. She came to treatment three years before the material now presented, due to high levels of anxiety, insomnia, and depression. She was the youngest of four siblings, two girls and two boys. *There was 10 years of difference between Beatrice and her immediate older sister.* She was previously in therapy for about two years but had to discontinue when her therapist moved to another city.

> Her discourse was very much the same for at least two years, and only in the last few sessions did a change start to appear. Usually she will

come, lie down, and complain about how stressed she feels, the high level of anxiety usually when she wakes up, of how little time she has for herself as well as her boss's irrational and inconsiderate demands; she usually expresses her complaints with a contrasting smile that seems to cover up a feared and concealed rage. She has also been dealing with her mother's diagnosis of cancer made three months before. From very early in her treatment we managed to understand the importance of the age difference with the other siblings, which provided her with a feeling of no importance. During one session she remembered a repetitious situation at dinnertime, when her parents and her older siblings would engage in political or philosophical discussions leaving her out, which made her feel painfully ignored. As a way to deal with such a continuous threat, she split the feeling of insignificance together with that part of her mind capable of thinking about it, and tried to free herself from the mental pain with the use of projective identification. The result was a continuous incapacity to resolve the conflict because not only did she lack the competence to think about the issue, but also she found the threat of insignificance in most of her everyday interactions. She came to analysis with the unconscious purpose of "borrowing" the analyst's mind in order to deal with her anxiety, as well as to be guided and told what to do, as if she were an inanimate object, a machine and not an alive person. In contrast to the patient described in Case 1, Beatrice brought few dreams, a condition that reminded me of what Scott[5] once said about self-envy, how the awake part envies the dreaming one. She complained of great anxiety every day as soon as she awakes, as if her omnipotent conscious mind finds it very difficult to delegate to her unconscious, or to postpone solving her problems until the next day, as if she feels bad about not being consciously present because she was away sleeping. Such inability to delegate represents the centre of the conflict in any chronic insomnia.

As a very early form of defence she resorted to excelling in any field in which she became involved, to such an extreme that she often got hurt. She started piano lessons at six years of age and did very well, winning prizes and being able to execute public performances with success; but she had to stop due to painful cramps in both hands. A similar story took place in her practice of gymnastics, which she also had to give up because of a serious injury to her back. She established with her piano teacher, old enough to be her grandfather, a sort of sado-masochistic relationship in which he manipulated their liaison in a rather perverse manner, with sexual manipulations and promises of complete success (supra-significant), combined with cruel threats and coercion of abandonment (insignificance), if she were not to abide by his demands. At the same time he became her "champion", or someone who was going to provide her with a complete manic triumph in her rivalry with the rest of her older siblings, now scattered worldwide.

The level of anxiety was always very high because of the superego demand of outshining herself in order to carry an envious vengeance against her parents and siblings, by projecting into them her feelings of insignificance. Therefore, consequent guilt and an unconscious need for punishment derived in a sort of circularity, which was always translated into a greater anxiety. With the years, this condition extended to all of her everyday activities and she would carry on with her life as if in a deadly form of competition. The feeling of insignificance always split and projected, remained hidden and threatening as if around every corner: at home with her parents and siblings, at work, with friends and in the analysis. At the beginning of every session she states how extremely anxious she feels about her work, her mother's condition, a presentation she will have to make to her boss, with her boyfriend, and so on. She never refers to whatever hypothesis we might have elicited during the previous session to explain her anxiety, although she gets involved and repeats with evident interest the content of the interpretation given at the moment. It seems as if she is extremely ambivalent, desiring to free herself from her anxiety, and at the same time feeling very angry and envious about what the analyst has to say and the powerful need to render the analyst completely "insignificant".

At one point, she says after a short silence that she was trying to remember something she wanted to talk about, something she thought about before coming. "I think that I am not able to remember because the days I come here I also have a massage, and I feel very cloudy, I cannot think very clearly but I also feel less anxious and more relaxed." I said that perhaps she does not need a mind, because she wishes for me to use my mind to give her a massage. "Well," she says, "I come to find directions of how to get rid of my anxiety." "The problem", I then add, "is that if you come to see me to give you a 'massage' in order to find directions to get rid of your anxiety, we will be leaving you out, and that, I think, will be rather unfair for you, because it will make me very important but it will make you very insignificant."

It was difficult for her to imagine that there was nothing in her everyday reality that could justify the amount of anxiety to which she was referring, meaning that she was unconsciously and incessantly inventing ways to torture and terrorize herself. At the same time, she wanted somebody else to find an answer to free her from the anxiety state she had created, but without her taking any active role in the search, and, even more important, attacking and destroying any possible hypothesis provided to her through the interpretation. Obviously, an important part of herself was very successful in generating a chronic state of anxiety, while at the same time splitting and projecting her "thinking apparatus" in order to use the analyst's mind with the purpose of rendering it useless. The problem, as I saw it, was that she was trying to free herself from feelings of insignificance by projecting them out into others to make herself significant; a sort of a metamorphosis from insignificant to super-significant; but done with such cruelty that her own state of well being was not considered, and she became paralysed with terrible anxiety and hopeless despair. But even this mechanism was insufficient, because she felt then like an "infra-insignificant" disguised as a "supra-significant", becoming terrified of being discovered, and always feeling false as an impostor.

On one occasion she pointed out a certain change. The first day she came back after the Easter holidays, she stated that she went away to Margarita Island with her girlfriend, Elisa, felt very good and had a wonderful time. While there, she met a nice guy, and at the end spent one night with him, something she had never done before in such a short time and with an unknown man. "Elisa is a very good looking and sexy girl, very successful with men, very different from me, because I usually feel uncertain, that they don't like me. This time it was the opposite, I don't know exactly why, but I felt more at ease and it seems that men were more interested in me than Elisa. The guy I am telling you about ... we were dancing at a discotheque, then he suggested going to another one, and I knew what he was planning but I went along with it. On the way he said to go to his apartment and I consented, feeling very relaxed. It was like a new experience, I was not frightened as I previously felt with men." I agreed that it was a new experience. Not only was she not complaining about feeling stressed or anxious as she did before on similar occasions, but also she did not feel she had to protect herself from men who were trying to use and hurt her so she would have to try to make them useless. She listened carefully to what I said and agreed with it, and then as if she had not listened, she added: "I think my mother wants me to stay there with her because she does not feel comfortable with my brother and sisters."

Case 3

Manuel was a fifty-five-year-old patient, married with three children, second of three siblings, the son of European medical doctors who came to Venezuela during the Spanish Civil War, when the patient was only five years of age. His parents settled in the interior of the country, due to government regulations, until the patient moved to Caracas to study medicine. Manuel was born with a congenital kidney defect that required early monitoring and later a surgical intervention. The patient often remembered the continuous preoccupation of both parents about his physical health, examining him often or requesting urine tests. He felt that in comparison with the other siblings he was overprotected, creating the feeling that he was different. Even to the present time he has a very poor relationship with them, especially with his younger brother. He came for consultation because of marital conflicts, unspecific anxiety, and depression. He had an extramarital relationship for several years with a colleague, with whom he felt relaxed and well understood, in contrast to his wife, who was described as very selfish and emotionally dependent.

I felt that any hypothesis presented as an interpretation was heard and discussed by the patient, but later on, during the next session, he did not mention it at all and continued repeating the same issues as if nothing had taken place, as if we were dealing with a sort of "deaf-mute" internal object. It seemed as if it were impossible for him to learn from his experience and to grow out of the repetitious pattern. For a long time the sessions were reiterative, almost boring, a feeling Manuel often complained about, as if there was an intense need to exercise an omnipotent control in order to maintain the status quo, where any change became a threat and elicited often a narcissistic rage.

I had very often interpreted that in the relation between his wife and his lover there was a replication of what he had emotionally experienced during his childhood in relation to both of his parents: emotions associated to his mother, that she was very selfish and responsible for his disease, were displaced on to his wife, and those related to his father were projected on to his lover, who, being also a doctor, was going to take care of and protect him as he felt his father did when he was a child. He was in analysis three times weekly and this session is from a Wednesday. He lay down and said: "I talked with Lilia about how bad our marriage is. I told her that I wanted a divorce; she reacted strongly, very angry, insulting me, calling me selfish and stupid She also questioned whereabouts was my kidney, referring to what I have told her *you said*, that I was repeating a conflict from my childhood related to my kidney problem. She also said that I was very aggressive against her and the children because I didn't care about any of them. To end my marriage terrifies me, to leave X (his lover) also, to have both or to have neither of them terrifies me as well.

He remembers a dream he had that morning.

> During the first part he is in an aeroplane going somewhere and he is sitting with me (the analyst) and another colleague who works with him at the hospital. Then he says to the analyst that there are no side effects with the medicine he is taking. Then there is a second part of the dream, where he is sitting in a park and sees his elder son. He looks older, aged, with a hard countenance, as if he had lost his childhood innocence. In the third part there are several men fixing a road, working very hard, dressed in tough clothes.

He associates the first part, about the side-effects, with something the analyst said about the kidney, that his parent's attitude and that of himself was that "here everything is all right, there are no side-effects", as if there were not psychological repercussions to the kidney problem. He said: I don't know how you could get inside the kidney problem and associate it to the troubles I have with my wife and X. Then I said: "Not how *I* could get inside." Then he said, interrupting, "Well, how *we* get inside" and I said, "Not that either, it will be better to say, how could *you* get *inside* of it yourself." Then he stated that the colleague in the dream is vegetarian, and the other day he invited her, together with other doctors from the hospital, to a meat restaurant, but then realized she was vegetarian and that he had to find some vegetarian place, which was not easy and made him angry at her. He thought that there might have been a reason why he felt that way. In relation to his son, his face in the dream reminded him of a friend from childhood who once told him that his father was rather ruthless and once, when he did not want to eat, his father very aggressively forced him to do it. His son—the one in the dream—is at this moment facing a difficult financial situation at his work, and Manuel feels that his son is losing his innocence. The third part of the dream he thinks is related to the work he had to do in the analysis to solve his conflicts, mostly his mental suffering. He recalls the myth of "Tantalus's punishment" and feels that he is in a similar predicament of not being able to drink from the water that is surrounding him, that every time he tries, it moves away. Then I said that he was trying to convince me and himself that his kidney problem did not have any side-effects, but he is aware that the vegetarianism of his colleague does have an unpleasant side-effect because he feels angry and has to go out to buy special food. He also associates me with his friend's father, as if I was pushing him into the "food of side effects" and was forcing him to lose his innocence, and, like Tantalus, he was trying not to drink, not to know. I also added that a "tough work", like that in his dream, was awaiting us ahead in order to repair the damage and to patch the absences. Perhaps the rough part was also related to an immense feeling of anger and envy against his parents, his mother who made him imperfect and different from his siblings, also his ambivalence about his father and me, who had not been able to spare him from his fear and suffering. In order to remain "innocent" and not to know, he has to become like Tantalus and not drink from his own history.

During the next session he stated that he felt anxious about giving a conference. It was not so much giving the conference, but preparing it could become a real torture. I said that since he got rid of his mind in order not to think about his kidney problem, he feels that he has no mind left to prepare anything. However, once he is there giving his conference he finds out that this is not true. At one point he said that he remembered a short dream featuring two pencils, and said that he thinks one pencil was his and the other was mine. I said that each of us was writing at the same time about two different issues, but the problem was that we were not communicating with each other. Then he remembered another dream, where he had booked surgery for two patients at the same time, and I added that perhaps he was telling us that he was becoming aware of the existence of the two different issues. He associated to a film, where someone invites a girlfriend to a country house and they try to cook lobsters but are afraid to put them into the boiling water, and they play, and the man, who is a photographer, takes pictures and they have a wonderful time. Later on, he invites another woman, but this time, when he tries to repeat the same situation as before, this woman is different because she is more serious and does not play at being afraid like the previous girl and just drops the lobsters inside the pan. I said to the patient that the two issues represented two parts of himself. One part plays like a child, making games out of serious matters, such as, for instance, not wanting to be aware that his wife might suffer a great deal if she were to know that he was having an affair with another woman and also his lover would suffer, too, because she was "entertaining marriage". At the same time, another part of himself could feel like acting like the second woman in the movie, throwing the lobster in the pan, when I make references about how difficult it might be for him to deal with a wife and a lover, or having experienced a kidney cancer. To become aware terrifies him, so instead he would prefer to make a game of the analysis There were also important envious feelings experienced by the "traumatic object" against any healthy sign given by anybody, which paralyses him, a trend very much present in the transference.

Notes

1. I have preferred to use "preconceptual" instead of "pre-verbal trauma", because I am not referring just to speech, but to conceptual stages of development related to symbol and ideograms formation. Using Piaget's theoretical model this would correspond to the period of "concrete operations", previous to "formal operations", meaning before the age of ten to twelve years.

2. Another explanation about the existence of a deaf-mute condition, was presented by Bion (1967) when he states, that in some patients, the question "why", which depends on causation, such as, "why the patient and the analyst are there", has been split off out of guilt, (perhaps related to death wishes, although Bion did not clarify this) and instead a superficial "what" might take its place (p. 102).

3. I have previously referred to this issue as "The forgotten self". See Chapter Two.

4. The association of corn with a penis could also be sustained by the fact that, unlike other food (vegetables) of similar shape, the way that it is eaten resembles an act of fellatio.

5. See Chapter Four.

Self-envy

From the point of view of "part objects" and "link" theory

"As a dog was crossing a river with a piece of meat in his mouth, he saw, as he thought, another dog under the water upon the very same adventure. He never considered that the one was only the image of the other; but, out of greediness to get the two, he jumped at the shadow and lost both. One because it had not existed, so he could not get it, the other because the current took it away"

(Aesop: *The Dog and his Shadow*)

"There are people whose contact with reality presents the most difficulty when that reality is their own mental state"

(Bion)

I have previously referred to self-envy (López-Corvo, 1992, 1995, 1996b, 1999, 2003) as a condition resulting from an envious interaction between different part objects composing the Oedipus structure. Let us suppose, for instance, that there is an important increment in the amount of envy that a child who is feeling excluded experiences towards his parents, and that this envy is mostly directed to what the child acknowledges as feelings of harmony, love, sexuality, creativity, communication, etc., between the couple. As the years go by, these feelings could become idealized and remain in the self as "foreign" elements not completely assimilated by the ego. When this child grows and becomes an adult, just like his parents, the envious element that remains unassimilated inside could again be reactivated, but this time, however, such elements previously envied in his parents are now part of himself.[1] This condition is always reflected in the transference as a sustained attack against idealized links between analyst and patient, experienced as a "creative", "productive", and "harmonious" analytic couple. This situation could either turn into a negative therapeutic reaction, or induce a premature disruption of treatment.

I specifically remember the case of a diabetic patient who, very often in the midst of the session when something relevant was taking place, would interrupt to go to the bathroom, as if there existed a direct connection between her mind and her bladder. The diabetes also became a model to understand how my interpretations symbolized food she did not use, similar to sugar in diabetics, which eventually is expelled through urine. A few months later, when holidays were close, she announced for the first time in four years that she wanted to discontinue her analysis. However, during the days that preceded the date of our departure, and together with the separation anxiety related to it, there were also new feelings, revealing a different use given to discoveries she obtained in her analysis. During one session she stated that in the past she thought nothing about what took place in the session; she would usually go to the bathroom, and then drive to a coffee shop where she "got something sweet in order to get rid of the bitterness of the session". However, lately she was doing it differently: "I was thinking about the dream I had yesterday[2] ... do you think that there could be more than one interpretation? I really believe that you are the one who appeared in the dream", and further on: "Last night I was drawing mandalas[3] from a book and in one of them, there was one that looked just like the crater in the dream."

What I think was important here was her new preoccupation with what was taking place during her analysis, even beyond the limits of the session, which was different from before when she was continuously trying to expel interpretations through her emunctories, or to neutralize with a candy what she felt was a "bitter criticism". However, it was very interesting to observe that now, when for the first time these changes of attitude were taking place, representing the beginning of a creative analytic couple, or the manifestation of a productive link that induced her to continue investigating on her own, that it was at this precise moment that her desire to leave the analysis also appeared. I felt that perhaps behind her acting out there were inner feelings of self-envy, as I have described above.

All envy is essentially a form of self-envy, because we always envy those elements that have been previously idealized internally, and then, when projected into others, we end up envying in them exactly what we originally had envied in ourselves. Understanding the dynamics present in self-envy is easy, thanks to the structure of the mind presented by Klein and followers; however, there are also views consistent with the concept of self-envy presented by Freud in 1932, when he referred to unconscious mechanisms of guilt, which we could now very well associate with envy between different part objects in the self. Freud stated:

I once succeeded in freeing an unmarried woman, no longer young, from the complex of symptoms which had condemned her for some fifteen years to an existence of torment and had excluded her from any participation in life. She now felt she was well, and she plunged into eager activity, in order to develop her by no means small talent and to snatch a little recognition, enjoyment, and success, late though the moment was. But every one of her attempts ended either with people letting her know or with herself recognizing that she was too old to accomplish anything in that field. After each outcome of this kind a relapse into illness would have been the obvious thing, but she was no longer able to bring that about. Instead, she met each time with an accident which put her out of action for a time and caused her suffering. She fell down and sprained her ankle or hurt her knee, or she injured her hand in something she was doing. When she was made aware of how great her own share might be in these apparent accidents, she, so to say, changed her technique, instead of accidents, indispositions appeared on the same provocations—catarrhs, sore throats, influenza conditions, rheumatic swellings—till at last she made up her mind to resign her attempts and the whole agitation came to an end. [1933a, pp. 108–109]

Freud explained the theory behind this conflict as follows:

There is, as we think, no doubt about the origin of this unconscious need for punishment. It behaves like a piece of conscience, like a prolongation of our conscience into the unconscious; and it must have the same origin as conscience and correspond, therefore, to a piece of aggressiveness that has been internalized and taken over by the super-ego. If only the words went together better, we should be justified for all practical purposes in calling it an "unconscious sense of guilt". Theoretically we are in fact in doubt whether we should suppose that all the aggressiveness that has returned from the external world is bound by the super-ego and accordingly turned against the ego, or that a part of it is carrying on its mute and uncanny activity as a free destructive instinct in the ego and the id. A distribution of the latter kind is the more probable; *but we know nothing more about it* [my italics]. There is not doubt that, when the super-ego was first instituted, in equipping that agency use was made of the piece of the child's aggressiveness towards his parents for which he was unable to effect a discharge outwards on account of his erotic fixation as well as of external difficulties . . . People in whom this unconscious sense of guilt is excessively strong betray themselves in analytic treatment by the negative therapeutic reaction which is so disagreeable from the prognostic point of view. [*ibid*, p. 109]

Klein's introduction (1946) of a new architecture of the self, formed by part object representations, together with primitive defence mechanisms, such as projective and introjective identifications, has established a better perspective to understand the existence within the internal world, of continuous reciprocal part object interactions. Following this dynamics, Heiman (1952) referred to "intra-psychic projections" to describe paranoid states:

. . . but I did not understand how such intra-psychic projection took place, until I came to appreciate the part played by the splitting mechanisms. In the light of Melanie Klein's concept of the paranoid/ schizoid position and through her presentation of the defensive processes of splitting in early infantile life, *I realized that intra-psychic projection is preceded by a split in the ego*. [p. 210, my italics]

Rosenfeld (1971) has described the existence of a complex destructive mechanism of different part objects which functions similarly to a "gang Mafioso". Joseph (1975) referred to patients "difficult to reach" in whom splitting of personality induced a resistance of the analysis, because one part tries to keep another more needed aspect away from treatment. Grinberg (1975) described the existence of intrapsychic projective identifications directed towards internal objects as a way to explain Freud's dynamics of the lost object in "Mourning and melancholia". Meltzer (1973) has referred to destructive narcissism as a part of the self that presents itself to another suffering good part, "as a protector from pain, as a servant to its sensuality and vanity and covertly as a brute and tortures" (p. 97) Steiner (1982) speaks of a "perverse relationship between different parts of the self", in patients in whom a narcissistic aspect of personality could acquire an exaggerated power and control over healthy parts, inducing them to form a kind of perverse alliance. When the intricacy of these inner relationships is taken into account, "self-envy" interaction between the representations of different self parts is quite understandable (López-Corvo, 1999, pp. 210–211).

"Attack on links that relate", present in a mind dominated by part objects instead of total ones, as well as by paranoid–schizoid mechanisms over depressive ones, could be an important way to understand what I have explained above. In this condition, the sense of total object or depressive mechanisms sensed in the external object will induce intense feelings of envy that will result in inner attack of the alpha function, in order to destroy painful awareness. This destruction will hinder the possibility of achieving the level of total object and as a result, the closing of a circular behaviour. "Self-envy" represents one stage in this chain of events, meaning the inner envious attack towards feelings of harmony, creativity, and aliveness present in human beings. It is responsible for experiencing objects as inanimate instead of total and alive. It makes it impossible to comprehend the sense of unconditionality present in links of love between human beings.

In his paper about attacks on links, Bion (1967) established that:

Observation of the patient's disposition to attack the link between two objects is simplified because the analyst has to establish a link with the patient and does this by verbal communication and his equipment of psycho-analytical experience. Upon this the creative relationship depends and therefore we should be able to see attacks being made upon it. [1967, p. 94]

And further on, when referring to a patient, he states:

The recurrent anxiety in his analysis was associated with his fear that envy and hatred of a capacity for understanding was leading him to take in a good, understanding object to destroy and eject it—a procedure which had often led to persecution by the destroyed and ejected object . . . I said that he felt so envious of himself and of me for being able to work together to make him feel better that he took the pair of us into him as a dead piece of iron and dead floor that came together not to give him life but to murder him. [*ibid.*, p. 97]

A clinical case

Raul is a fifty-year-old, brilliant and successful architect who came to analysis three years before the present material, because of chronic unspecific anxiety and bouts of paralysing depression. He was the eldest of three siblings of an upper middle-class family, whose father he described as aggressive and threatening, "a street fighter, who usually hit first and asked later"; while his mother was depicted as aloof and emotionally distant towards him, in contrast with what he felt was a more amenable response from his other siblings, especially his younger sister. Since the beginning of his analysis, he regularly brought books and papers from well-known authors, mainly philosophers, and read from them at the opening of the session, usually to prove something I had previously stated or to sustain something he wished to say. I felt this issue was so important that I even engaged in the subject when he demanded, until it faded away as we understood that such a ritual represented an important defence, used in order to read in others what he very much feared to read in himself. It was a mechanism used as a protection against castration anxiety induced by a persecutory object placed in the analyst.

Raul presented a circular history of extremes between successive financial accomplishment and consequent failures; a situation not referred to by him spontaneously, but which became obvious by the end of the second year of analysis. He also communicated, with great difficulty and shame, his compulsive masturbation, infrequent sex with his wife, and regular use of call girls.

When he was around eleven years of age his mother changed his room from the front of the house where his parents' and siblings' quarters were located, to an isolated room at the back of the house. This became a decisive issue that eventually marked an important dissociation in his personality. Although there is not a conscious explanation, it is quite possible that such a decision could have hinged on Raul's voyeuristic curiosity towards his sisters, together with some sexual apprehension from his parents. There were feelings of exclusion, desolation, impotence, resentment, frustration, and intense envy towards the group that remained together at the "front of the house". A powerful need for revenge grew to significant proportions and was acted out through voyeuristic phantasies, compulsive masturbation, passive aggressive acting-outs against his parents, as well as overt sibling rivalry towards his sisters. The "back of the house" space became a narcissistic conglomerate,[4] a sort of stronghold that was later incorporated as an anal element. At the same time, the "front of the house" issue became an idealized mirror image of the "back of the house", and was experienced by him as a place where loving, acceptance, harmony, and so on, was continuously taking place between his parents and siblings, and from which Raul felt completely excluded. Intense feelings of envy, as well as a powerful need to attack and destroy those particular forms of linkage, were established. A paranoid–schizoid interaction was created between both extremes "front–back" of the house, later incorporated within body zones, where "back of the house" was identified with the anus and the "front" with the genitalia.

Such identification maintained an unconscious communication between both, in such a manner that his penis was constantly used as a vengeful instrument to smear, debase, sadistically control, and to express his ambivalent feelings towards women. There was a regular phantasy of attacking and debasing anybody or anything that he felt was related to those attributes present in the "front of the house", in order to change them and place them in the "back of the house", meaning the anus. Anything experienced by Raul as an internal "back of the house situation", was experienced with a sense of failure and feeling of depression, as well as powerful feelings of "revengeful hope".[5] Consequently, the need to change the situation into a "front of the house" matter increased, and as soon as he experienced that he had "achieved" it, he felt triumphant and elated. However, there were also persecutory guilt feelings that eventually would induce in him the "back of the house situation", creating a tautological circularity of triumphs and failures. It was mostly an inner struggle between excluded envious and virulent anal aspects of the self, and links of love and concern for others, which were attacked and destroyed as a self-envy mechanism without ever measuring its consequences. Unconsciously, Raul experienced the same envy he once felt towards his parents and sisters as outside objects towards any form of interaction he now finds similar to that previous experience, although this time the issue takes place within himself—as a form of self-envy—in his relationship with others; and he attacks this interaction with the same sense of destruction he once did as a child against his parents and siblings.

He brings the following dream:

> He was in a bar having a drink and two stools to his left was someone he knew, Mr Z, a well-known architect who passed a note to him congratulating him for starting his new job. He looked at Z who greets him by smiling and nodding his head. Suddenly a very fat man stumbles in and sits between the two of them, blocking each other's view and taking half of his stool. He wakes up feeling anxious.

He associates Z with his own desires to achieve and do well, while the fat man represents the envious and self-destructive aspects that attack and destroy any attempt of communication with reassuring parts of himself.

Notes

1. It is obvious that these interactions take place between internal "part objects", and not against the self as a totality. In this sense, the name "self-envy" is not perhaps the most appropriate one; however, I have not been able to find a better expression than this one, originally used by Scott (1975).
2. There is more information and a full account of this dream in the previous chapter.
3. A Hindu or Buddhist graphic of a circle enclosing a square, as a symbol of the universe.
4. See Chapter Six.
5. See López-Corvo, 1995, about "Revengeful hope".

CHAPTER FIVE

"Nameless terror"

Roland: Seems clear that the attempt [to evoke the memory of the terror] is inherent to avoiding making conscious something that produces fear or terror, and that behind this, the object is nameless. There are many formulations of fear not formulated or ineffable.

(Bion, 1975, p. 77)

Wild or unthought emotions

Bion's notion of "nameless terror" represents a certain kind of dreadful, "unremembered memory" related to the ineffable or the thing-in-itself, and should not be confused with other forms of fears, like phobias for instance, that already carry the signature of the unconscious representation of the feared object, which could be eventually named. Nameless terror is mostly related to a state of "mindlessness" resulting from splitting, projection, and *murdering of the mind*, as I have already described it in Chapter Three.

Freud originally stated that all anxieties are traumatic and become chronic as the result of a state of alertness towards a possible danger continuously fabricated by the mind and related to childhood traumas. He said:

> Taking this sequence, anxiety–danger–helplessness (trauma), we can now summarize what has been said. A danger situation is a recognized, remembered, expected situation of helplessness. Anxiety is the original reaction to helplessness in the trauma and is reproduced later on in the danger-situation as a signal for help. [1926d, pp. 166–167]

There are other issues that contribute to maintaining chronic "signal anxiety", besides the sense of helplessness; such as the fear of doing nothing or giving up the signal anxiety, once the anachronism of a repeated but not remembered infantile trauma is recognized; as if doing nothing carries the risk of, in fact, succumbing to the imaginary menace. There is also a sense of omnipotence, of having to be continuously present and feeling completely indispensable in dealing with the imminent danger. As a consequence, this attitude induces incapacity to delegate, a need to be present and alert at all times, making it necessary to remain awake; thus it becomes very difficult to fall asleep. To these concepts, originally presented by Freud, Bion added a very significant mechanism, that anxiety produced by early trauma is incremented when the ego, as a form of defence against distress, resorts to minute splitting and projects the "thinking apparatus" as I have already described in Chapter Three, when I referred to preconceptual traumas. Phobias, on the other hand, are always the expression of projective identifications produced by the psychotic part of the personality, which fabricates bizarre objects providing the ego with a better control of the danger by localizing it in a specific time and place.

A crucial characteristic of chronic anxiety is the incapacity to "name" the original trauma, because of the existence of a trap with no way out, where there will be terror whether the trauma is named or not. This creates a kind of fear we might find in the Oedipus quandary.

Five months after commencing a three times weekly analysis, Deborah, a married woman, childless, in her mid forties, came to a session, and said: "I feel very tired this morning because I could not sleep last night. My husband was away and I was terrified that someone could break into my bedroom . . . I was raped, you know . . . when I was seventeen I went to Argentina and I was in a bar with a girlfriend, and it was a bit late. I was talking with the bartender. My girlfriend said she wanted to go because she was tired and the bartender said that he would walk me to my hotel that was around the corner. He might have put something in my drink because I couldn't remember what happened, but he abused me sexually and I couldn't do anything, and I don't remember either."

The question then, I thought, was: how had that bartender "raped her mind", in such a way, that for over thirty years he had remained cloaked in her memories, ready to jump and make himself present, immediately after she finds herself alone? Could his presence, after such a long time, be justified by the fact that she *did not want to remember* then what exactly happened that night, and that she still does not want to remember now? Is it because of what she does not want to remember that the bartender is not forgotten? And what is it that she does not want to remember in order not to forget? What exactly could be that pleasure derived from such a repetitious dilemma, for which she is willing to pay with the price of terror?

In Chapter Three, on "Deaf-mute objects and preconceptual traumas", I referred to early experiences that take place at such a primeval time that it is impossible to name them, because at that time, not only does language not exist, but it is created later on for different purposes. Bion uses Kant's expression of "empty concepts that lack intuition, or blind intuitions that lack concepts", which rapidly change into "black holes" (Bion, 1975) where, "turbulences and empty concepts float with scandalous meanings" (*ibid.*, p. 229).

From these remarks we could guess the existence of two main sources of nameless terrors: one deriving from preconceptual traumas, that I have described in detail in Chapter Three; another related to the paradox implicit in the structure of the Oedipus complex, such as the case of Deborah I have just briefly described. The following are clinical examples depicting both conditions.

Three clinical cases:

Case one

Sara is a forty-five-year-old woman, of Italian extraction, married with two children, the oldest of four siblings, three sisters and one brother. She came to analysis because of marital conflicts after finding out her husband was unfaithful and she was seriously considering the possibility of a divorce. Sara was an attractive, rather seductive, very intelligent university graduate and a painter. She was ambivalent about her father, although she openly stated she felt she was the most beautiful of her siblings and her father's favourite; she also often remarked she was envious of how "men did their things", in comparison to women. There was a form of feminine protest with masculine identification and phallic envy. She described her mother as very needy and dependent, like another child, or "the fifth sister, people referred to her as the baby", something that contrasted with the dominating and independent attitude displayed by her father.

When she was about eight years old, her mother was diagnosed with lupus erythematosus, and ten years later, after a series of acute crises and several hospitalizations, she died. For a while we investigated in the transference Sara's continuous dread of this illness in relation to Oedipus phantasies, her guilt associated to her mother's death, her identification with her father, and her ambivalence towards men. During one session she mentioned in passing, without further explanation, that her elder daughter was allergic to cold, something she had noticed for the first time two years ago, when she was bathing in the sea during the spring, and her body got all red and she felt sick. Countertransferentially, I felt she was concerned because of the relation between lupus and skin reaction to sunlight as well as temperatures. I felt for a while that her capacity for insight contrasted with her resistance to talking about her fear of lupus, particularly in relation to her daughter. In another session she referred to her husband saying she was afraid to link her sisters with lupus, and added that she knew this disease was related to women. Then I said, and she agreed, that she feared to name the lupus because if she did, it might happen; and she added that she was completely certain she did not have it.

After a short silence, she stated she was thinking of entering one of her paintings in an exhibition to compete for a prize, something that made her feel very anxious, because she never thought her work was that good. This is the first time she had attempted to compete with her work, something she considered real progress, but felt terrified of losing. I said that she confused her work with herself, that it was not her painting that was at stake, but herself. She answered that she feared her paintings were like "defective children" that would not be well liked. Then I said that she felt that her mother's "lupus defective uterus", attacked and destroyed by her, now existed in her, and was continuously threatening to appear any time and produce a defective child, demonstrated, for instance, by her fear about her daughter's allergy to cold. She cried silently, and then slowly stated that a few weeks earlier she had spoken to a dermatologist, who told her that it was better not to test her daughter, that it was better not to know. She also remembered that her mother never travelled in winter because her toes and fingers got purple and hurt a lot. She added that she found it very difficult to talk about this, because it terrified her.

Then I said that she replaced the lupus with her terror of not knowing what exactly she was suffering from, whether from lupus or from a nameless ineffable terror. "Lupus" could then represent the name of a nameless terror, possibly linked to matricidal feelings, that she or her daughter could either suffer the disease in order not to name the crime, or to name the crime, in order not to suffer it. The real terror, I said, was neither the crime she never committed, nor the lupus she and her daughter never have experienced, but continuously and endlessly to live imprisoned in that predicament. After all, the Oedipus complex represents a paradox, either having the intention of trying to avoid something you end up doing, or trying to do something you will never be able to perform. True acts of incest or parricide–matricide are not the expression of Oedipus pathology, which can be symbolized and resolved, but a psychotic acting out which represents the omnipotent expression of the "real aspect of projective identification",[1] where inner and outer worlds are confused and terror is split and then projected into external objects, which then, in turn, become bizarre objects.

Case two

I will now refer to a case related to preverbal trauma. Elizabeth was a young woman, married with two children, who came for treatment because of regular drinking binges. She was the only child because an older brother died very young when she was only three years of age; and it was around this time, and possibly due to the death of her brother, that her parents separated. Her mother, also an alcoholic, was a depressed woman who travelled often, leaving Elizabeth with maids and governesses but without friends to play with, in a sort of dejected environment she described as a parody of the "poor rich girl". The following is the last session before the Christmas break, and after eight months of analysis on a five times weekly basis. I had also told her four days in advance that it was going to be impossible for me to see her on Friday and that this session was our last. The patient said: "I went to the bank to look for your money, but the person who always changes it for me wasn't there, and I could not convince the other teller who was in his place to do it. I begged him, tried to seduce him, used my husband's name . . . but it was impossible; at the end I had to call my father-in-law to borrow money from him . . ." Countertransferentially, I felt she was talking about her resistance related to payment, possibly as a form of revenge because of the separation. She continued. "And Antoine (father-in-law) is like crazy with Vincent, my son, who asked him for a train as a Christmas present and he got it from Miami and waited for a month, and now everybody is trying to put it together. It is not like before when he never gave him something special but only gave him money." Then I said to her that perhaps she felt disappointed because I did not behave like Antoine towards Vincent or her towards me, doing all that she could to get my money, while instead I was abandoning her prematurely.

She remembered a dream:

> I am with Vincent in his room and there is a giraffe, a beautiful wooden giraffe. Vincent goes to bed, and an older man comes inside. He is like a mad scientist—like a madman—with a box, like a food container. Inside there is something horrible. It is like a piece of meat that moves by itself; it is throbbing, but only when I look at it. I feel he doesn't know what he is doing. And I try to leave the room, but he follows me trying to give me an injection. Then I am in another room and there is a lighted swimming pool, and they are doing experiments with monkeys, but I don't know what they are doing. They take a monkey and put it in the pool, and it explodes. Then they try to experiment with cold water, and ice starts to form in the water. A man jumps inside the pool and sinks to the bottom, and I start to feel anxious. I decide to look for him and jump in the water too. But when I reach the bottom, I realize that he is just a wire dummy.

She stated: "The giraffe was beautiful, but it was made only of wood, it was not covered with soft material as they usually are. The scientist could be you. The experiment with the monkeys reminds me of Harlow's movies. I don't like the smell of raw meat, it disgusts me, *and I am a vegetarian.*"

The dream shows a complex unconscious phantasy triggered by the separation, which portrays different fears: (a) it seems as if the separation put her in touch with something cold, like a giraffe without fur, similar to Harlow's monkeys, something that is also present at the end of the dream when she became aware that the "man" in the pool is a wire dummy. Also, the "drowned" part of herself she tries to rescue happens to be emotionless, dead, a wire dummy perhaps connected to childhood memories, as violent as her dream; (b) there is a distrust towards me since she feels I tormented and frightened her with interpretations and, similar to her mother, abandoned her. There could also be a degrading of the analyst in order to deal with separation anxiety, if I am a 'worthless mad scientist' who does not understand her and go away, it would mean a respite for her; (c) what appeared to be most threatening seems to be her inability to communicate to herself or to others what is taking place inside herself, something portrayed in the metaphor of the meat, that becomes "alive" only to herself, and cannot be understood or perceived by the analyst, similar to what I previously described as the "schizoid secret" (López-Corvo, 1995).[2] I believe that her remark about being a vegetarian could be related to her paranoid phantasies of having murdered her parents due to anger, envy, and revenge, and then finding out about her crime through the piece of meat, representing their despoilments. She feels trapped between her need that I should rescue her, her murderous anger about being again abandoned, and her need to degrade her memory of me. This condition, on the other hand, determines the transference and faces her with a terrible dilemma she cannot understand and cannot communicate to herself or others: she is terrified to value me because she will then miss me and will suffer the separation, but if she debases me in order not to lose me, then she will again feel terribly lonely and hopeless. This is exactly the core of the nameless terror she had experienced in relation to her parents, and as a way to deal with her guilt she had resorted to becoming a vegetarian.

Case three

Isabel is a young university student, who describes a repetitious dream, in which she feels threatened and very anxious about the picture of an immense avian clawed foot, like an eagle's or some other kind of large bird. We investigated the symbolism from different angles: as a phallic symbol, murderous Oedipus desires, rape phantasies, and so on. At one point, she shared the dream with her mother, and because Isabel likes drawing, she made a sketch of the foot. Her mother then pointed out to her that it reminded her of the base of a bathtub, where she used to bathe her when they were living in Paris. Apparently, during her pregnancy with Isabel, her mother showed symptoms of heart failure as a consequence of the rheumatoid fever she had suffered as an adolescent. When Isabel was around eighteen months of age, her father, of French extraction, decided to take his wife to Paris to get a second opinion. During her mother's hospitalization, Isabel was left under the care of a French governess who did not speak Spanish, and who used to bring her to the clinic during visiting hours. Often, when she was fit to do it, her mother bathed Isabel in a bathtub that rested on four legs simulating beautiful bronze eagle's feet, which the mother used to show to Isabel and make stories about them. In this case, the anxiety attached to this memory was related to the complete change of her entourage and surrounding that were then linked to separation anxiety, impotence, anger, and ambivalence. I would like to add that the discussion of the content of this dream made its recurrence disappear.

Notes

1. I will be referring to this issue in Chapter Seven.
2. I have described the "Eleusinian mysteries" in detail, at the beginning of Chapter Three, about the "deaf mute object".

CHAPTER SIX

Murdering "gangs" and narcissistic conglomerates

From the point of view of Bion's saturated–unsaturated theory

An attempt is made to clarify confusions related to the definition and metapsychology of narcissism, following statements made in classical theory in relation to primary and secondary narcissism, and by object relation theory about the introjection of ideal and bad objects. Pathological and destructive narcissism is considered following concepts introduced by Rosenfeld in relation to the death instinct, as an internal organization that *insistently and relentlessly commits murders of the self*. A differentiation between normal and pathological narcissism is attempted. Using these theoretical contributions, a description of what might be considered a "narcissistic unit" or "narcissistic conglomerate" is introduced. Finally, the clinical concept of narcissism is examined from the point of view of Bion's theories of "narcissism vs. socialism", "psychotic vs. non-psychotic part of the personality", as well as "saturated vs. unsaturated".

Narcissism

A series of misconceptions and misunderstandings have largely contributed to the confusion still present in the psychoanalytical notion of narcissism. There are, since Freud, at least two qualities that define narcissism. One refers to the quality of *fusion* between different part object representations, as opposed to separation or differentiation: a concept implicit in Freud's description of primary narcissism; the second and more important one within classical theory refers to the *expansive* quality induced by the incorporation, within the self, of libido attached to the outside object or object libido, just as it is clinically observed in what Freud described as secondary narcissism. From the point of view of object relations theory, secondary narcissism represents an impossible condition, because the drive–object relationship constitutes an unbreakable unit, meaning that there would never exist a clean cleavage between libido and the cathected object, because there will always subsist a meaningful trace of the original object. Such an idea induced Klein to prefer to rely more on the quality of the object introjected, and to explain the expansive quality observed in what has been described as narcissistic pathology as a consequence of the introjection of the "ideal" object.

Object relations theory broadened these conditions of "fusion" and "expansion" by considering two other qualities. The first is the inclusion of aggression as opposed to libido (ego instincts contrasting with sexual or death instincts as opposed to life instincts); the other quality, a consequence of the previous one although less investigated, attempts to include the "bad" object as opposed to the "idealized" one. In spite of the theoretical logic implicit in this last statement, there has been a clear opposition to consider also the introjection of the bad object within the self as an expression of a narcissistic form of object relation. As I have stated above, one explanation could be related to the association established by Freud and later on sustained by other schools of psychoanalysis, between narcissism as a clinical entity and the expansive quality produced by the incorporation of object libido, a condition where description of the so-called "narcissistic personality" pivots. There has been great resistance to considering the depletion or *contraction* (in contrast with *expansion*) of the self observed in the incorporation of the bad object during clinical depression, as equally narcissistic as the incorporation of the ideal object observed in what Freud described as secondary narcissism. From this perspective, narcissistic personality associated with the incorporation of the ideal object

or object libido would correspond to a descriptive or phenomeno-
logical description and not to a metapsychological one. Klein, for
instance, had the following to say:

> Another typical feature of schizoid object relations is their narcis-
> sistic nature which derives from the infantile introjective and
> projective processes. For, as I suggested earlier, when the ego ideal
> is projected into another person, this object becomes predominantly
> loved and admired because it contains the good parts of the self.
> Similarly, the relation to other persons on the basis of projecting
> bad parts of the self into them is of a narcissistic nature because in
> this case as well the object strongly represents one part of the self.
> [1946, p. 13]

In this line of thinking, introjection of the idealized object (libidinal investment of the self) as we observe it in narcissistic personalities (Kernberg, 1975), as well as introjection of the bad object as
seen in melancholic states, are both consequences of a narcissistic
fusion between self-representations and the internalized external
object. (These are organized as a structure which I will soon discuss
as the "narcissistic conglomerate".) From a metapsychological
standpoint the quality of *fusion*—as opposed to differentiation—
between different part object representations should, perhaps,
represent the most important feature that defines narcissism,
regardless of considering it as an expansion of the self as observed
in narcissistic states (because of introjection of the ideal object), or
with a contraction of the self in depressive states (because of introjection of the bad object).

    (A)   *Fusion*: In classical theory, only libido.

             In object relation theory aggression is added.

NARCISSISM

    (B)   (i) *Expansion*: In classical theory, corresponds to
              incorporation of "object libido". In object relations
              theory corresponds to incorporation of the "ideal"
              object
             (ii) *Contraction*: According to object relation theory,
              it corresponds to incorporation of the "bad" object.

Segal (1983) summarized Klein's contributions as follows:

... she [Klein] differentiates between narcissistic states and the narcissistic object relations and structure. The narcissistic states she relates to the withdrawal to *an idealized internal object* [my italics] ... The narcissistic object relations and structure she relates to projective identification. Her view of narcissistic object relations continues Freud's work on narcissistic object choice, but emphasizes also the elements of control of an object implicit in the concept of projective identification. [p. 269]

Although Klein's contributions to narcissism were scanty, one could infer from the little she said an important discrepancy with classical postulates, which, perhaps due to political reasons of the moment, were never completely ventilated. Even Segal's account, presented above, leaves out the notion of a "narcissistic state" also based on the "withdrawal to a *bad internal object*", as introduced by Klein in her previous quote. Such an oversight from a Kleinian added more to the confusion.

It is unfortunate that Freud described narcissism only in terms of his concept of libido and never revised the notion after 1920, when he began to emphasize the significance of the death instinct. This narrowly focused formulation of narcissism based on the idealizing quality of the incorporation of the object libido, in Freudian and ego psychology terminology, or ideal object in Kleinian language, is responsible for a persisting confusion over the artificial distinction between drive and object. According to Fairbairn (1952), the introjection of the idealized object that amounts to a "grandiose self" (as seen in manic states) requires the compulsion to project the bad object, which, when introjected—and this occurs very often (bipolar pathology)—changes into a depressive condition which in Kleinian metapsychology is also narcissistic.

Perverse and destructive narcissism

In the original myth, Narcissus, punished by Nemesis, falls in love with his own reflection, and remains helpless beside the water trying to touch his image. Unable to move himself away, he changes into a river flower. The prophecy of Tiresias the seer is then fulfilled: "that Narcissus will live a long life only if he never knows himself";

and never knows about himself like Dracula, unable to see his image on the mirror. This is the main characteristic of pathological narcissism.

I will refer to pathological narcissism only as the pathological form of the schizoid–paranoid position, where the intensity of the death instinct shatters the object into extreme parts of very good or idealized objects and very bad or persecutory ones. Originally, the ego idealized the good object as a defence to compensate for the pain induced by the frustration brought by the bad object (Klein, 1946). This explains why the idealized object so closely mirrors the bad one (just like Narcissus and his own image on the surface of the water). Even though both part objects are closely interrelated, they must also remain separated and distinct from each other to avoid the good object from being destroyed by the envy of the bad object. Omnipotent processes of projection, introjection, and identification guarantee such a separation. If a part object, bad or idealized, is introjected within the self, its congruent (mirror-image) counterpart must be projected into the outside object. In order to guarantee that such splitting will be preserved, projection must be supported by a mechanism of identification, meaning that both part objects, idealized and bad, should be anchored, not only within the self (introjective identification) but also in the outside object (projective identification).

In 1971, Rosenfeld suggested the need to discriminate between libidinal and destructive (aggressive) forms of narcissism, stressing that parallel to the idealization of libidinal aspects, there was also an idealization of destructive bad self-objects. These objects were usually structured following an internal Mafia-style configuration, which tyrannically controlled the mind by means of deceits and manipulations. Such domination of the idealized bad object was established according to the pleasure principle and following a complex and narcissistic organization, which tried to maintain, with great violence, an omnipotent control of the good objects - usually projected into the analyst—by means of a destructive and successive degradation. The main purpose of such pathological organization is to establish control of the internal world, a tyranny over the mental apparatus, preserving the organization and continuously destroying any opposition to it, by seduction, threat, coercion, deceit, and so on. Preservation of life, peaceful harmony, long-term tranquillity, and so forth are continuously denigrated and devalued to the point that not only is logical symbolism obstructed, but cause–effect relationships are also inverted. *Action is measured more by its intention than by its consequences:* after-effects of drugs are marvellous, all-night parties are fantastic, parents and authority figures are suspicious, injected drugs superb, etc. Secondary consequences are completely denied: loss of work or studies, robbery, troubles with the police, family conflicts, crime, prostitution, diseases, and so on. "Badness" is idealized and negative identification, such as delinquency, suicide, drug addiction, or any other kind of destructive acting out, is sold to the ego as an expression of the true self: "better to be someone by always saying *no*, than to comply with others and disappear by saying *yes*". Let us consider the following case.

A patient involved in a long history of delinquent actions and drug consumption had managed to change to the point of creating his own business and giving up drugs for three years following a long commitment to a therapeutic community. He had been in analysis for two years and was doing reasonably well, aside from some occasional acting out. We had managed to understand some of the processes of internal splitting—the existence of a part object we referred to as the "drugged one" representing the structure of the narcissistic "gang" or pathological narcissism; the inner struggle to deny any feeling of dependency; the exaltation of omnipotent behaviour; and so forth. We also explored the hypothesis that the "drugged one" was a revengeful part of him that tried to destroy the "good son" he felt his parents wanted him to be.

Two weeks before the summer holidays he brought the following dream:

He was walking with his girlfriend on a dark street and was afraid of being mugged, when suddenly three individuals jumped out of a corner, put a gun to his head, and said: "Don't you move, this is an assault." He was scared they would take a chain and medal he wore around his neck, which was very important to him because it was given to him by his mother when he was a child. The thought in the dream of the chain being taken away made him very depressed.

His associations brought memories from the time he was an assailant and had once tried to rob a drug dealer; he was almost shot by him, and was later caught by the police. He recalled, as well, a time when three thugs tried to mug him. He got into a fistfight with them and managed to disarm them, but was chased afterwards and feared being shot. The chain and medal he was wearing were associated with his good aspects: the good son his parents wanted him to be. I told him that he was very angry about me going away because he feared being mugged inside by the envious part object that we named the "drugged one", and robbed of the chain, meaning his desire to be the "good patient" he felt I wanted him to be, or again, the good son, a possibility that made him very depressed.

Narcissism vs social-ism according to Bion

I think perhaps Bion might have attempted to avoid further controversies in the definition of narcissism, like those induced by issues such as "fusion–expansion" and "contraction", by considering a different vertex. He classified instincts according to (a) the "purpose", by using the notion of a preconcept in search of a realization in order to structure a concept; or in other words, to unify the "instinct" representing the *noumenon* with "thinking" representing the *phenomenon*;[1] (b) Bion discriminates between individual (or narcissistic) and gregarious (or social-istic) kinds of relationship, depending on the "nature of the object relations". Narcissistic relationships would then represent the interaction with internal part-object representations that could be projected into the outside object, by means of projective identification, where there is not really an interaction with others as separated entities but only with those parts that have been projected into them. Bion distinguishes this from a "social" interaction with the "Other" as a separate being, something he illustrates by hyphenating the word social-ist.

Bion argues that a division of this kind, between individual and group, would be less conflictive than an ego and sexual instincts schism, as described by Freud. In an undated note written around 1959, Bion portrays a different form of narcissistic polarization, between a projected element and its introjected mirror counterpart, similar to what I have previously described as a "narcissistic conglomerate". He states:

These two terms [social-ism and narcissism] might be employed to describe tendencies, one ego-centric and another socio-centric . . .

They are equal in amount and opposed in sign. Thus, if the love impulses are narcissistic at any time, then the hate impulses are social-istic, i.e. directed towards the group, and vice versa: if the hate is directed against an individual as a part of narcissistic tendency, then the group will be loved social-istically. [1992, p. 122]

Saturated and unsaturated elements

Bion might have borrowed this concept from chemistry, and has used it to describe situations or states that remain completely impregnated with something if saturated, or the opposite, entirely free or empty if unsaturated. Frequently Bion uses the Greek letter κσι (*ksi*) to stand for an unsaturated element. For instance, "β elements" represent well defined closed objects or the "thing-in-it-self", which are completely saturated.[2] The mind of the analyst, on the other hand, must remain open, free from memory or desire, or unsaturated, similar to a preconception in search of a realization (Bion, 1963, p. 70). Bion states that psychotic patients often fear elements they experience as saturated, because they might not be capable of distinguishing between a high level of saturation and voracity. For instance, the patient could experience the analyst's own desires (saturated element) as an attempt to rob him of his sanity (Bion, 1965).

The "narcissistic conglomerates"

According to Bion, the baby gets rid of unpleasant or painful feelings by way of projective identification directed to the mother or, more specifically, into her breast. For the sake of understanding, we could imagine two extreme possibilities: (i) the mother contains the baby's projective identifications and modifies or detoxifies them to a less painful and more bearable experience. Once the baby incorporates this condition, it will result in the construction of alpha function. (ii) Not being capable of providing the previous option, the mother rejects projective identifications, refusing to become a depository of the child's feelings. Obviously, the first option eventually will be translated into mental growth and mental health and, evidently, it would not become a matter to be dealt with in the psychoanalytical room. The alternative, however, represents the conflictive side, the symptom-inducing part of the personality, which will determine the very substance of the transference—countertransference dimension. It is obvious, then, that the lack of reverie on the part of the mother will hamper the possibility of structuring an alpha function,[3] which eventually will metabolize raw sensuous experiences, or beta elements, and change them into alpha elements.

Pathological narcissistic structures represent the repetitive product of non-reverie forms of interaction between the baby and his/her mother. They constitute a certain form of beta elements I have previously referred to as the "narcissistic particle" or "narcissistic conglomerate" (Lopez-Corvo, 1994). These structures are made of a double fusion of part-self and part-object representations, placed internally (the "internal cluster" product of introjective identifications) and a congruent or mirror cluster, also formed by fused part-self and part-object representations, placed outside in the external object (the "external cluster" product of projective identification). In other words, an internal cluster plus a congruent mirror structure or external cluster forms a particular narcissistic particle or conglomerate. Clusters are integrated by fusion of part-self and part-object representations. The position of both clusters, internal and external, may exchange within the paranoid–schizoid position, but distance between them is always conserved. The need to preserve this distance will determine the clinical rigidity and pathological character of that particular structure. For instance, the patient I have previously described produces the phantasy that the analyst, like his mother, wishes for him to be a "good patient" worth wearing the chain and medal. However, an extremely envious internal object, the "drugged one", will mug and rob this alternative in order to attack and destroy the goodness of the object projected into the analyst. An "envious–revengeful–drugged–debased" part kept inside, and an idealized "good–medal-wearing son–patient" counterpart, projected into the analyst and conceived as the analyst's desire, will form the "narcissistic particle". Out of envy and revenge due to a threat of separation, the situation reverts: the revengeful part attacks and destroys the analytical couple, depicted in the dream as the mugged couple formed by him and his girlfriend. In the associations, the envious attack is represented by the attempt to rob a debased analyst portrayed by the dealer. An important change is that the manic triumph previously experienced by the attack on goodness and the idealization of badness now fails, and instead of experiencing manic feelings he gets depressed.

Another patient, for instance, might be struggling with the pain induced by the existence of an internal narcissistic cluster formed by an "excluded–abandoned–envious child", while at the same time projecting into the analyst a congruent and external cluster made of a "loved–abundant–independent object", experienced in the transference. Induced by the suffering, the patient might take holidays a few days before the analyst in order to invert the narcissistic organization.

Such a "narcissistic particle" that I am now considering would be equivalent, as I have previously stated, to Bion's description of "beta elements". They represent high-speed particles good only to be expelled, acted out, or used as material for projective and introjective identifications instead of material for thinking.

In summary, a closed, saturated, narcissistic conglomerate is made of two opposite mirror images: one introjected, which forms the inner structure; and another projected into the outside object via projective identification mechanisms. It could also be represented by the equation $+2-2 = 0$, or geometrically by a circle, similar to saying that two steps forward and two steps backwards amount to remaining at the same place. It represents an "equilibration by inversion" formed by two equal, but opposite movements. The "alpha function", on the other hand, changes beta elements into alpha elements by introducing among many other things an opening, due to the capacity to mourn and replace the absent object with symbolic representations.

Normal narcissism

Considering narcissism as synonymous with fusion makes it possible to also find normal situations that consolidate, by means of fusion between parts, in order to create a whole. Following Bion, in normal forms of narcissism, a preconcept establishes a realization to construct a conception, which requires blending with an experience to create a concept. This outcome differs from pathological narcissism, where parts fuse to preserve the splitting and always remain as part objects, without ever achieving a sense of wholeness. Fusion in this case will imply a mechanism of being completely shut down, whereas the normal kind of narcissism would entail fusion towards openness and greater growth, as well as more autonomy and sophistication.

Normal narcissism could be linked to "learning from experience" and to mental growth, representing a system completely unsaturated and open to new experiences. In other words, it would represent the consequence of a capacity to tolerate frustration, something that will allow the emergence of a preconception that, being unsaturated, would be open to saturation and to change into a conception. However, if frustration intolerance is too overpowering, then the person will react against the object out of envy and destroy it, remaining trapped between these feelings and persecutory guilt, giving room for a pathological form of narcissism to develop.

The difference between pathological and normal forms of narcissism will hinge precisely on the capacity to produce *symbols*. The process of symbolization is not just a cognitive procedure of naming the absent object but, most of all, it is a course of action that attempts to deal with destructive and omnipotent feelings experienced in relation to original objects, such as the breast or the penis. The omnipotent power exercised by the breast on the baby involves real and serious matters of life and death, normally experienced by the baby with great terror. The capacity of the ego to change original objects into others following a process of symbolization will result in "second-hand" objects experienced as less threatening because they have become more familiar, more private and domesticated. This process is achieved thanks to the mother's reverie function, which, from a Kleinian point of view, helps the baby move from the paranoid–schizoid to the depressive position.

For Bion, the "alpha function" is the mechanism responsible for changing closed and saturated beta elements into open, unsaturated alpha elements, by introducing the capacity to generate *symbols*. I believe, however, that other dimensions such as *space* and *time* are also of great significance. Space relates to projection, meaning discrimination between internal and external worlds, while *time* relates to transference or discrimination between past and present. These transformations also require certain ego proficiency, such as the capacity to reach a resolution of splitting processes, to acquire a notion of a total object and to achieve the level of a depressive position. In the course of moving towards mental growth, a process of mourning will be required to symbolize the space left by the absent object; or in Klein's words, to move from the paranoid–schizoid to the depressive position: "the way to the symbol, is always marked with mental suffering". Bion states (1962, p. 56) that the process of symbolization required by alpha function in order to change beta into alpha elements, is achieved by changing from *concrete* to *abstract* means, where abstraction represents the capacity to separate the particular or individual from the universal. Changing concrete to abstract could be similar to a shift from anatomy to physiology, or the difference between "what?" and "why?" "What" refers to something static and is related to the parts but not to the whole. "Why", on the other hand, implies a cause, a functioning, an interaction, a link, a relationship, or thinking. It would be like the difference between inanimate and animate or between the "dead" and the "alive".

A patient in his third year of analysis says, immediately after lying down, that the night before he was playing Scrabble with his wife, that she again won the game, and again he felt very frustrated and angry, to the point that he suddenly hit the board and threw the pieces all over the place. He explained that his wife was winning by adding a plural to a word he knew has no plural, because it applied to both singular and plural; but he could not remember which one was the exact word. I said that perhaps the problem hinged exactly on the quality of a word, which he felt had no plural, while his wife felt the other way around, and that he experienced such a dichotomy with his wife as something very threatening. It was like a word-thing that he could not pluralize. "I wonder", I said, "which word or thing could that be?" After a short silence, he said: "I know what you are thinking, you are thinking about the penis."

He was dealing with the phantasy of a phallic mother, related to his own childhood experience of an aggressive, domineering mother and a passive dependent father. Since there was no plural for penis, it meant that there was only one penis, either his or hers; or in the case of the Scrabble game, more hers than his. He felt his wife, like his mother, was dealing with something she knew well. At the same time he felt he was dealing with the absence of something he didn't know, meaning that the only way out of such a dilemma would be that "penis" could be pluralized by the opening provided by the abstraction of a symbolism. It was not a simple Scrabble game, it was a serious issue, because losing meant he had the absence and she had the penis. By destroying the game, he was also attempting to deal with the castration anxiety induced by identity confusion and unconscious dependent–homosexual desires related to his phantasy of a phallic mother. There were two issues responsible for his terror: his incapacity to abstract and symbolize the phallus, to pluralize it into an infinite number of penis(es): it could be anything, and the need to disavow the penis, not being able to have it in order not to lose it, or even better, being able to lose it in order not to need it; in any case, women have no penis and men do not lose them. It was similar to what Segal (1957) described as a "symbolical equation".

Notes

1. Noumenon is a concept used by Kant to describe "what is intuited ... the absolute reality for which we have no empirical or sensible knowledge, and can be grasped by intuition only". Phenomenon on the other hand, is defined as "everything that presents itself to the senses". For further description see López-Corvo, 2003.
2. "Beta elements" represent raw sensual impressions that have not been transformed by alpha function and are only good for projective identification. See López-Corvo, 2003.
3. "Alpha function represents an abstraction used by Bion to describe the capacity to change sense information into alpha elements as well as providing the mind with material to create dream thoughts". See López-Corvo, 2003.

CHAPTER SEVEN

Excessive projective identification

"Struggling against the call to be exactly where the projections bounce back"

(López-Corvo, 2006, this volume)

Introduction

Before attempting an investigation about the concept of projective identification, it would be important to comprehend what Bion implies when he discriminates between "the psychotic and the non-psychotic part of the personality".[1] The two parts, psychotic and non-psychotic, are always present in all individuals regardless of whether they are diagnosed as psychotic (schizophrenic, for instance) or are considered normal. In this sense, the discrimination between the two parts of the personality is based on the "contained–container" theory, in the sense of wondering which part contains which, meaning that there is a quantitative gradient between both parts. In the psychotic individual, for instance, the psychotic part "contains" the non-psychotic, whereas in the "normal" or non-psychotic person, the psychotic part is "contained" by the non-psychotic part. However, the dynamic inside the psychotic part itself, regardless of the diagnosis of the person, is always the same. In other words, what takes place inside the psychotic part of the personality—meaning the defences involved—regardless of the individual's diagnosis being psychotic or normal, has absolutely the same dynamic; what changes is the relation or the ratio between container and contained.[2]

Projective identification is related to a "splitting of space", which allows what is internal to be projected into the external; in this sense, such splitting determines the stuff that composes the countertransference. The transference, on the other hand, is the consequence of a "splitting of time" that changes early transient reality into permanent, repetitious, intrapsychic facts.[3]

When we attempt to define projective identification we find at least four important difficulties: the first is related to the tendency to associate the concept with some form of "mysterious" communication; the second refers to the tendency to describe this mechanism in relation to psychotic patients and not to the "psychotic part of the personality" as I have just explained above. There are also two different forms of projective identification, one pathological or destructive, and another normal or creative; similar to what has been stated previously in Chapter Six, in relation to pathological (destructive) and normal (creative) forms of narcissism. Usually, however, when we refer to projective identification we indicate pathological forms of projection and identification. The third difficulty refers to discrimination between "projector" and "recipient", an approach that leaves out the complementarity, or two-way interaction, giving the impression of communication moving in one direction only; the fourth difficulty refers to the differentiation between "projective identification" and "projection". *I do not believe that they can be separated, that there is such a thing as a "projection only", free from an identification process. I think "identification" is always present in all projections: identification is the "shadow" of projection;* and this I believe, was the real contribution of Klein.

An important characteristic of projective identification is related to the interaction between the part that remains inside and the part projected. There is an unconscious, forceful complementarity between the identifications involved, resulting in such an enormous and powerful paradox, as of having to search and find exactly that which, at the same time, is so much feared. *The struggle is with the powerful unconscious need to place ourselves in the exact place where the projections bounce back.*

Projective identification has been described as an attempt to free the mind from unpleasant or dangerous thoughts and feelings by unconsciously projecting them into other compatible minds, with the purpose of establishing some kind of communication, control, and action. Although "projective identification" is a fair term to define the process, it would have been easier to follow if Klein and followers had borrowed from physics a word like "resonance", to describe the implicit mechanism in the projection; perhaps a term like "projective identification by resonance" might have been useful. It is obvious that certain forms of unconscious resonance would take place between different individuals, when mutual or congruent internal objects are present that could make possible the process of identification in both. Let us think, for instance, of someone whose superego's threats and demands induce the need for a continuous projection of any internal object experienced as imperfect. If, at the same time, there is another person who internally shelters unconscious masochistic needs for punishment, because of Oedipal masturbatory phantasies, then this second individual could "resound" to the unconscious call of the first person, and then get involved in a mutual sadistic–masochistic interaction.[4]

I also refer to the inconvenience of discriminating between "projector" and "recipient", because such separation could create the impression that projective identification moves only in one direction, instead of being conceived of as the product of mutuality, moving between two minds in both directions; just as an exhibitionist could induce feelings in a voyeur, in the same fashion that the latter could induce desires in the former. The discrimination between projector and recipient can also get confused with the roles of victim and aggressor. For instance, we could interpret the destructive acting out of a delinquent adolescent (projector?) against the "good desires" of his parents (recipient?) as an expression of victimization. However, such a belief could impair the investigation from the opposite direction; i.e., the investigation of the unconscious dealings the family might be employing towards the adolescent, who might represent a depository of bad objects expelled by the family. This could be a way to avoid "good" objects remaining in their minds without facing the danger of being damaged by the "badness" projected, and then acted out by the delinquent acts of the adolescent patient. A mutuality such as this could also be observed in what I referred to as "iatrogenic splitting" (López-Corvo, 1995), a condition present in patients described as having "multiple personality disorder". In this case, a hysterical patient might present a degree of dissociation and exhibitionistic phantasies that could elicit, via projective identification, voyeuristic feelings in the therapist, that if counter-acted, would result in the creation of different "personalities" in the patient, in a rather progressive circularity, making it difficult to discriminate between who is the projector and who is the recipient.

Excessive projective identification

Bion defines projective identification as

> ... a splitting off by the patient of a part of his personality and a projection of it into the object where it becomes installed, some- times as a persecutor, leaving the psyche from which it has been split off correspondingly impoverished. [1967, pp. 36–37]

Initially, he refers to "excessive projective identification" in a way I believe could be considered quantitative as well as qualitative, giving the impression that he first elaborated the quantitative aspect based on Klein's similar observations and afterwards inves- tigated the qualitative aspect in relation to what he considered the "real" characteristics of projective identification.

Quantitative excess

The quantitative part has been used to describe the intensity of projection exercised by the *"psychotic part of the personality"*,[5] as a reaction to the "aversion to reality" resulting in projection of the apparatus for thinking, as well as judgement, verbal thoughts, links, and so on. The consequence in psychotic patients is the loss of boundaries between inner and outer worlds, the creation of "bizarre objects" and of delusional systems. One of the main characteristics of the psychotic part of the personality is based on the early and tenacious attack against the apparatus of perception. Bion states:

> This part of the personality is cut up, split into minute fragments, and then, using the projective identification, expelled from the personality. Having thus rid himself of the apparatus of conscious awareness of internal and external reality, the patient achieves a state which is felt to be neither alive nor dead. [1967, p. 38]

In the face of extreme mental pain, as in the case of clinical psychoses or early and significant traumas,[6] or better, in Bion's more synthesized fashion, "the psychotic part of the personality", the ego attempts to deal with unbearable persecutory anxiety by minute splitting of the apparatus of perception, sense organs, links, and verbal thinking; followed by projective identification of these splinters into the outside object, which narcissistically becomes undifferentiated from the inside world. This condition will provoke, among many consequences, the location everywhere of the internal objects projected, inducing phobic symptoms, absence of a "thinking mind" capable of metabolizing and "containing" the chronic sources of anxiety, and the incapacity to discriminate between animate and inanimate.[7] Transference of these patients will always portray an idealization of the analyst's spoken words and dependency towards the analytic process, similar to the relationship experienced with medical doctors, which Lacan has described as the "place of the supposed knowledge".

Qualitative excess

The qualitative aspect refers to what Bion called the "realistic" aspect of projective identification. He states that there is the "omnipotent phantasy" that it is possible to split off undesired, albeit sometimes valued, aspects of the personality in an object outside. However, sometimes the patient might be able to induce a real action in the object, to make the omnipotent phantasy a reality. This could be seen in someone who is struggling with the inner phantasy of killing the sexual internal parents in order to free himself from guilt and be able to love freely. It can also be seen in someone who is dealing with an internal persecutor and convinces a third party to murder someone else into whom he had projected the internal persecutor. Bion concludes: "I have suggested an emended version of Freud's pleasure principle theory so that the reality principle should be considered to operate co-existentially with the pleasure principle" (1962, p. 31).

According to Bion, when Klein refers to "excessive projective identification" she is not only referring to frequency but also to the omnipotent belief implicit in it. When a child, ruled by the pleasure principle and a "rudimentary consciousness" (as stated by Freud), attempts to free himself from bad internal persecutory objects by means of "omnipotent" projective identifications released into his mother, the digestion of such projection by the mother's alpha function (reverie) will be translated into realistic growth for the child (1967, pp. 112–113, 118). This means that it might be possible to induce a real action in the person (mother or analyst) into whom the projection has been made, which will then make the omnipotent aspect of the phantasy a reality. This is something that also can be observed in the act of communicating an interpretation to the patient that has been built on the material of a projective identification produced by the patient. Counteracting, or acting out the countertransference, is also an important example of the "real" aspect of the projective identification: a very attractive young woman, whose parents divorced when she was five years old, was fondled and masturbated as a child by a maternal uncle. When she was eighteen she started psychotherapy with a young and inexperienced psychiatrist who, not being able to deal with the powerful projective identification of a very needy child, and confusing the mouth with the vagina and the penis with the nipple, got involved in mutual sexual manipulation and intercourse. Eventually, the guilt involved due to the attack and destruction of the possibly therapeutic "solution", mostly experienced by the therapist, brought the clandestine relationship to an end. This outcome enraged and later depressed the patient who shortly after made a serious suicide attempt.

Michael, who has been unemployed for several months, is now investigating his rivalry with peers at work as an explanation for leaving his job, something he has previously experienced while holding other positions. He also referred to shameful and guilty feelings related to voyeuristic behaviour originally related to his younger sister. We have been trying to find symbolical connection between these two issues. On Monday's session he came early and, while waiting by the door, heard me calling my wife. As he lies down he says he heard me calling my wife, whose name he knows from a book I have written. Then he talked about memories from childhood related to peeping through a hole in the maid's bathroom, and I said he is also peeping and curious about my wife and me. On Tuesday, as soon as he lay down he says he thinks I am annoyed about his curiosity over my private life, and then adds that he feels the analysis is making him feel uncertain and he lacks the necessary liveliness needed to find a job. I said that he is projecting on me feelings related to his father, because I am not annoyed about his curiosity, but it seems to me that he came prepared just in case, when he states that analysis is robbing his liveliness; it will be like a protection against any supposed annoyance on my part. I also wonder if this mechanism, of feeling threatened and then attacking, could be related to his difficulties at work, that he might feel that he said something and that this annoyed somebody, and although it was not like that, he attacks the person before this person has anything to say. Then the person, in fact, reacts to his attack and counterattacks. What started as a phantasy and a projective identification changes into reality.

Normal projective identification

Bion discriminates between "pathological" forms of projective identification, used primarily as a means of omnipotent control and evacuation, first described by Melanie Klein in 1930, and "normal" projective identification, used as a primitive method of communication between the infant and his mother. He considers it to be not only an omnipotent fantasy in the infant's mind, but also the infant's first method of communication. Referring to Klein's (1946) description of the "introjection of the good breast" as a "precondition for normal development", Bion concludes that:

> ... there is a normal degree of projective identification, without defining the limits within which normality lies, and that associated with introjective identification this is the foundation on which normal development rests. [1967, p. 103]

Bion described the mother's "reverie function" as the paradigm for normal projective identification, capable of inducing in the child an increment of normal growth, ego autonomy, and capacity to learn from experience; this is similar to the purpose present in analytical therapy, where the interpretation as a form of projective identification attempts to induce in the patient, similar changes as those achieved by the mother's reverie. The difference between normal and abnormal forms of projective identifications seems to hinge more on the "intention", than in the "format" of the communication itself. Normal projective identification is ruled by love and gratitude, inducing positive growth, life (animate) and freedom; while the abnormal is ruled by envy and revenge, exercising imprisonment, death (inanimate) and negative growth.

Growth, represented by Bion by the letter Y, was defined as a preconception in search of a realization, which, when directed towards the outside, towards reality (or social-ism) will be considered positive: $+Y$; but when directed towards the inside, egocentric or narcissistic, it will then be conceived as negative: $-Y$. But growth could be a difficult issue that might change depending on the vertex form in which it is being considered. A soldier capable of defending himself during a war and of inflicting heavy casualties on the enemy might be considered, based on his capacity to destroy lives, as an efficient, reliable, and autonomous person. It has been expressed by some historians that Columbus divorced his first wife and married the daughter of a cartographer in order to have access to new maps; also he left his son Diego under the care of monks in order to be free to travel and fulfil his dream. He achieved lasting fame, but, obviously, was neither a faithful husband nor a responsible father.

A twenty-eight-year-old patient with an important oedipal dependency on her parents remains single, unemployed, and still lives at their home. When she was twenty-three she met a man with whom she established an important loving relationship that lasted almost five years. Then he decided to break the attachment because he felt too young for a serious relationship and wished to travel on his own. She complained bitterly, accusing herself of not doing things the right way, felt abandoned and a complete failure. What was unfair in her superego accusations was that since an important part of her wished to remain at home, she was able to choose (from among many men) the one who was not going to end up offering to marry her, and thus force her to break her oedipal dependence. Which one of her parts should we consider in order to measure her success, the one that wished to leave her house, which obviously failed in her choice of a man; or the successful part that managed to choose the right man—among so many—that allowed her to remain at home? After all, any one of these choices is as good as the other; they only portray different but unavoidable consequences. Bion states that in order to find out which of these outcomes would be equivalent to "positive growth", we should use the vertical axis of the Grid, which will be found in Chapter Fifteen.

Notes

1. I have also dealt with this subject summarily in the Introduction to this book.
2. It would be something similar to the comparison between a broken piece and the total picture of a hologram, where both enclose exactly the same image. (See Lopez-Corvo 2003.)
3. Splitting of space and time also takes place in the body, the result being the cancer cells that detach themselves from the original organs and invade others (splitting of space) while at the same time they multiply (splitting of time) forever. Cancer cells die because the host dies, otherwise they would be eternal. See, for instance, the experimental cancer called the "Walker tumour", which was used continuously for more than fifty years to innoculate rats all over the world.
4. We could also think of sea waves, where there is independence between water molecules and the apparent progress of the waves. The former moves extensively vertically, but little horizontally, around only 1% of the movement of the wave. This process was understood by Leonardo da Vinci, who compared it with the progress achieved by the wave produced by the wind in a wheat field, where the wave progresses but the plants remain rooted.
5. See that I am referring to the "psychotic part of the personality" and not to "psychosis" as a clinical entity, meaning that these mechanisms are present in everybody, psychotic or normal. See Note 1.
6. See Chapter Three, "Preconceptual traumas and the "internal traumatic object".
7. See Chapter One, "Murdering the mind".

CHAPTER EIGHT

The relativity of the vertex

From the point of view of a binocular vision

Introduction

I n his work on transformation (1965) Bion presents arguments to explain situations where patients could alter their position in relation to outside objects by changing their view-point as a result of splitting of time and space dimensions. Bion refers to this mechanism as "reversible perspective", where the patient's time and space operates in a different dimension to that of the analyst, similar to Rubin's vase, where you can see either a vase or two faces looking at each other, depending upon what you choose as a figure and what as its background.

Bion also refers to a "binocular vision", such as, for instance, the capacity to consider the breast and its absence as two different spaces, an attitude possible only when there exists the capacity to symbolize the absent object; because, after all, to observe the absence of the object and to name it at the same time is precisely the result of a binocular vision. Such form of vision is absent in psychotic patients (or, following Bion, in the psychotic part of the personality) because thinking is then dominated by a blind void that Segal (1957) has referred to as the "symbolic equation". It is also indispensable for the analyst to keep a binocular vision about the session, in relation to transference for instance, with its twofold time component about what has occurred in the past and what is happening now in the session; or in similar terms, between unconscious and consciousness, or between phantasy and reality.

Bion has used the concept of "correlation", meaning the character of two correlative terms, where one cannot take place without the other, such as, for instance, between tall and short, good and bad, etc. In geometry, for example, two quantities are correlated when the value of one variable determines the other, like the diameter, which is correlated with the surface of the circle. Bion refers to correlation in relation to splitting as observed in projective and introjective identifications, or in what he also referred to as "reversible perspective", where two fragmented parts correlate with each other, such as seen in addictive behaviour, where the perverse aspect correlates with the part that, due to guilt, repents (López-Corvo, 2003).

A soldier from country "A", at war with country "B", is suddenly overwhelmed by an excess of bravery and in the midst of the battle kills a great number of enemies. Without any hesitation, his peers and high ranking officers will consider him a true hero; however, the parents of those soldiers who died in the confrontation will believe otherwise, and the warrior responsible for such a deed will be thought of as a true criminal. There is a certain relativity depending on the vertex or point of view that we take, which could make someone either a hero or a criminal. Patients very often shelter fragmentations inside their minds, resulting in different parts that relate with each other like two countries in conflict, mimicking the war situation I have just described, and should be considered, as Bion stated, with a binocular vision.

Rosemary's Baby *and other cases*

Susan is a thirty-two-year-old married woman who consulted because of chronic anxiety and uncontrollable bouts of rage. She was born out of wedlock and did not know her father until she was a late adolescent. After a short time in analysis it became clear that her main traumatic issue was related to early separation, because when she was a baby her mother had to leave her with her grandparents, who at that time were living in one of the Caribbean islands. When she was four, her mother came to pick her up and brought her to live with her in her country of origin. Two years later her mother moved in with a man who had four children of his own: fourteen-year-old twins, a nine-year-old boy and a little girl around her own age, whom she felt to be very aggressive. She said she hated but feared them, and remembers one occasion when the twins cut the tyres of somebody's car with a knife. "There were four people against two, if my mother agreed with me, otherwise it was myself alone. When I met my stepfather the first thing he said was not to call him 'daddy' because he was not my father." She said she did not feel she was very feminine and referred a recurrent dream where she is chased by very good-looking women. I told her she feared the femininity in herself. She often wonders if her father would have been more loving if she had been a boy. At one point in her analysis she reported a dream:

> She was having sexual relations with her husband when suddenly they were interrupted by her mother, who came into their room. Next they were shopping and suddenly realized that her mother was following them. She turned towards her very angrily and told her to leave them alone.

She stated that at this time her mother was thinking of separating from her husband and began seeing a therapist. I said that an envious internal "mother part" in her was attacking her desire to become pregnant, just as she might have done as a child towards her own mother. As a mechanism of self-envy, now she is both the envious child she used to be as well as the pregnant mother she wants to be. She answered that she was indeed attempting to become pregnant; she stopped taking her contraceptive medication but feared she will not become pregnant after all.

Two months later she stated that the nurse called to inform her that her blood test was positive, although she did not present any sign of pregnancy. She fears delivery because it could be too painful, or she could have a miscarriage, or the baby could be deformed, like having six fingers, Down's Syndrome, or cleft lip. I said she is pregnant with twins. She asks how do I know, and I explained that she is telling me that she carries two babies, one in her uterus and another in her mind. The one in the uterus is just "news" on the telephone; the other in her mind seems to be an envious, murderous baby who wishes to get rid of the baby in her uterus. Perhaps she experienced similar envious feelings towards her mother as a child, when she feared she could have become pregnant with a baby brother or sister from her stepfather.

Two sessions later she presented a dream that corroborated what I had previously interpreted

> She had given birth to a beautiful baby, who suddenly turned black. She asked her husband if he had any black genes in him; something he denied. Then she looked at the baby closely and realized that the black colour disappeared and the skin turned white when she rubbed it.

She stated that she does not know why she had a dream like that; there are no blacks in her family. She remembers that the island where she lived as a child with her grandparents was a Caribbean Island where the majority of the population was black. "Some of them worked as maids in our home. There was a little girl, the daughter of a woman who worked for my grandparents, and I could have thought she was my sister, or perhaps that her parents were my own, because after all, my grandparents looked too old to be my real parents." She also remembered a woman teacher when she was at university, whom she liked very much and had phantasies that she was her mother. She even followed her once to see where she lived. After a long pause, she stated that she still feels she could have a miscarriage, also that a friend told her breast feeding was very painful and she is very sensitive around her nipples. She needs to have an operation on one of her teeth because she could lose it, but also fears the medicine she will need to take, like penicillin, decadron and another she does not remember the name of, could be harmful to the baby. I again repeated that she seems to be pregnant with twins, that the baby in her mind looks like a little envious, murderous, black baby who wishes to poison the baby in the uterus in order to destroy it. She recalls the film *Rosemary's Baby*.

Another patient complains of not being able to fall asleep, of going to bed at four o'clock in the morning and waking up at 11 a.m. every day, and states that he wishes me to give him sleep medication. I said that he wishes to make me an accomplice to a part of him that does not consider the other part of him that wishes to go to bed late. Another patient I will refer to as Mike comes for treatment because of an important marijuana dependency he wishes to give up. He explains that every day after work he comes home, has a light supper, smokes pot, and watches pornographic movies. He also states that to smoke marijuana is bad and that he would like to stop it, but, so far, it has been extremely difficult for him to do so. The patient is divided, although he is not aware, between a part of himself—I will call it part A—that compulsively consumes marijuana without being able to stop it, and another part of himself—I will call it part B-that is completely the opposite, that will like not to take the drug because it makes him feel very guilty. There is a dissociation between an "ego ideal" that offers to the ego an ideal model to which it must continuously submit but cannot ever fulfil, and a realistic aspect that becomes debased, feels shameful, and remains hidden. This "ego ideal" functions in a way that resembles Procustes' bed,[1] that, regardless how you do it, it will never be satisfactory.

Another patient I will call Irene suffered from acute anxiety attacks, which incapacitated her for work, although she was able to finish her studies as a computer technician. Her sister, one year younger, has managed to find a job and has moved away from her parent's house, while Irene, still living at home, is having difficulties finding a suitable work position. She often communicates about her search for work, how people often like her portfolio but never call or offer her a job. It is as if she is split between a part (A) on the one hand, that wishes *not* to find a position in order to stay home and be looked after, while, on the other hand, there was also part (B) that wants, like her sister, to leave her house, to "be successful", to take chances, to make money and to be independent. Up to a certain point, she remained at her parent's house, had not found a job and was clear that her desire to leave was more of a wishful thinking, a powerful phantasy but not a reality; while at the same time remaining at home and feeling protected by her parents was obviously the "real" acting part of herself.

I said to her that she was split in two: part A was true but hidden, while part B was obvious but was not true; that she felt ashamed of part A and felt like hiding it, like someone who felt ashamed of a relative and kept him out of sight. I also added that I wondered what was so bad about wishing to stay at home with her parents and do nothing, if after all, it seemed that this was what an important part of herself preferred to do; whereas if she had wanted to act part B, she would have been already working by now, like her sister was. In the transference, the situation was very similar; it became rather difficult to help her to acknowledge that it was absolutely necessary for her to make her treatment her own affair and not something that belonged to her parents or to myself. It took quite some time to convince her to come at least twice a week, as well as for her to understand that she was not a car or a machine brought to the mechanic to be fixed.[2]

The issue was to rescue and approve the part of her that wished to stay at home and remain forever as my patient, wanting for me to take over, to become pregnant with her and to help her to be born again, problem free. The conflict, I said at one point, is that the "regressive" purpose of this phantasy is against the laws of nature, because we are all fatalistically condemned to grow and therefore, it is essential to invite this regressive part to therapy, to make it legal and find out what exactly is registered within this aspect of her. At the same time, the analyst faces the risk of responding—or counter-acting—to the intensity of the patient's projective identification, which continuously attempts to convince both—patient and analyst—that phantasy A is real and part B is not true and does not exist. I often say to the patient that such a statement is rather unfair, because part B represents a successful aspect of herself and not a failure. The real problem is the difficulty, because of unknown reasons, to openly acknowledge such a success instead of debasing it as an expression of failure.

Gerry is a twenty-six-year-old, intelligent patient who, due to a chronic dependence on marijuana, was unable to go beyond the first year of university. Significant paranoid feelings and a debt of around $40,000 forced him to move from the campus to his mother's house and to begin working as a helper in a flower shop. He brought a dream:

> He was driving around with his mother, listening to rock music, which he likes and which his mother was very much enjoying too. He drove her to the backyard of a house where Justin, a classmate from high school used to live. On his way to the back of the house, he passed a window where he could see his friend's parents working. He was afraid of being caught while in the backyard, where he tried to show his mother some beautiful flowers. Two other friends, also from high school, arrived and said that they were attending a party to celebrate Justin's graduation and, since Gerry was not attending school, he was not invited, something that made him feel left out and very upset.

He said his mother got divorced when he was very young because his father was a bum. His mother, on the other hand, is an artist, a photographer, very accessible and understanding, different from other mothers. He had shared with her his own experiences about different perceptions under the effect of hallucinogenic mushrooms. Sometimes, while at work, he sees beautiful flowers and thinks she might like to take pictures of them; also, he can from his work spot Gerry's house, the one in the dream. He remembers that Justin's mother was very strict, "she never liked me, and Justin came to school with swollen eyes because his dad, who was really his stepfather, used to beat him." About the friends that came around in the dream, they were like Justin, finishing their university studies, one in engineering and the other in medicine. He then complained about feeling bad because, unlike his friends, he could not finish his studies, "I feel I am a real failure."

Then I said that he was unfair to himself. If he were to try to get away in a rocket either from the moon or from Saturn, from where did he think it was going to be easier? "From the moon," he said, "because there is less gravity." I continued: "You might have a similar problem, because it was easier for Justin to move away from his strict mother and his aggressive stepfather, it was like moving away from the moon; but for you, to get away from such a nice, understanding, sensible mother would be like trying to get away from Saturn." He was unfair with himself because he had been continuously using marijuana for many years, and marijuana is a drug that specifically acts upon the brain, and the brain is the most important organ needed to get a university degree. In other words, the part of him that tried to remain with his nice, powerful, and understanding mother, by means of a chronic use of marijuana in order to destroy his capacity to learn, was extremely successful.

Notes

1. A mythical giant, killed by Theseus, who was a thief and murderer; he would capture people and tie them to an iron bed, stretching them or hacking off their legs to make them fit.
2. See Chapter One.

CHAPTER NINE

The unconscious

Denouncing consciousness's fear of truth

"We are concerned not with what the individual means to say so much as with what he does no intend to say, but does in fact say"

(Bion)

"Le á traduire primordial, nous le nomons: l' inconscient"

(Laplanche, 1992, p. 139)

An epistemological notion of the unconscious

What exactly is the unconscious made of? According to classical theory the unconscious represents a reservoir of repressed unfulfilled impulses, which are continuously pressing to achieve satisfaction, albeit not always capable of attaining it due to strong rejection from super-ego demands; as a consequence there will be a continuous reappearance of its disguised derivatives. Restricted by a static quality, the unconscious lacks the possibility of reaching consciousness by itself, and will require the help of preconscious mechanisms in order to mutate "thing repre-sentations" into "word representations" (Freud, 1915e).

We now seem to know all at once what the difference is between a conscious and an unconscious presentation. The two are not, as we supposed, different registrations of the same content in different psychical localities, nor yet different functional states of cathexis in the same locality; but the conscious presentation comprises the presentation of the thing plus the presentation of the word belong-ing to it, while the unconscious presentation is the presentation of the thing alone. [*ibid.*, p. 201]

Later contributions made by Fairbairn and Klein changed the Freudian notion of the unconscious content, that is from a pure decathected drives notion to the notion of the unconscious as a reservoir of early narcissistic *object relations* repressed memories. These representations could interfere with ego growth and integra-tion processes by compromising and eventually withholding and isolating split part objects, which will then be capable of interacting with outside objects by means of projective and introjective identi-fications.

Using Saussure's (1916) structural contribution to language, the French school of psychoanalysis has argued the veracity of Freud's notion of "word representation" by stating that the unconscious is, by itself, capable of the attributes of a language. Ricoeur (1970), for instance, referring to dreams, stated that language and not wishes should be placed at the centre of analysis. Lacan, on the other hand, stated, "the unconscious is structured as a language". According to Laplanche and Leclaire (1960), the Saussurian *signified* takes the place of the "drive in search of satisfaction", and the intimate rela-tionship between *signified* and *signifier*, just as observed in any spoken language and represented as follows: S/s, is broken in the condensation or metaphor where a new relation is then established: the *signifier* S is replaced by a new one S', now represented as: S'/s, but the previous S, instead of being suppressed takes the place of the *signified*, which now could be represented as S/S, and the derivative now represented continues as such, like a latent sequence of *signifiers*. Now a more complex formula could be set up as a chain:

$$\frac{S' \times S}{S \quad s.}$$

The bar that separates *signifier* from *signified*, on the other hand, represents a dual notion of repression and condensation, because, after all, metaphor is a direct consequence of repression.

Meltzer (1983) appears to take a similar direction when he conceives dreams as an expression of unconscious thoughts:

> The most lucid sequence would seem to require the definition of the dream-process as one of thinking about emotional experiences, after which the way would be clear to examine what Freud calls the "considerations of representability" (by which we will mean symbol formation and the interplay of visual and linguistic symbolic forms) and the "dream work" (by which we will mean the phantasy operations and the thought processes by which the emotional conflicts and problems seek resolution). [p. 51]

Matte-Blanco (1998) had developed a model based on mathematical logics in order to explain some characteristics of the unconscious as they were originally described by Freud: presence of reciprocal contradictions and denials, displacement, condensation, absence of time, and the switching of external and internal realities. Matte-Blanco argues that conscious and unconscious logics are completely different in relation to the capacity to establish symmetrical and asymmetrical reciprocities. For instance, if I were to say that A is B's father, its symmetrical opposite, that is, B is A's father, could never be true, unless we are referring to an unconscious construct, where such symmetric incongruity could be possible. Matte-Blanco states that unconscious processes are dominated by symmetry and conscious processes are dominated by asymmetry.

Ontological characteristics of the unconscious

To conceive the unconscious structured as a form of language, to know about its logic, about its different forms of association and particular syntaxes, represents an important contribution to the epistemological understanding of its true nature. There is, however, a very important perspective that has not received the same

attention. I am thinking about the ontological aspects of the unconscious. "We infer the unconscious", said Freud in 1933, "from its
effects, but of its true nature we know nothing" (1933a, p. 70). What
is the unconscious made of? What is its true purpose? Why do we
need an unconscious as classical analysis suggests? Is it a reservoir
of *repressed* and undesired drives? Why does the unconscious speak
in a cryptic language, making it difficult to understand its messages? Is the unconscious an organ that continuously secretes truth
and denounces conscious lies? Why is the unconscious completely
autonomous, and why does it operate entirely by itself without
conscious intervention?

The unconscious functions like a regulating agent, which automatically maintains equilibrium by adjusting consciousness's
appreciations of internal and external realities perceived by the
sense organs. The unconscious could be considered as an organ that
continuously reveals truth, or as an adaptational and self-protective
instrument that attempts to correct conscious lies.[1] The fact that
perception by sense organs is influenced by the pleasure principle
will make it biased and unreliable because not always will it be
fastened to the truth. In this sense, the unconscious is indispensable
for life preservation, for it would operate in relation to consciousness, as an ecosystem intended to maintain an equilibrium, or
homeostasis between lies and truth, similar, for instance, to how the
pancreas controls the amount of insulin discharged into the blood
stream, depending on the existing level of glucose. On the one
hand, the unconscious is an organ of hybrid qualities. In order to
produce messages it uses a syntax formed by symbolic and meta-
phoric ideographs, which are very similar to conscious language,
instead of using the biochemical language present in involuntary
organs such as the pancreas, for instance. On the other hand, the
unconscious is completely autonomous and involuntary, just as
other involuntary organs are, capable of manufacturing and
"secreting" truth without any conscious intervention.

The main difficulty of the unconscious is its use of a cryptic
language, as it is observed in the component images of dreams, in
parapraxis, or, more difficult to observe, underneath any spoken
word during the process of free association in any analytical hour.
The truth has already been thought by the unconscious, the analyst
is only an exegete who practices the hermeneutic of a symbolic text.

The unconscious is always present, even when we are completely awake and consciousness dominates our mind, analogous to the stars that become invisible during the day while still present.[2]

Lacan has stated that the unconscious is the "discourse of the Other",[3] where the "Other" means the mother (Lacan, 1966, p. 16). In this sense it could be understood that Lacan's unconscious is related to super-ego and ego identifications with the mother, leaving out the intuitive aspects of the unconscious so well emphasized by Bion's concept of O, or in Lacan's own terms, by the "imaginary order".

How does the unconscious think?

In 1925 Freud added a footnote to the "Secondary revision" section of his *Interpretation of Dreams* (1900a, p. 506n), introducing the hypothesis that dreams could represent "a particular form of thinking". From this assertion we could infer that, for Freud, the unconscious, besides being considered as a "reservoir of unsatisfied wishes", was also an organ capable of thinking. How is the unconscious able to express itself in such a manner for its message to be revealed and eventually used? Visual images become the best possible choice for the unconscious to reveal itself during sleep, because vision is the only sense available, given that voluntary muscles are inhibited and audition is compromised to alert in case of danger.[4] Visual images are used by the unconscious, instead of words, in order to create messages, like ideograms or symbolisms, but lack the exactness of written or spoken lexis.

Being deprived of a speech organ, as Benveniste (1971) had stated, the unconscious communicates its messages in a similar way to that used by explorer bees to indicate to other bees the location of flowers, and also similar to how signal language is used by deaf-mutes, or how, in miming games, players attempt to pass a message without the help of speech. If someone alien to this game were to observe players from a distance, he or she might find it difficult to understand the players' grimaces and contortions intended to lead to the interpretation of the concealed message. In a similar fashion, visual images are manipulated by the unconscious in order to represent a message, and will disregard other meanings implicit in the image, like actors representing a character in a play would, for they would necessarily disregard their own personal identity that, if used, would become an impediment. This can explain "dream distortions", or why dreams do not follow conscious logic and instead often present themselves as very odd and with obscure unfolding. The narrative sequence of images in a dream will be determined by its symbolic meaning. Images might be loaded or pregnant with significance, depending on the message implicit in them, and will never be established by any conscious reasoning.

Since Freud, the unconscious—due to its elusive and ineffable characteristics—has been "defined by absences", comparing it to consciousness and to outside reality, and referring to those attributes that are missed in it, such as time, space, and mutual contradictions. Only mechanisms of condensation and displacement can be considered as true characteristics of the unconscious, which Lacan, in order to sustain that the unconscious is structured as a language, has made equivalent to figures of speech, such as metonymy and metaphor, respectively.

I believe that if dimensions such as time, space, contradictions, and asymmetrical logic were present in the unconscious as they are in the real world, they would not only become absolutely unnecessary to the unconscious intentions, but would constitute a total hindrance to its purpose of sending a hasty message to consciousness. All unconscious mechanisms must be subordinated to a prompt and efficient form of communication. If it were to have the same consideration of time, space and so on, indispensable to consciousness and reality, the unconscious process would lack the same pace and effectiveness that it requires. It would be similar to actors in a play who, instead of acting their assigned character, would insist on being themselves and addressing their own personal interests and conflicts, thus obstructing the play representation.

When Egyptians invented hieroglyphics, they did it with the purpose of communicating, of portraying clear and useful messages in order to be understood, and never with the intention of making them puzzling and unintelligible; the obscurity of hieroglyphics, however, is a direct consequence of ignorance brought about by history, which, up to Champollion's intervention, made them only decorative and irrelevant. In a similar fashion, *repudiation* (repression) makes unconscious creations—like dreams, for instance—decorative and irrelevant, just as hieroglyphics once were. The unconscious is quite accessible during childhood, but loses its clarity afterwards, as "fear of truth" progressively takes over with the progress of time and socialization. We become "unconscious illiterates", and then require a psychoanalyst special translator in order to help us tame consciousness[5] and make the unconscious an essential tool for survival. It could be conjectured that such unconscious illiteracy represents a natural kind of barrier that protects us from the anxiety—not to say the terror—generated by truth, for we are not capable of understanding the message portrayed by the unconscious until the ego is prepared to "contain" the impact of truth. It would perhaps be like giving the ego the chance to choose between "knowing" or "ignoring" long before being primed to do so. The unconscious will only perform in close connection to the ego's level of development; or, in other words, everyone has the unconscious they deserve. Such a barrier created by natural illiteracy is perhaps similar to the existence of the hymen in women, which creates a barrier in young girls to prevent the danger of premature pregnancy, for the fear of pain would post-pone penetration until they are better prepared and more capable of sustaining motherhood. The story of the Sphinx in the Oedipus myth carries a similar connotation, because the Sphinx, meaning "to squeeze" in Greek (Σφυγε), committed her crimes by strangula-tion. She killed herself when the truth of her riddle was revealed by Oedipus, entailing, in other words, the violence implied by the truth.

There is another interesting aspect related to the notion of *repres-sion*. If you were not allowed admittance into an exclusive nightclub because the porter recognized you as the same person who, a few hours earlier, was protesting against the club's possible immoral practices, you might say that your entry was denied because you were considered suspicious or dangerous, but you would not say that you were "repressed". If messages from the unconscious denouncing conscious lies were not admitted by the preconscious, this would not mean that the unconscious content is repressed. A similar situation takes place in therapy with some borderline pathologies, when certain kinds of splitting allow the patient to repeat an interpretation giving the impression that a proper insight has been achieved, but a few sessions later the same conflict reappears, as if the interpretation and the apparent insight have never taken place. Deafness is commonly present during the analytical hour: the patient hears without listening.[6]

Instincts or preconcepts?

Freud's conception of the unconscious as a reservoir of impulses or instinctive drives searching for satisfaction was influenced by both Darwin's ideas and the invention of the steam engine machine. Fairbairn and Klein proposed that the aim of the impulse was towards objects, instead being towards indiscriminate satisfaction. Furthermore, Bion added a *mind* as a sort of container, which determines the ultimate limit of all mental operations. Based on Kant's (1781) idea of "empty thoughts", he introduced the notion of "preconcepts", which I believe changes the notion of drive or impulses as established in classical psychoanalysis. Therefore, according to Bion, preconcepts represent a state of expectation comparable to the innate or *a priori* disposition babies have towards the breast. In other words, when the baby (preconcept) gets in touch with the breast, a realization takes place that could be translated into a concept, which Bion represents as a form of container–contained relationship. After birth, those preconcepts or empty thoughts are immediately fulfilled with realizations—meaning experiences with real objects—and then accumulated as memories in the mind. Depending on whether or not frustration is tolerated, preconcepts can either be discharged as projective identifications, or move forwards and be metabolized by a mechanism Bion has referred to as the alpha function, which will then change them into concepts.

Denouncing lies, or a reservoir of undesired impulses?

Conceiving the unconscious as a reservoir of undesired drives provides a completely different scenario than perceiving it as an organ that denounces conscious lies. To perceive it in the latter scenario would be like vindicating the unconscious from an ominous, unfriendly, and threatening nature, to a more gracious, positive, and valuable one. The other possibility is the existence of a progressive change from one extreme to the other as the ego grows and unconscious–conscious communication improves. Details of this aspect are presented in Chapter Eleven.

Dreaming: the unconscious true language

I will be referring to dreaming in more detail elsewhere.[7] Now, however, I am mostly concerned with the concepts of "dream work" and "dream thoughts". Following classical theory, dream work is conceived of as a repressive mechanism that will change the apparent content of a dream into something obscure and confused. Freud described four mechanisms: condensation, displacement, considerations of representability (or elaboration), and secondary revision. Bion, however, took a different view to that suggested by Freud and proposed that it is conscious material, instead of unconscious, that is subject to the dream work. According to Bion, the conscious material is stored as memory and later used to manufacture dreams as well as to make transformations from the paranoid–schizoid to the depressive position. He says: "Freud says Aristotle states that a dream is the way the mind works in sleep: I say it is the way it works when awake" (Bion, 1992, pp. 43, 47).

Initially Bion referred to "dream work α", but he later wanted to change it for he felt it could create confusion if it were to be used in a manner different from what Freud had initially created it for (*ibid.*, p. 73); however, he continued using it in the same manner even after making such a remark. The term "α-function" was used for the first time in *Cogitations*, in a note possibly dated to the end of the 1960s, which allowed Bion finally to discriminate between dream work proper and alpha function. To build this theory he used concepts from Freud's *Interpretation of Dreams* (1900a) and "Formulations on the two principles of mental functioning" (1911b), as well as Klein's notion of guilt, superego, and paranoid–schizoid and depressive positions.

Alpha-function represents an abstraction used to describe the capacity to change sense information into α-elements (Bion, 1992, p. 63), as well as to provide the mind with material to create dream thoughts that could allow discrimination between being asleep or awake, between being conscious or unconscious, and to give a sense of identity and selfness (Bion, 1967, p. 115). The brain never rests. What takes place is a fluctuation between states of consciousness and unconsciousness, thanks to the α-function and to the permeability of the contact barrier that allows one side to remain awake while the other is asleep. Before he discriminated this function from dream-work, Bion stated that a series of steps were essential: (i) to pay attention to sensuous impressions; (ii) to store these impressions in the memory; (iii) to change them into "ideograms"; (iv) and, depending on which principle dominated the mind, either to store them and to remember them if the reality principle dominated, or to expel them under the ruling of the pleasure principle. Dream-work represents the way in which the preconscious works in relation to the unconscious's contents, and it depends on whether the "contact barrier" or the "screen of beta elements" dominates.[8] For Bion, thinking is a consequence of thoughts and not the other way around. Thinking represents an obligatory development of the mind that is produced by the pressure of thoughts.

I would like now to refer to a dream brought up by a woman during her second visit. What I found then to be very interesting, and I think many therapists might have encountered similar appreciations, was the contrast between a rather primitive and concrete framework in her mind and the beautiful metaphors produced by the labour of her unconscious dream-work.

Z was a widow in her late fifties, who developed symptoms associated with a reactive depression with suicidal ruminations. Z was brought for consultation by N, her only daughter, recently married to H, who, due to financial restrictions, was forced to move back to Z's home. N was in analysis with a colleague who had given her my name in order to evaluate her mother's emotional condition. There were some differences and arguments between Z and H, which N ameliorated and perceived as the expression of mutual adjustment. Z's husband had died suddenly from a heart attack about five years before the time of consultation and, according to N, her mother might have been reacting either to another anniversary of her father's death, or perhaps to the proximity of her menopause. Educationally, Z had barely finished primary school, and her thinking was usually dominated by magical and omnipotent reckoning. She believed, for instance, and did not hesitate to explain it to anyone who asked her, that following a series of rather simple adding and subtracting calculations, she could with great accuracy foresee the winning number of the lottery, although she had never been able to achieve it.

At the beginning of the second visit she presented the following dream:

> There was a woman lying dead and a man beside her who appeared rather unconcerned. He was drying his hands with a towel that he then threw with scorn over the face of the woman. She opened her eyes as if she was not dead. She was pale and her breasts were small like a little girl's. She then climbed over a high wall and threatened to jump.

Z provided no associations and stared at me in silence, waiting for me to say something. I said that her dream seemed to put emphasis on a sort of scornful or inconsiderate attitude of men towards women, showing no respect for a dead woman. "It is true", said Z, and added hastily: "But he [the character in the dream] did not know she was alive"; meaning perhaps that she was not a fool, that she was "alert". Then, as some kind of protest, she started to generalize the attitude of being unconsidered by all men, stating that her husband used to be like that with her, as well as H, her son-in-law, who often displayed a similar behaviour towards her daughter, N. Even her father, who died when she was only eight years old, was also very disrespectful towards her mother. She then remembered that, after her father's death, her mother, not being able to look after all of the children, placed her together with other siblings in a boarding school for two long years.

While listening I thought, but said nothing, that perhaps the woman on the wall wanting to jump might have represented the intense mental pain she had suffered because of all the losses and feelings of desolation she might have endured, something unconsciously experienced again at the approach of the anniversary of her husband's death. She wished to be dead, but she was alive, alert, and in pain. I felt the central issue of the dream was related to a series of unresolved mourning situations: the death of her father when she was only a child (the child-like aspect represented in the dream by the woman's lack of breasts), her being placed in a boarding school at such a tender age, and, finally, the sudden disappearance of her husband when she was a grown-up woman. She was very angry at men's lack of consideration, because they died and left her so desolated. To this situation we must also add that N and her husband moved into her place, a situation that triggered intense feelings of envy related to Z witnessing the love and company N and H provided to each other, in contrast to Z's loneliness and hopeless ageing. Z was angry with H because he was "unconsidered" by being alive, in comparison to those men in her life who had disappeared. An attempt to introduce some of these ideas failed because Z was unprepared for such an amount of truth.

It was surprising and fascinating to observe the way in which the unconscious was capable—and always is—to find beautiful representations in order to denounce Z's history and continuous suffering. Her ambivalence, suicidal ideas, loneliness, envy, anger, and powerlessness had already been experienced by Z in the past, and were still enduring with great intensity. During a matter of seconds in a few condensed images of a brief dream, behind a conscious that was almost illiterate and dominated by primitive, magical, and concrete thinking, the unconscious portrayed the whole tragedy.

Notes

1. Ancient Latin knew about consciousness's capacity to deceive (as observed in illusions and hallucinations), and registered such discovery by providing a common root to designate the words "mind" (*ment-e*) and "lying" (*ment-*ire).

2. Sir Henry Wotton (1568–1639), in his poem: "you meaner beauties of the night", expressed a similar interest:

> You meaner beauties of the night,
> That poorly satisfy our eyes
> More by your number than your light;
> You common people of the skies,
> What are you when the sun shall rise?

3. "Other" with a capital O, (or A, because "other" in French is *autre*). Different from the other, or *petite autre*, representing the ego in the imaginary order or narcissistic relationship with the object.

4. In other conditions such as psychosis, the unconscious floods consciousness while awake, making it difficult to distinguish between sleeping and wakefulness. During this stage, projected unconscious contents that reach the external objects give place to hallucinations and

what Bion has named the "bizarre object". In this case (while awake), vision is usually engaged to alert danger while audition, being less compromised, is often chosen as the available sense to reveal the unconscious by means of auditory hallucinations.

5. See Chapter Eleven: "The three faces of the preconscious".

6.   See Chapter Three: "Preconceptual traumas and the "internal traumatic object".

7. See Chapter Fourteen.

8. Bion defined "contact barrier" as an imaginary membrane that separates–unites unconscious and consciousness, composed of alpha elements and responsible for discriminating between sleeping and wakefulness, among other states. It is different from the "screen of beta elements", composed of an agglomeration of beta elements and responsible for the presence of psychotic states. For a better definition see López-Corvo, 2003.

CHAPTER TEN

Interpreting or translating the unconscious?

Introduction

Referring to dream analysis, Meltzer (1983) has questioned the use of "interpretation", because this term seems to suggest that the analyst has added some meaning of his own; a sort of theoretical sin of which no analyst is ever innocent. "Formulation", according to him, might be a better choice, because the process of formulation implies the acknowledgement of a transformation, which in dreams, for instance, will imply the change of a visual image into a verbal language. Along the same lines, *Webster's Dictionary* defines interpretation as a way "to conceive on the light of an individual belief, judgment or circumstance". "Formulation", the word Meltzer suggested, would connote "change from one place, state, form or appearance, to another." The psychoanalytic act of making conscious the unconscious would imply all of these actions: clarification, formulation, interpretation and translation.

Originally Freud used the word *deutung*, very close to *deutlich*, meaning "clarification", although different from interpretation. *Deutung* was initially conceived as *tramdeutun*, meaning "clarification or dream interpretation", a concept that was already implicit during the time of the cathartic phase, when interpretations, influenced by the dynamic of the steam engine model, were used to induce a "discharge of accumulated libido", while the symptom would act as a pressure valve. It was an instrumentation close to neurophysiology and to mechanisms originally described in the Project, when the analyst was conceived as not different from a medical doctor, responsible for a symptomatic resolution and a future cure. At the same time, the influence brought to bear by Darwin's theories made the instinct's need for an immediate satisfaction the main purpose behind any animal behaviour, including that of humans. In this way, dreams were considered a simple satisfaction of repressed instinctive wishes, or, in other words, its interpretation or *traundeutung* was given by its *deutung* (direction or sense), because it would always be known that the meaning of a dream represented the satisfaction of a repressed wish, something that, as a consequence, left "anxiety dreams" without any logical explanation.

New discoveries that followed shed light on the complex organization of the mental apparatus, like the interaction between the id, ego, and superego, as well as the preconscious and conscious. The tragic fatalism present in the Oedipus complex became the centre of any mental suffering, together with the polarization between death and life instincts. The ego turned into the central character of the drama, pulled by three opposite agencies: the instincts' immediate satisfaction, the superego's moral restrictions, and the unavoidable weight of reality. Repression became the model of all defences, representing the most economic way out from the pressure exercised by the three agencies. The introduction of the transference and the countertransference concluded the picture.

During that time three important features guided the interpretation: (i) the attempt to subdue the resistance and lift repression to id's contents; (ii) to restore childhood memories: (iii) Freud's continuous investigation about the secrets of the mind, something present in the narration of the Rat Man and the Wolf Man. The need to investigate in order to empirically validate new hypotheses induced Freud to interact directly with his patients in order to explain the purpose of his discoveries. His notes from the Rat Man's first four months of treatment are paradigmatic, and although we do not have any proof that he might not have continued such a methodology, we do not know that he did otherwise either. It is obvious that dream interpretation played a fundamental role in the systematization of the interpretation, as we can read from Freud's article "The handling of dream-interpretation in psychoanalysis" (1911e).

In 1933, Nunberg (1965), an important personality within classical psychoanalysis, stated, following Freud's steps, that interpretations directed to the ego usually induce revelations of id contents as well as the reconstruction of instinctive development. An id interpretation, on the other hand, often illuminates certain characteristics or habits and allows a reconstruction of their meanings (p. 347). I agree with this statement, but I would add that interpretations directed to the ego's specific point of view or perspective often will be translated, in the ego awareness of its particular splitting, as a form of defence against the anxiety induced by this kind of mechanism. On the other hand, emphasis placed on historical reconstructions or on id contents often carries the danger of stimulating transference idealization, dependency, or persecutory feelings. A precise "confession" of fantasies is no longer as important as to assist the ego to deal with the anxiety induced by the splitting produced by unresolved historical issues. The solution is no longer based on revelation of intimacy, but on the conflict experienced by the ego in the face of a fragmented self, projective identifications, reality demands, and the importance of achieving a state of ego autonomy. A patient brings books that she tries to read at the beginning of the sessions; one could address the issue by saying that the patient must stop reading and talk about her history, or one could address the interpretation to the ego conflict by saying that she is having difficulty knowing whether to read from a book or to read from her. The first approach could elicit persecutory feelings and dependency, the latter, although addressing the same unconscious conflict of avoidance, also portrays the ego's freedom to choose. After all, the practical problem is not so much from where to read, from the book or from her; the true issue, I think, is to know that, although she is free to choose either way, she will have to face different consequences related to either choice.

From this perspective, that of where the interpretation should be directed, Fairbairn's and Klein's approaches would have been better named "ego psychology" instead of "object relational". For them, the internal world was no longer ruled by repressed instinctive energy struggling to achieve satisfaction. Neither was the ego conceived as a device for opening and closing valves, thereby regulating the restricting libidinal pressure. The internal world was instead organized as an active memory compilation of primeval object relations, stored as object representations without any possible distinction between instinct and object. Such relations then would be unconsciously multiplied in the transference, where they would be capable of performing, not as repressed or discharged gaseous entities, but as phantasies that could be attacked, damaged, split into small or large pieces and, most of all, projected into the outside object or again reintrojected as powerful identifications. I think that a crucial contribution to psychoanalysis is depicted in Klein's notion of the self, conceived as an obscure and protean interaction of part object relations within the complex geography of the internal world. Such conception obviously had an immediate influence on the construction and purpose of the interpretation, no longer essentially directed towards repressed id contents, but towards the ego's immediate complications brought about by the existence of interactive forces between different part objects, as well as the ego's manic or depressive attempts to repair damaged objects.

The introduction by Bion in 1962 of the phenomenology of an apparatus for thinking thoughts, in order to understand psychotic defences was very influential in clarifying the purpose of the interpretation.[1] Bion understood that a common mechanism in psychotic patients was their abhorrence of reality that induced a need to split the thinking apparatus and to project it outside the self. Such a mechanism induces in these patients the need to require from the analyst the use of his/her thinking apparatus in order to think for them,[2] something often observed in patients who expect to be guided or told what to do. An important rationale of the interpretation in these cases would be to help the patient to deal with their fear of reality and to become aware of this process of splitting and projective identification of their apparatus for thinking thoughts. In Chapter Three, about "deaf-mute object and preverbal trauma", I refer in detail to this mechanism and also provide extensive clinical material.

The interpretation as a theory

Two different attributes could be considered in relation to the aim of the interpretation: (i) the interpretation represents an epistemological outline in the form of an hypothesis, which attempts to make sense of or translate the latent content behind the manifest discourse; (ii) the interpretation also contains implicitly a therapeutic intention, attempting to reduce the level of mental suffering. Bion (1963), for instance, stated that psychoanalytic interpretation could be understood as "theories" held by the analyst about methods and models the patient has about the analyst, and that when meaningful in expression as well as content, it could have a therapeutic effect. The interpretation could also be considered as "wild thoughts" never before being thought by the analysand and, often, not by the analyst either.

The act of formulating an interpretation in order to translate the latent content, involves a series of complex, automatic, and intuitive actions that we could summarize as follows.

1. To listen in a state of floating attention (Freud, 1912e), without memory, desire, or understanding (Bion, 1970).[3]
2. To establish a kind of comprehensive identification with the patient, referred to by some as: "duplicated resonance" (Weiss, 1950), "empathy" (Beres & Arlow, 1974; Kohut, 1982), "at-onement" (Bion, 1965). This kind of automatic implementation should be differentiated from the mechanism of projective identification (Sandler, 1993), because the former represents a "normal kind of narcissism", open and unsaturated; while the latter corresponds to a pathological narcissistic state, closed and saturated, that imprisons.[4] Intuition plays a definite role in seizing what Bion has referred to as "O," or the capacity of the analyst to be able to capture the patient's unconscious with his/her own unconscious and then transform it into knowledge (K) in order to manufacture the interpretation. In this sense, the phenomenon disclosed by the interpretation could increase knowledge, although never unveil the unconscious reality, incessantly becoming, which is continuously changing like the water in a river. It should first be intuited and then comprehended.

4. To sustain the expectation, waiting for "that substance" that reiterates, like Poe's "Purloined letter", or the continuous return of the "repressed"—in classical terms—or the "repudiated", as I suggest. "An interpretation", says Bion, "should not be given on a single association; a single association is open to an enormous number of interpretations" (1992, p. 210). Just as two different points might determine the direction of a line in Euclidian geometry, two different associations (or more) might also provide the direction the interpretation would eventually take. From the point of view of topology, there is also, along the same lines, what is known as a "homeomorphic transformation", meaning that in spite of a continuous change, something remains unaltered.

Bion states that O should be gathered with an "act of faith": "Through F [act of faith] one can 'see', 'hear', and 'feel' the mental phenomena of whose reality no practising psycho-analyst has any doubt though he cannot with any accuracy represent them by existing formulations" (Bion, 1975, pp. 57–58).

Trying to explain the concept of F ("act of faith"), Bion (1970) remembers what Freud once said in a letter to Andreas-Salomé, where he mentioned his method of achieving a state of mind that would provide clarity when the subject of investigation was particularly obscure. "He speaks [Freud] of blinding himself artificially, as a method of achieving this artificial blinding I have indicated the importance of eschewing memory and desire" (p. 43). Bion also states that the hypothesis then established should be organized around a "selected fact" that will provide a sense of meaning and cohesion to the interpretation, representing a "constant conjunction". In this sense, the interpretation represents a theory, a deductive scientific system that provides order to the initial chaos of observations. Any given scientific system must require the presence of at least three functions: (i) that a private event could be made public; (ii) that it could resist a reality test; and (iii) that the events group themselves in a way that makes sense, or, in Bion's own terms, "to have a common sense", meaning that all the senses of the analyst agree as well as those of other persons who happen to observe.

Bion approaches the interpretation from the vertex of different theories, such as, for instance, the "theory of functions", which conceives the interpretation as a transformation of sense impressions related to an emotional experience, into alpha elements, that would proliferate, become organized around a selected fact and change into a narrative. From the point of view of container–contained theory, Bion discusses the capacity of a patient to learn from experience by making use of the message given by the interpretation, and to associate it with past experiences. Bion refers to this situation as a "commensal" kind of container–contained interaction, where three instances are involved: the interpretation ($\male$), the patient ($\female$) and the knowledge (K) resulting from the association. This could all be represented as: $[+(\male+\female) = +K]$. However, when the interpretation representing a positive message ($+\male$) meets a negative environment where envy prevails, represented as ($-\female$), the interpretation might be denuded of every meaning, leaving only an insignificant or useless residue, like a simple noise; the equation in this case could now be represented as follows: $+\male+(-\female) = -K$, producing what Bion refers to as a "*withoutness*" or negative knowledge: $-K$ (Bion, 1962, pp. 96–99).

The interpretation: translation or transformation?

Mahoney (1980) says,

> Freud should be ranked among the world's major theoreticians of translation . . . for he ascribes to the concept a scope and depth that appeared nowhere before in history. His understanding of translation is truly a semiotic contribution . . . Nevertheless, the question remains for us as to what kind of difference might be legitimately posited between translation and transformation. [pp. 471–472]

Bion has stated that all interpretations represent "transformations" of representations that contain invariables within a specific psychoanalytic theory, in such a way that the comprehension of an interpretation would depend on the invariables involved. For instance, understanding impressionism as the transformation of a landscape into a picture could be similar to the dynamic present in the "interpretation", when conceived as a transformation of a series of unrelated elements surrounding an individual behaviour (landscape), which could become understood with the use of the dynamic of the Oedipus complex (picture). As stated above, Bion also defines interpretation as the transformation of raw sensuous impressions—beta elements, the thing-in-itself or "O"—into alpha elements.

I think that the interpretation is both: (a) *translation* of unconscious cryptic messages into conscious semiotics, and (b) *transformation* from a certain kind of unconscious set to another conscious set, as a form of topological or homeomorphic change. I think the main difficulty hinges on several issues: (i) whether it is a personal or individual message; (ii) whether the syntaxes used by the unconscious to communicate its messages are obscure and its codes too imprecise like the Oracle of Delphi;[5] (iii) the emotional quality of both persons present—analyst and analysand—induce mutual undesired but unavoidable emotional responses, according to the transference and the countertransference, which contaminate the purpose of the analysis. Such an outline implies that the *psychoanalytic clinic is secondary to the initial didactic purpose of psychoanalysis to teach auto or self-analysis.*

Freud's great intuition induced him to invent the couch and to place his chair behind his patients, not only with the purpose of avoiding continuous and strenuous scrutiny from his patients, but also because it was the best and most unique form of obtaining a sort of presence–absence of the perturbing but necessary existence of the analyst in the analytical room. It was similar to the facility provided to translators during a conference, a sort of cabin where they hide and work, making themselves present only by their voice. The patients, on the other hand, must dissociate and play two roles, that of "speaker" by associating freely their inner thoughts, and at the same time that of "audience", who listens to the interpretation provided by the analyst–translator. To conceive the analyst as a translator would help to deal with several confusions present in psychoanalytic practice, such as the demand made by patients to the analyst to initiate the session, as if a translator could commence a translation before the speaker initiates his/her speech; or to pretend that the analyst asks questions before the patient starts to speak, as if a regular interpreter could answer questions about the content of a presentation, ahead of the speaker reading the text. I think that when both participants of the analytic dyad understand the dynamic of this form of interaction, the progress of the analysis will be facilitated. It could also be useful to clarify countertransference confusions, such as the compulsion of the analyst–translator towards a cure, to provide the proper answer when pressed by the patient to give advice, to ask questions, or to say something.

Violence in the interpretation

The main purpose of the interpretation is to translate unconscious messages portraying truth that consciousness has rejected but might be prepared to accept or to interact with. I have stated in the chapter referring to the unconscious that perhaps we are born "unconscious illiterates" as a way of being protected by nature from the violence of truth, making an "unconscious translator", such as a psychoanalyst, utterly necessary. This violence is depicted, for instance, in the myth of Oedipus and the Sphinx, where the latter (representing the unconscious) demands from men approaching (representing consciousness), the solution of a riddle whose answer is "man"; the failure to decipher it, would end in being killed by the monster (the Sphinx) by strangulation.[6] The appearance of Oedipus, *portraying the hero, the psychoanalyst*, who is capable of providing the right answer, ends the criminal action of the Sphinx who, notwithstanding the weight of the truth, kills itself. Every night we are presented with a similar dilemma, when the unconscious, revealing itself through the riddle of dreams, is either ignored and a possible "awareness" or "insight" is "killed" or, with the help of psychoanalysis, the truth is disclosed, and that particular unconscious revelation of a dream, once unveiled, would, like the Sphinx, disappear or die away.

The interpretation, by continuously revealing the truth and contrasting it with conscious lies, carries with it a certain amount of violence. Lies outline the "psychotic part of the personality" in Bion's terminology, representing a narcissistic and pathological structure that stubbornly opposes and fears those changes disclosed by the interpretation. Patients are always dissociated between: (a) the "non psychotic part of the personality", which might desire a change from the suffering induced by a narcissistic structure, where the patient feels trapped by compulsively repeating it; and (b) the psychotic part of the personality, ruled by lies and the need to preserve the status quo, in spite of the suffering implicit. For this latter part, changes induced by the interpretation would represent a threat, robustly opposed by the narcissistic structure. In other words, what is desired by the "non-psychotic part", is at the same time rejected by the "psychotic part", representing the core of the ambivalence within the pathological paranoid–schizoid position, present, with more or less intensity, in all psychoanalytic therapy.

Bion has referred to "catastrophic change" as those side effects induced by the interpretation over the structure of the pathological narcissistic organization; "catastrophic" because it is often accompanied by a sense of disaster, if feelings produced by changes in the narcissistic structure can not be "contained" by both participants. We can follow this process in the case of Jane, a twenty-five-year-old phobic patient who had been in analysis for about three years when this material was produced. After a short Easter holiday to the beach, she came rather enthusiastically because she was able to drive her parents' car back and forth, something she has never tried before. She also dared swimming in the ocean, and managed to struggle with inner feelings of remorse and persecution she had always experienced before, in similar circumstances. She brought two dreams, in the first of which she was with a man from the university and she felt scared. She used to find him very attractive, although he exhibited some odd, crazy, dangerous behaviour, like cutting his face with a razorblade or stapling his hands. She associated her memory of this man at that time with fear and a certain respect for being able "to have the guts to do those things". I then said to her that for no clear reason a part of her seems to feel that those changes she was experiencing, like being less afraid, driving, and so on, were also experienced as something odd and dangerous. I added that she fears a new part in her that could be so daring, but that perhaps could make her crazy. She remembered a second dream:

> She is driving back from the beach to her house and she stops and is trying to park the car when she bumps into a car behind. The man who is driving this car looks Mexican. He is nice and tries to provide information, when someone who is in the parking place tells her to be careful with this guy, because he cannot be trusted. Then she realizes that the Mexican had put a "joint" inside her backpack. His mother is also

there. She looks like a nice person, and the patient says to her that her son is trying to plant marijuana in her bag.

She associates the Mexican with me, because I am Spanish-speaking, and states that she does not trust me because she does not know if I am interested in her, or her money. She provides no further associations, and I said that although there is something she trusts, or at least feels that she could talk about—because the Mexican's mother is nice and she is able to complain to her—there is at the same time, as she said, something suspicious because the Mexican put something "bad" inside her "back-pack", meaning her mind. It seems as if there is a part of her that feels that my interpretations are suspicious and dangerous.

Bion states that "catastrophic changes" occur when a transformation that has taken place cannot be contained—following the container–contained theory—like the case of a psychotic patient who felt that acquisition of verbal thoughts through psychoanalytic therapy has brought suffering and depression, inducing the need to free himself from it with the use of projective identification. The patient directed powerful feelings of hatred against the analyst, accusing him of making him insane by making him aware of his own disease (Bion, 1967, pp. 32–34).

The three dimensions of the interpretation: extra-transferential, transferential and intrapsychic

In 1947, Binswanger referred to three different interacting worlds: *unwelt*, referring to the relationship with the external world; *mitwelt*, related to the interaction with others; and finally *eigenwelt*, depicting the internal world, and in this way related with what we might refer to as the "intrapsychic". Binswanger then made a remark that could still be considered very fitting: "Classical psychoanalysis has only a shadowy, epiphenomenal concept of *mitwelt* and no real concept of *eigenwelt*" (1947, p. 49). Considering this statement, I have previously expressed:

If I were to extrapolate these notions and compare them with the different forms of interpretation as they are known today, *unwelt* and *mitwelt* could correspond to extra-transference and transference interpretations respectively. *Eigenwelt* seems to be left out of

this picture, at least concerning the metapsychology of the interpretation . . . [López-Corvo, 1999]

And further on:

By intrapsychic I am not referring only to a concept synonymous to
"inner world" or "reality structure", but also to the complex and
dynamic interaction of inner part objects within the self, in a
manner similar to Freud's expression—although never elaborated
further by him—that "all the interplay between an external object
and the ego as a whole . . . may possibly be repeated upon this *new
scene of action within the ego*" (1921, p. 130, italics added). [*ibid.*, pp.
209–210]

I also referred to the "intrapsychic interpretation" and stated
that from a theoretical point of view, we could conclude that if the
purpose of the extra-transference interpretation were to move to the
transference, the aim of the latter will be to move to the intrapsychic, in order to comprehend the complex interaction between part
objects within the self. Transference after all, does not constitute a
true reality, but an accidental complication of the continuous repetition of infantile traumas projected into the analyst, in the experimental setting promoted by the psychoanalytic process. The
intrapsychic, on the other hand, constitutes the true location where
all these part object interactions take place, representing the true
scenario from which the transference, as a mirage, comes from. I am
not implying by any means, that extratransference and transference
interpretations are not significant. My purpose is to emphasize the
existence of a further step, represented by the genuine space where
conflicts and the patient's suffering take place. There are at least
three situations where the intrapsychic interpretation is absolutely
necessary: (i) where patients are showing important signs of the
mechanism of self-envy; (ii) where there is a danger of transference
collusion; and (iii) in situations when superego objects are projected
into the analyst, inducing significant feelings of persecution and the
possibility of experiencing transference interpretation as accusatory.

About the silence

Silence represents the mute component of the interpretation, not as
an absence, but as the presence of an absence. Bion has said that the

"art of conversation" just as it takes place during the psychoanalytic interpretation, requires and demands an extension of the "no-conversation" (1990, p. 190). In the past there have been psycho-therapies based on silence, and during the 1950s there was the joke that prolonged silence, during psychoanalytic therapy, was intro-duced by postwar European *émigrés* because they had problems understanding their English-speaking patients.

There are at least six reasons responsible for an analyst's silence during a session: (i) because the analyst does not understand the latent content behind the manifest; (ii) because he/she does not wish to interrupt the flow of associations; (iii) to allow patients to build their own hypothesis after an interpretation; (iv) to avoid transference collusions with paranoid pathology; (v) as a form of counter-acting, when the analyst's mind is contaminated with outside interferences; (vi) also as a form of counter-acting, when the analyst uses silence with the purpose of forcing the patient to "confess" unshared material. In relation to this last statement, I believe that the "patient's intimacy" should not be a concern of the analysis, except for when it is used as a form of resistance, and then it should be interpreted along lines similar to any other form of defence, but different from the analyst countertransference needed to induce the patient to "confess" (Racker, 1969; Reik, 1948).

The difficulty in tolerating silence, frequent in the patient as well as the analyst, represents a form of resistance, sometimes resulting from confusion between medical procedures and psychoanalytic intention.[7] Often patients at the onset of a psychoanalytic process take a rather passive attitude and try to force the analyst to talk, expecting that the analyst should know more about the reasons behind their mental suffering and should provide a ready-made answer to their conflicts, a form of resistance Lacan refers to as the "place of the supposed knowledge".

During one of his conferences in Rio de Janeiro Bion, who made frequent references in his work about the silence, has this to say:

> . . . a patient comes into the consulting room and does not say a word; perhaps he keeps on coming for six days, or six weeks, or six months without saying anything. If one can stand it, then after six months one might begin to think, "I have an idea about the pattern of his silence. I wouldn't like to say at any given moment why his

silence today is not the same as his silence on Friday, and it won't be the same tomorrow. But I think that if I can go on listening to him being silent"—in the way that Freud talks about the importance of going on being present in the consulting room with the patient for long enough—"I begin to be aware of a pattern". Although we cannot say whether we have heard anything we could say, "It has an effect upon me—not on my countertransference—and I think I have had a respect for the silence of the session". If we cannot respect the silence—"I can't be bothered with this person; I can't come here day after day and have him lying on the couch saying nothing"—then there is no chance of making any further progress. It is difficult to explain to someone not present why we think that we could hear the difference between one silence and another. The patient, however is present. [1974, p. 94]

Francesca Bion (1995), on the other hand, repeats comments made by Bion about the patient who is silent all the time, as follows:

... restricting ourselves to verbal intercourse won't get us far with this kind of patient. What kind of psychoanalysis is needed to interpret the silence? The analyst may think there is a pattern to the silence. If he cannot respect the silence, there is no chance of making any further progress. The analyst can be silent and listen—stop talking so that he can have a chance to hear what is going on. [p. 20]

And on another occasion:

Some silences are nothing, they are 0, zero. But sometimes that silence becomes a pregnant one; it turns into 101—the preceding and succeeding sounds turn it into valuable communication, as with rests and pauses in music, holes and gaps in sculpture. [*ibid.*]

Notes

1.   A full discussion of Bion's theory on thinking is discussed in Chapters Nine and Eleven.
2.   Lacan has referred to this mechanism as "the place of the supposed knowledge".
3.   These steps are also described in Chapter Twelve.
4.   A difference I have already examined in detail in Chapter Six.

5. History says, for instance, that Croesus asked Delphi's Oracle if he should go to war with Cyrus, king of Persia, and the oracle responded: "If Croesus goes to war with Cyrus he shall bring down a mighty kingdom." Satisfied with that, the king returned to his country, took his army and invaded Persia, but was defeated. He returned to Delphi to express his anger at Apollo for misleading him. The priest of the temple pointed out that the god did not mislead but spoke the truth, only that he did not specify which kingdom.

6. Sphinx = sphincter, or something that squeezes.

7. See Chapter One.

CHAPTER ELEVEN

The three faces of the preconscious

From the point of view of Bion's theory of functions

"Nothing is totally under our control except for our thoughts"

(Descartes, 1614)

The three faces of Amarna

The village of Amarna, some time located between Memphis and Thebes in Middle Egypt, has been lost under the sand of the Sahara desert for the past three thousand years. Early in the 1800s fragments of unknown pottery, beautiful modelled statuettes, and mud walls of buildings began to be found, together with pieces of glassware, cartouches, stone or clay tablets covered with unfamiliar writing, and names of kings never revealed before. Carried by the enthusiasm of tourists and later instigated by Baron Alexander von Humboldt himself, the Germans started excavating the place around the middle of the year of 1800. The fragmentary mutilation of all the sculptures, the systematic suppression of all the names, including those of Akhenaton, Nefertiti, and Tutankhamen from all the walls, graves, and public monuments, induced the reflection that it might have been a methodical aggression directed towards the city, its treasures, and its inhabitants. Amarna had not vanished as other cities from the past had, due to entropy, abandonment, or natural disasters; instead, it was suppressed, totally abolished by men's unmerciful vengeance and pitiless envy.

In 1987, while an Egyptian woman from a nearby town was digging fertilizers out of one of the sites excavated by the Germans, she discovered in a corner some rotted wooden chests. One of them had lost its alabaster cover and it contained hundreds of little inscribed clay tablets. The woman, despite being illiterate, thought she had found something important. She put all the pieces in a bag and thought that by surreptitiously breaking up the bigger ones, she could earn much more from them, and so that is what she did. She then took the pieces to a nearby town, El Amarieh, from where they were sent to the Cairo Museum to be evaluated by the *"des Antiquités"* French service which, after examining them with little interest, declared them a total fraud.

An antiques merchant bought what was left of the tablets for a few coins and then resold them as souvenirs. By the time the Cairo Museum authorities found out about the lost treasure's significance, there were only 377 pieces left, which, after many years, permitted experts to reconstruct the tragedy suffered by Amarna. Most of them were letters written to Akhenaton and to the beautiful Nefertiti by the kings of Babylon, Nineveh, Canaan, and Mitanni. Someone's life was risked during the last moments of the city's final attack in order to save the king's correspondence; perhaps it was a clergyman or Aye, Akhenaton's father, or Nefertiti herself. Thanks to that we know today about the queen's preferred games, songs, jewellery, flowers, and perfumes, as well as about the history of Akhenamon's building of Amarna, who changed his name for Akhenaton, which means one who adores the sun as the sole God, and thus invented monotheism, later repeated by Moses in Judeo Christianity.

What is it exactly that makes the preconscious appear as if it behaves in different and contradictory ways? First, it performs as a "repressive agent" or, better, as a "repudiating agent" that rejects unwanted unconscious messages, imposing total suppression at all costs; the consequence is a form of "reversible perspective between the unconscious message and the preconscious ignorance, just as happened to the abolished city of Amarna. Second, it behaves as a "denouncing agent" of the "repudiated" through its derivatives, lapses, other linguistic forms or somatic syntaxes, especially through dreams, which sometimes whisper and sometimes scream—as in anxiety dreams—but lacking enough ego substance capable of decoding their text, similar to the negligence shown by the Germans who excavated the city of Amarna and the ignorance of the Cairo Museum Frenchmen. Last, the unconscious can turn into a consulting textbook whose private hermeneutic enables each individual to know about his/her ultimate truth, or Bion's O, and thus reconstruct the past, just as the already decoded letters facilitated the account of the suppressed Akhenaton and Nefertiti history.

The unconscious and the messages it sends are always unique, just like the city of Amarna; it is not its content that changes, but the attitude with which the preconscious relates to those unconscious contents, similar to the Egyptian excavators. *If the preconscious is not ready for the truth presented by the unconscious, it will experience it as a kind of projective identification and will react against it*. It will be similar to the resistance presented by a patient to an interpretation provided by the analyst, whose content might be true but premature in its revelation.

Interaction between the unconscious and consciousness

In "Learning from experience" Bion (1962) stated that Freud's theory (1911b) about consciousness being the only sense organ of psychic qualities, was not satisfactory. His argument was not against the validity of such an asseveration, but against the fact that it did not discriminate between the different kinds of interactions that take place between the conscious and the unconscious. According to Bion, the correct model would be depicted by the existence of a capacity, similar to the one given by binocular vision, whereby two sights of the same object are correlated. In psychoanalysis, the use of both conscious and the unconscious to look at a "psychoanalytic object" is similar to binocular vision. In order for images to superimpose without generating double vision, one must look inwards with the unconscious eye with much the same enthusiasm that the conscious looks outwards.

In the first place, the existing interaction between the preconscious and the unconscious is a container–contained relationship,
similar to the one observed between the baby and the breast or the
psychoanalyst and his analysand. In other words, it would represent the interaction between a preconception and its realization,
resulting in a conception (López-Corvo, 2003). The baby's instinctive and natural needs, similar to the unconscious, represent a
biological truth that is universal, predetermined, and irrevocable.
The main differences in the interaction between "container" and
"contained" would be determined by the oscillations (plus or
minus) within the maternal reverie and never by the baby's biological demands. The contained ($\circlearrowleft$) is always the same; what changes
is the container's ($\circleddash$) attitude. Bion states:

> If mother and child are adjusted to each other projective identifica-
> tion plays a role in the management through the operation of a
> rudimentary and fragile sense; usually an omnipotent phantasy, it
> operates realistically. This, I am inclined to believe, is its normal
> condition. [1967, p. 114]

I believe this model can help us understand the relationship that
exists between the unconscious and the preconscious as a part of
the internal side of consciousness. The unconscious, as a continuous source of truth, is always becoming, like the water's infinite
motion in a river. It is also unknowable, it cannot be grasped, but
can be intuited, like Bion's O; it can be represented more as an attitude than as a *fait accompli*, and its main purpose appears to indicate a repeated exposure of the individual's truth in relation to
conscious lies. The fact that the truth is not well received or that it
might represent a threat, will depend not on the truth itself, but on
the person who receives or disregards it. If the truth, disguised as
dream derivatives, walks on tiptoes in order to repeat itself without
having to disturb sleep, the displeasure induced by its presence
would be a problem for the preconscious, stirred up by the
conscious fear, and never a problem of the truth itself. It is not the
absence of truthfulness that makes the unconscious argue, but the
presence of lies, of their destructive, omnipotent power and the
danger they can impose even upon life itself. Ancient Latin had
already established that consciousness lies, for the words "lie"

(*mentior*), and "mind" (*mentis*) have the same root. The rejection or *repudiation* of a message presented by the unconscious would end up in a *reversal of perspective*, meaning that there will be no communication between them.

An obsessive patient said that she repeated in her mind many times some of the interpretations I had given her "in order" (according to her) "not to forget them". Then I said, trying to parody her truth, that she tried to take possession of what scared her from what I had said, turning it around without swallowing it, like children do who are compelled to eat, in order to get rid of it later when parents do not notice it. When leaving, she did not look into my eyes as she usually did. Instead she turned her head away, looking in the opposite direction and I had the impression she did not want me to see how she was trying to expel my interpretation through her eyes. In this case, both the message of truth carried within the interpretation and the unconscious content were experienced by consciousness as an intrusion, as a disturbing "projective identification" she tried to free herself of.

If the unconscious represents an organ that is continuously transcribing the truth (and I do not mean that it thinks about it, because the truth does not need a "thinker"), and is constantly denouncing lies, and, if the relationship between this instance and the conscious is similar to the one between the baby and the maternal reverie, conceived as a container–contained ($♀♂$) relationship, we might then consider a spectrum of different possibilities. Such possibilities will lie on a continuum, going from an extreme characterized on the one hand by total rejection,[1] as in psychoses where the unconscious has taken over the conscious and overflows it, or on the other hand by total acceptance, like the extreme portrayed by the psychoanalytic setting. The unconscious represents to the psychoanalyst an organ that continuously reveals the truth and, when contained by the analyst's reverie, it reveals the unconscious phantasy that will point out the path to follow in order to create the interpretation. In between the extremes there will be intermediate situations like the neuroses and borderline states dominated by omnipotent and magical thinking. Therefore, there will be, as in the history of Amarna, a progressive gradient that could be summarized by the following three possibilities.

1. Good ego capacity for frustration tolerance, which allows the negative realization of an absent breast to be changed into a thought about an absence; it also allows the creation of an apparatus for thinking thoughts and to learn from experience. Truth revelation is well taken making it possible to learn from experience and to induce positive growth.

2. Increased ego weakness, which will determine little frustration tolerance, and in turn trigger mechanisms of evasion, but not as much as to allow a complete dominance over the reality principle. Faced with the negative realization of an absent breast, the ego will attempt to deal with the painful experience by means of omnipotent beliefs which conceal the difference between true and false. Bion states: "Omniscience substitutes for the discrimination between true and false a dictatorial affirmation that one thing is morally right and the other wrong" (1967, p. 114).

    Truth is imposed by dictatorial and capricious means, learning from experience is seriously hindered and growth becomes languid.

3. When the inability to tolerate frustration is almost absent, thought development, as well as the creation of an apparatus for thinking becomes impossible. Realization of the absent breast is dealt with by means of excessive projective identification,[2] destined to evacuate the psyche from an accumulation of bad internal objects; a mechanism sometimes performed with such power that the whole mind is split and evacuated at high speed, like missiles to annihilate the space, creating what Bion refers to as "bizarre objects".[3] Truth and reality induce terror, learning from experience is threatening, and mental growth is regressive.

The three faces of consciousness

According to Bion's theory on thinking, sense impressions represent un-thought thoughts or the "things-in-itself", undigested facts like unspoken emotions that cannot be thought and are only good for being expelled by means of projective and introjective identifications, for which Bion reserved the name "beta elements". These elements can be metabolized with the help of a special process or "alpha-function", which will change them into thoughts or alpha-elements that can then be used for thinking. Incapacity to metabolize beta elements into alpha ones will result in an increment of the former that will be located at a preconscious level and will generate what Bion has called a "beta screen". If, on the contrary, beta elements are continuously changed into alpha ones, they will then accumulate by taking the place of the former and will result in what Bion has called the "contact barrier". Obviously, there will be a continuum between these two extremes, and we might consider now, just as we did before, the existence of three possibilities.

1.   *Psychoses*. Due to a lack of the alpha function, the preconscious becomes subject to a screen of β-elements, which is incapable of translating or metabolizing unconscious messages. However, it *senses them as a threat* and treats them in much the same way as dangerous projective identifications, undistinguishable from internal persecutory objects. Dominated by β-elements, consciousness is not capable of reasoning or containing either the external or the internal world; it is just a muscle, an organ for discharge where acting out and the pleasure principle dominates over sensible reasoning and the reality principle. At the same time, such a refractory or negative attitude of the preconscious towards unconscious messages of truth (similar to the abolition of Amarna), induces the unconscious to complain by screaming, invading and crossing with its syntaxes the boundaries of consciousness, thus resulting in a symbol confiscation and reduction of words to concrete things. It represents the typical psychotic symptoms, a reversion of the unconscious semantics where things (images, for instance) are words[4] and the internal world is confused with the external one. The unconscious, which in psychotics is so evident that it can be easily observed, fails in its purpose due to massive preconscious *repudiation*.[5] It represents such a ferocious deafness towards unconscious contents that paradoxically, the unconscious, in a way similar to the pandemonium produced by a mountain's slide which has dammed a stream, invades and floods consciousness. This concept was already clearly

considered by Freud as early as 1894, as well as many years latter, in 1934, when he states:

In psychoses, however, the turning-away from reality is brought about in two kinds of way: either by the unconscious repressed becoming excessively strong so that it overwhelms the conscious, which is attached to reality, or because reality has become so intolerably distressing that the threatened ego throws itself into the arms of the unconscious instinctual forces in a desperate revolt. [1933a, p. 16]

It reminds us of the paradox implied by the old medical aphorism which states that "the organism, in trying to find a cure, makes itself sick". The unconscious message of truth is perceived similar to the violence of a projective identification that terrifies the ego, which Bion has characterized with the sign −K. An important aspect—for it defines the relativity of projective identifications—is that this mechanism does not solely depend on the intentions of the unconscious or on its content, but mostly on the attitude of the preconscious as a receptor. Repudiation of unconscious contents due to preconscious terror of truth, forces the unconscious to overflow the conscious as well as to hinder its capacity to discriminate phantasy from reality, mostly because projections in the external world will induce a dialogue of the ego with itself, according to Bion's notion of the "bizarre objects".

2.   *Borderline and neurotic patients.* They represent a gradient between "psychotic and non-psychotic parts of the personality", in the sense that the healthy part of the ego is barely sufficient to contain the psychotic aspects of personality, sometimes being successful but at other times failing. Such a situation will induce some form of continuous alternation between the extremes of the psychotic part of the personality, be it the contained or the containing non-psychotic part. In this case, terror of truth does not achieve the extremes reached by psychoses, allowing the ego to take enough distance to be able to negotiate and make transactions, by means of fragmentation of the mind, anxiety dreams, somatic language, symptoms, as well as mechanisms of *magic* and *animism*. Such states of mind represent what Bion refers to as a *"rudimentary conscious"*, a

sort of "child mental apparatus" that requires a mother's or analyst's reverie in order to transform sense impressions into alpha elements.

There exists an interaction between the β-screen and the α-elements contact barrier, where the latter might sometimes show a continent capacity towards the truth denounced by the unconscious, although at other times it might also fail. Contact barriers also facilitate discrimination between what is unconscious from what is conscious, as well as dreaming from waking life.

Suppressed unconscious language gaps are filled with *somatic language*, generating symptoms, often culturally conditioned, which will determine the neurotic profile. *Animism* or magical thinking is a consequence of the incapacity to conceive the dimensions that total objects are made of, and of exerting the paradox of denuding life from what is alive and projecting it into inanimate things; it represents culture's potential violence—as in wars—not to distinguish what is alive from what is not. It constitutes a flat, bidimensional perception of the world, where there is neither a true sense of identity nor a feeling of belonging, and analysis is equal to a mechanical intervention, as if patients were identified with machines.[6] In other words, there is no difference between Cartesian dimensions of *res extensa* and *res cogitans*, because the body takes over the mind.[7] The body carries the potentiality of being distant and alien, it could be somebody else's affair, but the *mind* is where true selfness takes place; it is the only route towards ego autonomy. Even though α-function enables people in this category to know about their unconscious, the difficulty of "containing" the still present reverential fear of the truth prevents, as in the Amarna civilization, the translation of its language: *they ignore its syntaxes and remain unconscious illiterates.*

I will now examine some clinical material.

M is a young, married, childless patient. She was referred because one of her sisters ("my father's favourite") had recently moved back with her husband to her parents' house, something the patient felt to be terribly unfair and rather painful. She described her father as seductive, a womanizer, and someone who often consumed liquor; "My poor mum must have suffered a lot, but she was like another daughter, just like the oldest daughter." When she speaks, she looks serious and cries.

I ask myself why would she still be so affected by these things since she is already married and living on her own? She talks about difficulties with her husband, especially in relation to sex; he desires her more but she rejects him and does not wish to be touched, although she is capable of giving in. "Maybe I am furious because he is too selfish." At this point I have the countertransference feeling of two kids playing. She says she went to a sea aquarium at Miami and a whale purposely splashed some kids that were watching it who were right next to her; this made her cry and even now when she is talking about it, she cries again. She remembered once when she was little that a whale also splashed her and then she cried again.

I believe that the "splashing whale" represents the centre of her discourse, what Bion, parodying Poincaré (1908), has referred to as a "selected fact", for it makes clear and gives sense to the whole session. When the whale purposely splashes a child, it means that this child has been chosen; it makes her cry because she remembers all the times that she has not been chosen. Her parents were not good "splasher whales", her mother was not capable of splashing for she was competing to be splashed by the father. Besides, M chose and married a man who was also incapable of splashing her, therefore she had ambivalent feelings: she wished her husband were a whale of such splattering capacities that she could use him in order to take revenge against those who, like her sister, she felt were then splashed and were still being splashed. She would have liked to arrive at her parents' house and say "watch what a husband I have, watch how he splashes me", but sadly this was not the case, and it fills her with rage and impotence. Something of this sort I told her and she then produced a dream, in which an image of a pregnant woman takes a little girl by the hand. All she says is that she believes she could be that little girl and that the woman is really pregnant because she is immense. I ask her: "Like a whale?" In tears, she *smiles*. (At that moment I feel Bion's O has illuminated us.) It seems like a narcissistic condensation, where she represents all the roles: she is pregnant with herself and takes herself by the hand. It is a tautological and eternal scene: it is a "self splattering whale" that becomes part of a manic mechanism in order to avoid the terrible pain produced by exclusion. "After all", I said to her: "you continue to 'splash' yourself in tears." She openly smiled.

3.   *Binocular vision and contact barrier*. If the preconscious is dominated by a contact barrier, thoughts coming from the unconscious revealing a truth will be well received by consciousness.

It would be a situation similar to the receptiveness of a psycho-analyst's mind, which listens carefully to the analysand's discourse in search of a revelation of the unconscious; or similar to the receptiveness of a conscientious mother's mind, which is attentive to her baby in distress, in search of ways to contain her child's anxiety. This would be an ideal condition, where the ego would place itself above the difference between unconscious and preconscious, with a double vision that will allow it to sense reality on the one hand, and to intuit the unknown on the other.

Bion (1970) states that whatever the situation of the analysis, O is always there like a possibility for both the analyst and the patient (p. 102) In this way, he concludes, in psychoanalysis any O that is not at the same time common to both analyst and patient and, therefore, is not available for the transformation of both, must be ignored as irrelevant for analysis, for it will not be feasible to investigate it. What cannot be calculated, the "absolute fact" that has taken place in either a session or an artistic creation, or in an illuminated state, due to its very nature cannot be known (K), except if it evolves to the point that it could be known. This should be feasible when the transformation of O has been able to combine its invariant in such a way as to make it possible to communicate it to others (*ibid.*). An example would be the feeling felt by the artist when faced with his/her own O, which is able to be transmitted to the audience that listens to (music) or looks at (painting) his piece of work. To discover O represents a process feasible through the combination of two mechanisms: (i) knowledge of the unconscious, cryptic, syntactic language furnished by the analytic training, which allows its *translation* (López-Corvo, 1999); (ii) intuition achieved as a consequence of the above, through *not knowing* which paradoxically contains the risk of *knowing*, characterized by Bion as an *act of faith*. This mechanism can also be seen outside analysis, in privileged people capable of such truth revelations. For example, Einstein formulated his relativity theory after visualizing $E=MC^2$ in a dream (Lindon, 1966). Also in a dream, Otto Loewi was capable of understanding the role played by acetylcholine in the chemical mediation of nervous impulses. While he forgot this after waking up, he fortunately repeated the dream the next night. The same happened to Poincaré who, after fifteen days of arduous work was able, in a night of insomnia, to prove the existence of the Fuchsian's functions, to then forget them and recall them later when he was putting his foot on the step rest of a carriage. Robert Louis Stevenson (see Broks, 2003) was inspired by his dreams to write, as was Eugene O'Neill, who visualized the full scenes of his plays. There is nothing I could say about Freud or Jung that we do not know already.

Notes

1. See Chapter Nine on the unconscious.
2. Bion clarifies that "excessive" is not only a quantitative qualification but qualitative also, and refers to omnipotence present in the process of evacuation (1967, p. 114). See Chapter Seven, "Excessive projective identification".
3. See Chapter Three, "Preconceptual traumas and the "internal traumatic object".
4. It is similar to endometriosis, a condition that takes place when phallic envy prevents the menstrual period, creating a mental sphincter that closes the external path and deflects endometrial fluids towards the abdominal cavity, which in turn attack internal organs flooding them as a malignant tumour would.
5. Lacan has introduced the word "foreclosure", which I think is similar to what I am trying to say. He defines foreclosure as different from repression in that the element is not buried in the unconscious but expelled or repudiated by the preconscious.
6. See Chapter One, "Murdering the mind".
7. Or psychiatry takes over psychoanalysis.

CHAPTER TWELVE

Listening to "O"

"Take, for example, this piece of wax; it is quite fresh, having been but recently taken from the beehive; it has not yet lost the sweetness of the honey it contained; it still retains somewhat of the odor of the flowers from which it was gathered; its color, figure, size, are apparent (to the sight); it is hard, cold, easily handled; and sounds when struck upon with the finger. In fine, all that contributes to make a body as distinctly known as possible, is found in the one before us. But, while I am speaking, let it be placed near the fire—what remained of the taste exhales, the smell evaporates, the color changes, its figure is destroyed, its size increases, it becomes liquid, it grows hot, it can hardly be handled, and, although struck upon, it emits no sound. Does the same wax still remain after this change? . . . no one doubts it, or judges otherwise. What, then, was it I knew with such distinctness in the piece of wax? . . . nothing of all that I observed by means of the senses, since all the things that fell under taste, smell, sight, touch, and hearing are changed, and yet the same wax remains"

(Descartes, 1641, Mediation II)

"Aut tace, aut loquere meliora silentio"

(Salvator Rosa)[1]

"The psychoanalyst has to learn how one mind speaks to another beyond words and in silence. He must learn to listen 'with the third ear'"

(Reik, 1948, p. 144)

Psychoanalytic listening

Bion has used, like a metaphor, the myth of Palinurus as narrated by Virgil, in order to emphasize the stubbornness present in many therapists during the act of listening to patients. In *The Aeneid*, Virgil describes how Palinurus, after the storm, led the pilot ship followed by the rest of the fleet commanded by Aeneas. The exhausted sailors had now lain down on the benches. The God of Sleep, disguised as Phorbas, sat beside Palinurus who remained alert and alone, with his hands stubbornly fastened on to the rudder. Phorbas attempted to convince him to go to sleep, saying that he would sail the ship in his place. Opening his eyes, Palinurus responded:

"Me dost thou bid to trust the treach'rous deep,
The harlot smiles of her dissembling face,
And to her faith commit the Trojan race?
Shall I believe the Siren South again,
And, oft betray'd, not know the monster main?"
He said: his fasten'd hands the rudder keeps,
And, fix'd on heav'n, his eyes repel invading sleep.

At this moment Phoebes shook over his head a branch dipped in Lethe's waters, capable of inducing sleep and Palinurus, in spite of his effort to remain awake, plunged into the sea with such a force that he tore away the stern with the rudder. He called in vain for help and ended by drowning himself. Bion compares the pilot's stubbornness with the analyst's inclination to cling to classical positions present in medicine, such as taking a clinical history in order to provide a classified diagnosis, thereby contaminating listening with previous memories and desires about the patient, such as the intent to cure or to understand. The analytic setting, on the other hand, is strictly a private act, representing the relationship of an individual with her/himself, where the analyst's presence constitutes an indispensable "noise", a strange but necessary escort. The main role of the analyst is that of a translator of the unconscious, one who attempts to teach the patient the ability to read and to comprehend the cryptic syntaxes of the unconscious, something analysts have learned during their own analytic training.[2]

Listening: between Tiresias's blindness and Dionysius's ear

Tiresias reunited the contradiction of being a "blind seer" and perhaps became sightless, as stated by Callimachus, because he dared to see Athena naked, who then, in compensation, and because of the appeal from his mother, the nymph Chariclo, made him a soothsayer.[3] Freud emulates Tiresias when, in a letter addressed to Lou Andreas-Salomé dated 25 May 1916, he described a method he felt would provide an advantage to compensate for the "darkness surrounding an object of investigation". The method consisted in "blinding himself artificially", with the purpose of concentrating all the light in only one obscure passage. In 1948 Reik borrowed from Nietzsche the term "third ear" to describe the intuitive component present in what Freud described as a "state of floating attention". This statement is reminiscent of the intensity and effort exercised by Dionysius, the tyrant of Syracuse, who built a complicated system of pipes that connected his house with the local jail for the purpose of listening to his political enemies in prison and keeping himself well informed about any possible conspiracy.

Bion implicitly describes listening as a situation where the analyst, similar to Tiresias's blindness, must free himself from any preconception. It could be compared to a state of pure ingenuity that, if roughly translated into words, could mean not to know in order to make room for a preconception that will illuminate the problem which might have excited curiosity (Bion, 1965, p. 47). Afterwards Bion added the term "patience", synonymous with Klein's paranoid–schizoid position, although free from its pathological components, but related to feelings of suffering and of frustration tolerance at the act of listening during the psychoanalytic session.

Listening should be free from any "understanding, memory or desire" and, when dealing with psychotic patients in a state of "hallucinosis", it requires a constant discipline, a state of alertness and self-observation that will allow the appearance and evolution of truth or, following Bion, the evolution of O into K. When materialization of "ultimate truth" takes place and is subsequently assumed, it will then be connected with an "act of faith" in order to be used as the essential substance to create the interpretation (Bion, 1970, p. 124).

In notes written on 29 September 1959, Bion (1992) makes the following confessions about how he listens:

> Drowsiness is coming to me; it is part of the relaxation I have to achieve if my ideas are to be accessible. I must dream along, but then I risk going fast asleep. I have had to shut my eyes because they sting. Then I nearly went to sleep … I must not know anything about. A wrapping up and packing of the goods I wish to remove from the environment. [p. 82]

Further on:

> … essential that the creative worker should keep his alpha function unimpaired, it is clear that the analyst must be able to dream the session. But if he is to do this without sleeping, he must have plenty to sleep. [*ibid.*]

Bion also explains that suppression of understanding, memory, and desire could bring the analyst to a state of stupor or sleepiness that is not desirable. Such a state demanded by Bion is not an easy thing to exercise and tolerate continuously either by the analyst or by the patient. It will require a state of alertness and of constant discipline. Bion provides the following recommendations about how to keep memory absent:

> *Memory*: Do not remember past sessions. The greater the impulse to remember what has been said or done, the more the need to resist it. This impulse can present itself as a wish to remember something that has happened because it appears to have precipitated an emotional crisis: *no* crisis should be allowed to breach this rule. The supposed events must not be allowed to occupy the mind. Otherwise the evolution of the session will not be observed at the only time when it can be observed—while it is taking place. [1992, pp. 381–382]

"Desire", on the other hand, saturates the capacity to listen in relation to the future, in the same manner that memory saturates listening in relation to the past. *The analyst's desire imprisons the patient,* who might then feel the urge to provide the analyst with whatever he feels the analyst desires. A good example is the phenomenon of "multiple personality", which patients produce in order to fulfil the analyst's scopophilia. A prelude to such a condition could be observed in the analyst's need to maintain the patient's dissociation; for instance, remarking that the patient is not talking about what he/she is "supposed" to talk about, as if there were two different discourses, one forbidden and another permitted. Another example would be allowing the patient's need to keep away from the session certain forms of behaviours, performed either immediately previous or subsequently to the session, such as making remarks or talking about certain issues, routinely going to the bathroom, and so on. Also, an analyst's desire, such as a need to "cure", or to behave in a certain way, could trigger in the patient either negativistic or compliant tendencies.[4]

The analyst's reverie function

According to Bion, the baby gets rid of unpleasant or painful feelings by way of projective identifications directed to the mother, or more specifically, into her breast. For the sake of understanding, we could imagine two extreme possibilities: (i) the mother contains the baby's projective identifications and modifies or detoxifies them to a less painful and more bearable experience, a condition that, when incorporated by the baby, will result in the construction of alpha function; (ii) not being capable of providing the previous option, the mother rejects projective identifications, refusing to become a depository of the child's feelings. The first option will be translated eventually into mental growth and mental health and, obviously, it would not become a matter to be dealt with in the psychoanalytical room. The alternative, however, represents the conflictive side, the symptom-inducing part of the personality, which will determine the substance of which the transference—countertransference dimension is made.[5] It is obvious then, that the lack of reverie on the part of the mother will hinder the possibility of the baby structuring an alpha function that eventually will metabolize raw sensuous experiences, or beta elements, and change them into alpha elements. It is this part of the personality that becomes the material for analysis, and represents a dynamic that has been further discussed in Chapter Six, which deals with narcissism.

I believe that when choosing the word "reverie" to name the mother's capacity to tune herself to her baby's essential needs, Bion was recognizing in such a faculty, a dynamic similar to the analyst's ability to grasp the presence of "O" during the analytic hour.[6] Another aspect I wish to consider refers to the capacity to the mother's reverie to provide her baby, among all of the other endowments I have just referred to, with a sense of *unconditionality*, indispensable in discriminating between animate beings (alive) and inanimate things (not-alive); in order to acquire an inner sense of feeling love for what the baby *is* and not for what the baby *does*.[7]

Listening to "O"

The notion of "reversible perspective" represents one of the several attempts made by Bion to alert us to the danger of candidly believing that there is communication in the analytical setting when, in reality, the situation might be dominated by incomprehension, reproducing a dialogue between the deaf. "True distance and separation", says Bion (1992), "is not represented by the space that separates us from the galaxies, but in what separates comprehension from incomprehension."

How do we know exactly what a patient is communicating? Reik (1948) attempting to deal with this issue, borrowed from Nietzsche (2001, Part VIII) the notion of the "third ear", and stated that, "The psychoanalyst has to learn how one mind speaks to another beyond words and in silence. He must learn to listen 'with the third ear'" (p. 144).

Bion inferred implicitly that such a third ear was an "ear of intuition", listening not to the patient's external discourse, but to the internal revelation such external discourse would have intuitively induced in the analyst, when listening with an empty mind.

For Bion, the purpose of listening during a session is directly related to the intuitive revelation of "O", conceived as the noumenon, the thing-in-itself or the unknown; its recognition will imply a transformation from O to K, from the unknown to the known or from the noumenon to the phenomenon. This is an occurrence that should become automatic, like a habit; after all, once we learn how to walk we forget about it. It will be like "learning from the heart", says Bion, so that we can walk without having to remember how to do it.

Bion does not explicitly distinguish between O and countertransference, but it is obvious that this subject represents an important theoretical matter to be considered.[8] I think that what some analysts have pondered as countertransference, Bion believes to be O, while for him, countertransference portrays something unconscious to which we do not have access unless it has been analysed, similar to what others have referred to as the "analyst's transference". He states:

> One of the essential points about counter-transference is that it is *unconscious*. People talk about "making use of their counter-transference"; they cannot make any use of it because they don't know what it is. There *is* such a thing as my emotional reaction to the patient; I can hope that through my awareness of the fact that I have human characteristics like prejudice and bigotry I may be more tolerant and allow the patient to feel if my interpretation is or is not correct. [1980, p. 16]

Bion proposes the existence of some kind of function that could cast down a "constant conjunction"[9] he refers to as a "constellation",[10] capable of catalysing the fusion or "at-one-ment" with O. Such a fusion could be public, such as the interpretation made to a patient during the analytical hour, or the feeling experienced by artists in relation to their own O, which is then transmitted to the public who view their work or listen to their music. It is as if O, like Descartes's wax, could make itself present regardless of the number of existing variables that might result from the transformation of the object. "O" could be interpreted as the unconscious's continuous becoming. For instance, regardless of how extensive our experience as psychoanalysts might be, we could always face unknown dilemmas as we try to understand our dreams, something Freud (1900, p. 111, n. 1) referred to as the "dream's navel".

There cannot exist a becoming based on falsehood. O is the absolute truth of anything at any particular moment, because O is continuously becoming, similar to Heraclitus's theory of the "universal flux": "You cannot step twice in the same river, and today's sun is not the same one as tomorrow's".[11] In a similar fashion, O of today is not the same as O of tomorrow. Hence, it could not be known, because, if known, it is no longer O; or in other words, just when it is known, it would be no longer known and it is only known once it is not. It is neither a position nor a condition, but a possibility that might or might not be, even though it is always becoming. The analyst does not identify with O because he/she should be it (at-one-ment), and through this exercise the analyst will be able to know events that are the evolution of O (Bion, 1970, p. 30). For Bion, O has the following qualities: it represents the ultimate truth, be it good or bad. Who inhabits O is of no importance, regardless of whether it lives within God or the Devil; it is neither good nor bad, it can be neither loved nor hated. The only thing we can do is to be it. However, to identify with it will mean to be distant from it. In classical psychoanalysis, O's inaccessibility will be equal to resistance.

Bion distinguishes between the patient's O (Op) and the analyst's O (Oa). To ask, for instance, what is Op, implies to ask what the patient is talking about. Regardless of the analytic situation, any O that is not, at the same time, common to the patient and to the analyst and cannot be used in the transformation of both, should be ignored as irrelevant for the analysis, because it would not be useful for any form of investigation (1965, p. 48). In psychotic patients, the space where projection is directed could have infinite dimensions, and the analysis could be grasped as a transformation, where an intense and catastrophic emotional explosion of O has taken place. Elements of personality, links, emotions, and so on, are instantly expelled from their point of origin into vast directions, following a mechanism Bion refers to as the "hyperbole".

Although Bion did not explain it in this manner, we might conjecture that capturing O at a given moment could be equivalent to a transformation of O in K, similar to what Klein refers to as the "unconscious phantasy", although perhaps more complicated, touching an intuitive depth some religious persons describe as an "act of illumination". I believe, on the other hand, that it has also been erroneously described as an absence equal to zero. Let us look at a clinical example.

> A woman in her forties, who is married and works as a teacher, was having some difficulties with her husband, which reflected signs of childhood rivalry with her older and only brother. She started the session referring to problems related to her husband's management of an autistic child he had from a previous marriage and who was now living with them. She felt very critical of the way her husband was handling the child as well as the continuous rebelliousness exhibited by the child towards household rules. She was sitting up and wearing a pink sweater, to which I did not pay special attention. She had a dream:

>> She was attempting to have a meeting with three other women, another teacher from her stepson's school, a psychotherapist, and a neighbour. [At this point, I have the image somewhere in my mind, as a peripheral vision, of these women wearing pink sweaters like that of my patient. However, I do not pay not full attention to this matter until she had finished the dream.] She realized that there was no tablecloth on the table and decided to look for one, but became aware that the walls were all covered with papers written by her husband giving her foolish directions. Then she went upstairs to fetch the tablecloth but there was a step missing in the stair and some chairs blocking the way. She suspects this is also the work of her husband.

> At this point, I realized I had in my mind, since the beginning of her narrative of the dream, that all women from her dream were wearing pink sweaters as if they were her clones. I think that they represented her feeling of omnipotence, of wanting to be mother, teacher, and therapist of her stepchild, at the same time that she ridiculed her husband–brother; a mechanism she might have used as a child in order to compete with her older brother. I make the whole interpretation around the colour of the sweater, which I think represents O.

Transformation of O into K is necessary during the act of structuring the interpretation;[12] a condition that also requires from the analyst a previous capacity to transform K into O. Freud formerly voiced this situation when he referred to the notion of "floating attention". To apprehend O requires a trust in the phantasy that emerges while listening to the patient's discourse, and requires following of the patterns that make sense and seem related to the content of the patient's associations. The belief and use of such phantasies requires what Bion refers to as an "act of faith". Being able to reach such an attitude will depend on the analyst's discipline while avoiding using any memory or desire.

The "act of faith"

The "act of faith" represents an action of courage and self-assertiveness, and a belief that whatever the analyst is thinking while listening to the patient's material might be relevant to the understanding of the unconscious side of the discourse. Through the act of faith, says Bion,

> One can "see", "hear", and "feel" the mental phenomena of whose reality no practicing psycho-analyst has any doubt he cannot, with any accuracy, represent them by existing formulations. [1970, pp. 57–58]

O and Zen Buddhism

In his description of O, Bion introduces a different dimension not well followed or understood by occidental thinkers; it has a distinguishable flavour related to *intuition* and Oriental philosophy, specifically Zen Buddhism.[13] Although Bion never explicitly stated that there was any relationship between some of the concepts he portrayed and what was being said in Zen Buddhism, it is not difficult to establish a relation between this form of thinking and some of Bion's ideas. In the Kena-Upanishad, for instance, we can read passages that are very similar to the definition of O:

> "It is conceived by whom does not conceive it
> Who conceives it does not conceive it
> Those who understand it do not understand it
> It is understood by those who do not understand it."

Zen Buddhism, according to historians, was initiated in India around 2000 BC, and disseminated in China and Japan afterwards. At the beginning it was associated with religions such as Hinduism.

However, it soon became an independent form of philosophy of intuition. The main purpose of Zen is the search of at-one-ment with the universe, something that, if viewed from an Occidental vertex, might represent some kind of oceanic depersonalization, or a state of personality dispersion absolutely dominated by the unconscious, to which Zen Buddhists refer to as *satori*.

If the purpose of psychoanalysis is to make the unconscious present with the use of consciousness, the Zen purpose is to achieve unconscious domination by getting rid of consciousness. Methodology of investigation also runs in different directions; in Zen, for instance, it goes from intuition to theory, but theory is not well viewed, and is even regarded with a certain scorn. It has been mostly occidental researchers who have provided it with a greater relevance, as can be observed in the publications of Valliet (1971), Fromm and Suzuki (1963), LaSalle (1975), Herrigel (1953), and so on. Psychoanalysis, on the other hand, moves from theory to intuition, disregarding the latter, with the exception of Bion, who tried to make intuition a determining aspect within the analytical practice, a contribution that has induced regular misunderstanding and criticism of his work.

Zen masters search for a form of illumination they refer to as *satori* or awakening, through long-term daily meditations known as *zazen*, in an enclosed special place designated as *dojo*. Meditation stands for a voluntary state that attempts to free the psyche from any thought, memory, or desire and, after continuous practice, achieves a "nirvana" state of mind. Although meditation could be practised alone, it generally requires the presence of a Zen master, whose non-directing attitude bears a resemblance to the psychoanalyst's neutrality. Suzuki (1981) illustrates this: "A monk from Sun Dynasty named Chosui Shiye, asked the Zen master Roya Hyoryo: "How could the mountains, rivers and the immense earth sprout from the Originally Pure?" To which the master answered: "How could the mountains, rivers and the immense earth sprout from the Originally Pure?" (p. 48).

Curiously, Zen gives no importance to the analysis of dreams, using in its place a kind of riddle designated as *koan*, which students try to solve by following a similar intuitive approach that Bion referred to as "transformations in O". A well-known *koan* presents the following riddle: "the sound of one hand that applauds", and the solution, I think, might be "the sound of silence".

An analytical patient brought a dream that made me think of the relationship between *koan* and dreams. During a session we were investigating her unconscious need to lie to herself and to others, in relation to her ambivalent feelings of resentment and painful guilt, which the patient experienced in relation to her son's drug dependency and delinquent acting out. At one point, she referred to the fact that the proprietor of her condominium made a comment about how could someone as decent and good-looking as her son be involved in such behaviour. Then she produced a dream where someone, whom she could only see from behind, was making flattering remarks to her son, similar to those expressed by the proprietor. Then the person turned around and she realized that this man had "glass eyes". I thought this dream condensed the matter we were dealing with, that, similar to a Buddhist *koan*, it simply portrayed the "lie": how can someone with glass eyes be capable of making flattering remarks?

Bion advocates the use of intuition during the analytic session, in a manner similar to that which the Zen masters advocate throughout the practice of meditation or *zazen*. Buddhists say, for instance, "The obscurity of a cave changes into illumination when a torch of intuition burns".

Notes

1. "Say nothing, unless what you have to say is better than silence." In Salvator Rosa's (1615–1673) portrait, National Gallery, London.
2. See Chapter Nine.
3. There are two other versions to this myth. One states that Olympus's Gods punished Tiresias because he revealed secrets entrusted to his mother. The other version is from Hesiod, who states that Tiresias hit two serpents that were in coitus, wounding the female. For this the Gods changed him into a woman. Ten years later, when walking through the same forest, he found the same serpents, but this time he hit the male and was then restored to his original gender. Due to this experience, of being both man and woman, Zeus and Hera asked him to intervene in a dispute they had about who would have a more pleasurable orgasm. Teiresias agreed with the former by stating that

satisfaction was much greater for the woman, because if orgasm were divided into ten, nine were for women and only one for men. Finding herself betrayed, Hera got so angry that she made Teiresias blind, and Zeus, in compensation, provided him with the capacity to foresee the future.

4. See Chapter Two: "The forgotten self".

5. I refer to this last aspect as the "narcissistic conglomerate" and describe it in detail in Chapter Six.

6. See Chapter Twelve.

7. This issue is investigated in Chapter One.

8. The relation between O and countertransference is discussed in more detail in Chapter Thirteen.

9. Term taken from philosopher David Hume referring to facts joined by chance. (See López-Corvo, 2003, p. 67.)

10. See *ibid.*, p. 68.

11. According to both Plato and Aristotle, Heraclitus expressed extreme views that led to logical incoherence. For he held that (1) everything is constantly changing, and (2) opposite things are identical, so as a consequence, everything is and is not at the same time. In other words, "universal flux" and the "identity of opposites" theories entail a denial of the Law of Non-Contradiction. However, such contradiction could be entirely apparent, because things are always changing in order to remain the same, as Descartes tried to prove; an understanding that places Heraclitus well above Plato and Aristotle.

12. See Chapter Ten regarding the "interpretation".

13. When I mentioned this presumption to Francesca Bion, she remembered that Bion, while in California, purchased a copy of Alan Watts's book *The Way of Zen*, that she felt he might have bought second hand, because she realized it looked so tattered.

CHAPTER THIRTEEN

"O" or countertransference?

"An electron moving between orbits would disappear from one and reappear instantaneously in another without visiting the space between. This idea—the famous quantum leap—is of course utterly strange"

(Bohr, 1913)

"Think, what a testimony of spiritual elevation we might express, if we reveal that we are made of the same material of those we shape"

(Lacan, 1966)

More than one countertransference

As far as I can tell, Bion has not provided a specific and elaborated account on the subject of countertransference, only isolated statements in some of his conferences or perhaps implicit in other contributions. From his experience in groups and later in his seminars in Brazil (1974–1975) and New York (1977), he discriminates between those feelings experienced by analysts towards their patients of which they are conscious and thus are able to use in interpretations, and those feelings of which they are not aware and thus are unable to make use of. In the latter case there is no other alternative but to make these feelings conscious with the use of psychoanalysis. This last condition is what Bion refers to as countertransference:

> It is my belief that these reactions are dependent on the fact that the analyst in the group is at the receiving end of what Melanie Klein (1946) has called projective identification . . . the experience of countertransference appears to me to have quite a distinct quality that should enable the analyst to differentiate the occasion when he is the object of a projective identification from the occasion when he is not. The analyst feels he is being manipulated so as to be playing a part, no matter how difficult to recognize, in somebody else's phantasy. [1948, p. 149]

Several years latter, in 1974, during a visit to Rio de Janeiro, Bion maintains a similar criteria:

> Countertransference is a technical term, but as often happens the technical term gets worn away and turns into a kind of worn out coin which has lost its value . . . *The theory about a countertransference is that it is the transference relationship which the analyst has to the patient without knowing he has it* [my italics] . . . One cannot make use of one's countertransference in the consulting room; it is a contradiction in terms. To use the term in that way means that one would have to invent a new term to do the work, which used to be done by the word "countertransference". It is one's unconscious feelings about the patient, and since it is unconscious there is nothing we can do about it. [1974, pp. 87–88][1]

But we could observe, however, that Bion did not always think in these terms, because previously, in 1953, he stated:

> Evidence for the interpretations has to be sought in the counter-transference and in the actions and free associations of the patient. Counter-transference has to play an important part in analysis of the schizophrenic, but I do not propose to discuss this to-day. [1967, p. 24]

Unfortunately, he never "discussed" this issue afterwards. In his later appreciations he is close to Gitelson's (1952) discrimination between "the analyst's reactions towards the patient as a whole", to which he refers as "the analyst's transferences", and the analyst's reaction towards partial aspects of the analyst, to which he refers as "the analyst's countertransference". Bion is also close to Freud's original statements:

> We become aware of the "counter-transference", which arises in him [the analyst] as a result of the patient's influence on his unconscious feelings, and we are almost inclined to insist that he shall recognize this countertransference in himself and overcome it. [1910d, pp. 144–145]

Freud said little about countertransference because, at this time, it was a touchy subject linked with political issues related to the therapist's pathology, and the difficulty finally to accept that therapists should undergo psychoanalytic treatment. "He [Freud] did not doubt" says Gay (1988), ". . . that countertransference was an insidious obstruction to the analyst's benevolent neutrality, a resistance to be diagnosed and defeated."

Nunberg (1965), in his recount of Vienna's Wednesday Minutes, stated:

> . . . the blind spots caused by his own conflicts interfere with the ability of such a man fully to understand another. In order to eliminate such weak spots in the analyst's understanding of his patient, Freud—as these Minutes show—suggested at an early time that analysts be analyzed. This clearly demonstrates Freud's realization, soon after he began his work, that not only can the doctor exert an influence over his patient, but that the patient can influence the doctor as well. When the patient's conflicts coincide with those of the doctor, the latter may not see them; he may misunderstand them or identify with the patient. This phenomenon, which belongs to the sphere of what later was called countertransference, was an early topic of discussion in the Society (pp. 156–157).

From Nunberg (1965) we also find out that, in 1918, at the Psychoanalytic Congress in Budapest, the motion for the need of future psychoanalysts to undergo treatment was introduced, but it was rejected, and it was not until 1926, during the Bad Homburg Congress, that the motion was finally accepted. It is obvious that, at this time, neurotic traits present in these early therapists induced the need for a structured form of training that included treatment; later on, however, when this was no longer the case because proper psychoanalytic treatment became compulsory, psychoanalysts realized the existence of other essential angles about countertransference, different from the original conflict pioneers had to face.

Works such as those by Heiman (1950) and Racker (1969) introduced a different alternative from that of Freud. They argued that some feelings that patients could elicit in the analyst could create profitable outcomes, because these feelings could allow for further understanding of the patients unconscious phantasy. Heiman in 1950 states:

> This rapport on the deep level comes to the surface in the form of feelings which the analyst notices in response to his patient, in his "counter-transference". This is the most dynamic way in which his patient's voice reaches him. In the comparison of feelings roused in himself with his patient's associations and behaviour, the analyst possesses a most valuable means of checking whether he has understood or failed to understand his patient. [p. 82]

Racker (1969), on the other hand, discriminated between a kind of countertransference he referred to as "concordant", representing a form of commiseration or empathy towards the patient's feelings, where his id needs, ego conflicts, and superego demands induce conscious identifications with similar aspects in the analyst. This response constitutes the useful aspects of countertransference. Racker also distinguished a second form of countertransference he called "complementary", related to the projection into the analyst, via projective identifications, of internal objects from the patient, capable of inducing in the former identifications with those objects, giving place to a kind of countertransference that complements the inner narcissistic representations of the patient.

Bion does not explicitly discriminate, like Racker, between two forms of countertransference; however, it is obvious that he refers to a kind or experience related to unconscious aspects of the analyst that will require further psychoanalytic investigation, which he named "countertransference", and another form he specifically and emphatically referred to as "O". We will come back to this issue further on.

There has also been a kind of misconception, about what exactly was meant by the use the counter-transference during the analytic session, mostly in the North American practice, when analysts, in a rather naïve approach, confess to the patient irrelevant issues of their own, which will only add confusion to the outcome of the analytic process, representing what could be considered a form of "wild countertransference" (Sandler, 1993).

During the International Psychoanalytic Congress No 38 that took place in 1993 in Amsterdam, a very productive discussion took place as a consequence of an article presented by Jacobs (1993) about "The inner experiences of the analyst" and the discussion provided by Green (1993) on this paper. Jacobs referred to experiences or phantasies that took place within himself at the same time and in a parallel mode to the patient's free associations. Jacobs did not clarify whether the reason for the use of his associations was made with the purpose of capturing the patient's unconscious phantasy. It appears, instead, as if it was some form of "confession" he spontaneously shared with his patient. He said: ". . . certain thoughts, feelings, fantasies and physical sensations that I became aware of during this hour arose in response to unconscious communications from my patient (p. 7).

During this session, Mr V, the patient, started by criticizing his brother and a friend, for being "false", because lately they became very religious, sort of "pious Jews". The patient adds: "Now they are pillars of the Synagogue, big contributors who have their names on plaques in the sanctuary. On Friday night the Ks said prayers and lit *shabbos* candles. It was a farce" (*ibid.*, p. 10).

A number of disjointed recollections started to flow in the mind of the analyst, and he started to share them in detail, until an enigmatic memory took place: he remembered the mezuzah—a small object religious Jews place on their door—which belonged to his grandparents and he has now placed at the entrance of his office, where his patient was coming for the first time. Jacobs associates that Mr V's claim about the religious and false character of his brother and of his friend was related to the patient having subliminally noticed the mezuzah on his door. He writes:

... Now I think about it and wonder why these images are arising. As I do so, I have a sudden conviction. Mr V has seen the mezuzah on the door. On some level—perhaps subliminally—it has registered in his brain and through his associations to the religious objects in Mr K's home (which included the specific reference to a mezuzah), he has made reference to it.

On the basis of this hunch, which, I recall, was experienced with a sense of conviction, I ask Mr V if he noticed anything on the front door of the office as he came in. In response he is silent for a few seconds.

"You have something in mind", he replies after a bit, "but I don't know what it is."

I remain quiet again and Mr V lapses into silence. Then, finally, he speaks.

"Hey wait a minute", he says. "Do you have one of those Jewish things on your door? I think you might . . ."

Here we could speculate about the moment when Jacobs confuses his own feelings with those the patient's transference might have elicited in him. Why was it so important that the patient could have noticed the object on his door? How could the analyst's association have been used to understand the patient's unconscious phantasy and in this manner, also used to create the interpretation? If the therapist, as a consequence of his conviction of the patient having seen the mezuzah on the door, was suspecting a transference reference that he was also false, he could have then phrased the interpretation in those terms, instead of asking the patient if he had noticed something. He could have said for instance, "perhaps you feel that I, like your brother and your friend, am false too"; or "perhaps you feel trapped between your desire to trust me and your fear that I could also be false like your brother and friend".

'O' or countertransference?

Since I have already referred to "O" in more detail, I will now only pass on briefly, and guide the reader to the previous chapter. It is my feeling that, although there is a growing interest in the psychoanalytic community about several of Bion's contributions, his description of O is not a popular one. It has produced opposite reactions in Latin American psychoanalysts to those observed in North American colleagues, that is, it is of great interest amid the former while usually ignored and never mentioned among the latter. The Symingtons (1966), for instance, stated that when Bion introduced the concept of O, "some in the Klein group were quick to dissociate themselves from his thinking from that time onwards"; and later on, after he published *Memoir of The Future*, many British analysts, according to the same authors, considered that Bion had mentally deteriorated after leaving England to the point that "everything he wrote subsequent to his departure was to be dismissed as the rambling of a senile man" (Symington & Symington, 1966, p. 10). For Bion, the use of O during the analytic therapy, together with the absence of memory, desire, and understanding, stands for an essential instrumentation that eases the grasp of the unconscious message.[2]

Not all the associations that appear in the analyst's mind during an analytic session are induced by the unconscious production of the patient. Elucidating between those phantasies that are the product of the countertransference and those induced by the transference, is not an easy task. For Bion, this operation is absolutely indispensable, and O must be picked up with an act of faith and then transformed into K in order to construct an interpretation. How is one to know, then, if the phantasy that appears at a given moment in the analyst's mind is an expression of O, instead of an unconscious pathological element that is now surfacing? Attempting to avoid this dilemma, I use a simple rule: if I hear the material absolutely concentrated without memory, desire, and understanding, all the phantasies that appear could represent O, but if, while listening, I get lost in my own associations and do not follow the thread of the patient's production, then my own countertransference might be responsible for whatever is causing my distraction. I have also found it useful to observe that sometimes such distractions take place with some particular patients.

I remember, for instance, the case of Helen, a thirty-three-year old married woman in analysis for seven years, referred by her GP because of anxiety, agoraphobia, and suicidal ruminations. She was the eldest of five siblings, and her mother, who was adopted, grew up, according to

Helen, as a sort of "Cinderella", often displacing her own childhood sufferings on to her children in the form of a strict and frequently unfair discipline. At one point, at the beginning of her analysis, Helen remembered how her mother forced her and her siblings to remain in the garden after school until it was time to go to bed, with the excuse that they would dirty and mess the house up if they were to remain inside. From the beginning of the treatment, I started to observe that I had great difficulty concentrating on the material presented by Helen, often finding myself lost in a multitude of associations. During one of her sessions, seconds after lying down on the couch, she started to talk about the difficulty she had in parking her car in front of my house: "It seems that your neighbours are very busy", she said. "I had to wait until your previous patient left to be able to park and at the end I had to park in front of a garage. I hope I will not be obstructing anybody wanting to get out of the house . . . I hate to be in somebody's way, I don't really want to interfere . . ." After a long pause she continued talking about her father-in-law, who discriminates against women, saying that their place is in the house having children and looking after them.

At this particular moment I started to have phantasies about what to do in order to change some investments to have better dividends; and I also felt that these phantasies were not related to the patient's discourse, because I remembered being previously in a similar predicament, even though the material brought then by the patient was completely different. Becoming aware that I was on the verge of losing the thread of my patient's associations, I tried to concentrate again, but I found it extremely difficult, almost painful—similar to previous sessions—to give up the mental tactics I was applying in order to "improve" my finances. Although the contents of my phantasies were my own, the repetitious need to disconnect from this patient's discourse and the painful difficulty in keeping my concentration on her communication made me wonder whether there was something in the form of a projective identification I was dealing with, but was not then aware of. In other words, I thought there were two different issues taking place at the same time; on the one hand there was a "needy" element of my own that was concerned with improving my investments, representing my countertransference in Bion's terms; on the other hand there was also an emotional counterpart product of a projective identification that required an investigation in order to understand the true nature of its meaning.

My patient spoke about a young sister-in-law who was still living with her parents and was very much emotionally dependent on them. At this moment, it came to my mind what she had said at the beginning of the session, that there were too many cars in front of my house, and she had had to wait until my previous patient left and that she had parked in front of somebody's garage. I then felt certain that there was a relationship between these aspects of her discourse and my difficulty concentrating. I had the feeling that I was abandoning her, leaving her alone to talk to herself, while I absented myself, as if the interaction between us was very painful. I also thought that there was an important schizoid aspect about her, since I often have the phantasy that I could have abandoned the office without her noticing it. I felt it was like a revelation of something that had been going on in the session for quite some time, without my being able to figure it out. In other words, I thought it was like capturing Bion's O.

Then I said that I believed she felt threatened by other patients–siblings and their "busyness"; she imagined I was "sharing" with them something that made her feel painfully excluded and filled her with anger to the point that she wanted to stop the "exit" (like parking in front of the garage) of other siblings–patients; that perhaps she felt so threatened by the birth of so many brothers and sisters after her that she might have tried to continuously ignore them. She was silent for a while and then said that not only was she the oldest of all, but she was five years older than the brother who was the second eldest, and that there was only one year difference between him and the next. She stated: "They were always together, always playing among themselves and never allowed me to participate, I always felt left out." When her sister was born, she remembered thinking that perhaps, since she was a girl, this sister could be a good playmate, but the difference in age was so great that this was impossible. She remembered growing up alone, discriminated against not only because she was the eldest but also because she was a girl. Her voice at this moment was significantly sad, and I was, unlike at other moments, extremely attentive and receptive of her emotions, listening to her gloomy account about her feeling of exclusion, always lonely and with a considerable amount of envy towards the capacity of her siblings to play with each other. She was talking in a low voice, frequently interrupted by quivers and sudden bursts of crying. She also referred to her own nine-year-old daughter, who is an only child, and to her fear of having other children because she did not wish to expose her daughter to the presence of other siblings, as had happened to her. I thought that my difficulty following her associations was related to a projective identification that attempted to protect her from a painful history of continuous exclusions and mistreatments, of feeling neglected and uncertain, as if she did not have a place of her own or the right to "be". What I experienced in the countertransference was the presence of an absence, the feeling of someone cast off in her own phantasies, which induced again her childhood experience of being left completely isolated without a companion to play with.

The next session was the fourth and last of the week. She described in detail her daughter's birthday party, while I struggled again with my tendency to turn to my own phantasies. Then she mentioned—almost at the end of a session where I had remained completely silent—that her doctor, the one who had referred her to see me, had sent me his greetings, and she added with a certain tone I perceived as a kind of reprimand, that I should not forget my friends. At this moment I felt present for the first time in the session and tried to build the interpretation around this issue. I said that she wanted not to forget about me and that I did not forget about her either, that I had been absent from the whole session without saying anything, that she wanted to make me present, however, since this desire frightened her. She preferred to talk about other things, perhaps because this made her remember painful matters from her infancy.

On the next session she started to talk about her work, with the same previous monotonous details, and again I experienced the same difficulty following her. Suddenly, she became silent and remained like that for a long time; I felt uncomfortable and felt the need to say something. After twenty minutes I said that it seemed to me that she was very determined to make me present, in a way she had never tried before. She agreed and added that she was feeling the struggle to see who was going to remain silent longer. She also remembered that her mother often would order her around or give her directions and that, in reality, her mother did not care if what she ordered was accomplished or not, for it seemed that the important thing for her was to make herself present and to show who the boss was. She continued: "My mother talked to me with the sole purpose of debasing me, as if I did not exist. Then I started to do the same with her, to talk in order to make her disappear, just to say anything in order to get rid of her, so she would leave me alone. I often thought that it was dangerous to try to make her know what I wanted; it was very painful to feel that I meant nothing to her, that I was only someone with whom she could practise being the owner. It was easier to ignore it all and to remain distant."

During the next session she saw, through the office window, a cat that was walking through the garden and expressed that she did not like cats, "They are distant, very clean but ungrateful, not very friendly, interested only in what is convenient for them, different from dogs which are friendly, faithful, and grateful." She remembered a dog she had had when she was a child. This dog always followed her through the garden as she moved inside the house. Every morning, it wagged its tail, looking for her attention, "like saying good morning". As she talked, I remembered about something she had previously said about her mother forcing her and her siblings outside of the house; that she could have felt like the dog, moving around the garden trying not to be ignored by those that were inside of the house, painfully aware and trying not to be forgotten.

Then she remembered a dream and explained that they were really two dreams. In the first dream,

> she felt a deep feeling of longing, sadness and nostalgia, because her husband was away on a trip. The second dream was related to her work. She was told that her programme at work, where she was a supervisor, had changed. The supervision was going to take place during different hours, something she felt was not right for the personnel because it was not providing her with enough time to prepare for it. However, she also thought that this change was convenient for her because it did not interfere with playing tennis.

She provided no associations and I said that it seemed as if the dream was portraying the existence of two different parts in her, one was like a "dog part": grateful, aware, friendly, and so on; and another one like a cat part: aloof, distant, ungrateful, and concerned only with her things. That these dog–cat parts were similar to these two dreams, which also seemed to represent both parts, the first dream depicting a dog part and the second one the cat part. In the first part she is deeply taken by the absence of her husband, by how important he is for her, and by how much she cares for him. The second part is impersonal and based on insignificant details about what might or might not be convenient. It was similar to what she talked about during the previous session, when, under the influence of the "cat part", she attempted to ignore my presence, projecting the "dog part", needy and sensitive, in order that she might avoid suffering, or when feeling excluded, I might become like a forgotten dog and attempt to think about other things, similar to what she said she did in order to protect herself from suffering, when she felt mistreated or ignored by her mother. Also, she could project the "cat part" into me, and then we could both become distant and ignore each other, like being and not being together, or trying to make an analysis without really doing it. The problem, perhaps, was the difficulty in allowing us to become the dog part even if it implies suffering. She approved and started a recount of painful childhood memories about feeling abandoned and ignored and how she learned to feel numbness in order not to suffer.

I am completely convinced that it would have been much more difficult to understand her inner tragedy, or perhaps it would have taken more time, if I had used the transference only, instead of using my countertransference feelings—or O in Bion's terminology—in order to build the interpretation, in the way I have just described it. After this revelation, the analysis followed, for both of us, a completely different course, ending in mutual agreement a year or so later. From time to time I hear about her from our mutual friend, the physician who originally sent her for treatment. After several years she appeared to be doing well with her family, remaining completely free of her original symptoms. She continued her work as a recognized historian and even published a book.

Notes

1. Three years later, while in New York, he repeats the same concepts almost with the same words (1980, p. 16)
2. Some have compared Bion's O with Lacan's Real. However, the latter does not carry the practical importance and essentiality Bion has given to O at the moment of seizing the unconscious phantasy in order to create the interpretation.

CHAPTER FOURTEEN

Using the Grid

The more I investigate the Grid (see over), the more I become aware of the presence of a genius. It grants a sense of guidance, support, and strength approximating to what Gaea provided to Anteaus, a structure and conceptualization that carries the competence of clearing the mind. Bion, similar to Pythagoras, attempted to apprehend the two sides of the psyche, on the one hand the noumenon, the intuition or the ineffable, which he has referred to as "O"; and on the other hand, the phenomenon, or the observable fact. Bion tries to portray this in the Grid, perhaps inspired by Mendeleyev's Periodic Table. The Grid is a true monument to Bion's greatness, but as a monument can only be looked at and admired, and nothing else.

There are two combined axes, one horizontal, and another vertical, which can be read from left to right and from top to bottom. There are a total of fifty-six squares, eight verticals, and seven horizontals, most of them already filled by Bion, with the exception of a few left to be filled, according to him, "by someone in the future".

The Grid does not represent an indispensable element for the understanding of how the mind works; it stands more as a curiosity, as a brilliant attempt to reticulate what has been said during an

	Definitory hypothesis 1	ψ 2	Notation 3	Attention 4	Inquiry 5	Action 6	... n
A β-elements	A1	A2				A6	
B α-elements	B1	B2	B3	B4	B5	B6	... Bn
C Dream-thoughts Dreams, Myths	C1	C2	C3	C4	C5	C6	... Cn
D Pre-conception	D1	D2	D3	D4	D5	D6	... Dn
E Conception	E1	E2	E3	E4	E5	E6	... En
F Concept	F1	F2	F3	F4	F5	F6	... Fn
G Scientific Deductive System		G2					
H Algebraic Calculus							

analytic session; there is however, a particular issue that I will consider later,[1] related to the appraisal of "mental growth", a concept very much contingent upon the relativity of the observer, which could be measured in a more reasonable fashion if the vertical axis of the Grid is used. There is a common dismissal by analysts and students of Bion towards understanding how the Grid works, perhaps more as a form of resistance than a justified view, because, once its ways and reasoning are properly understood, the Grid becomes an easy and interesting tool to follow. Bion often sustained a sort of ambivalent manner in relation to the Grid, very optimistic at the beginning, but rather pessimistic in later years. In 1974, during a conference in São Paulo, he stated:

The Grid is a feeble attempt to produce an instrument. An instrument is not a theory. It is made up out of theories, just in the same way as a ruler, which is marked in inches and centimeters, has been made in conformity with a number of theories. But the ruler can be used by different people for all sorts of purposes. When I was a boy at school the teacher would say, "hold out your hand" and then use the ruler to strike the palm . . . That is about all I can claim for the Grid. Some people may be able to use it for different purposes . . . I think it is good enough to know how bad it is, how unsuitable for the task for which I have made it. But even if it inflicts a certain amount of mental pain I hope you can turn it to good account and make a better one. [1974, p. 53]

Later on, in 1977, he stated that the Grid allowed him to maintain a critical and illuminating attitude about his work; while the same year in New York, he also remarked that "As soon as I had got the Grid out of my system I could see how inadequate it is . . . the satisfaction does not last for long". And when asked how difficult it was, he responded: "Not for me, only a waste of time because it doesn't really correspond to the facts I am likely to meet" (1980, p. 56).

The horizontal axis

Bion also referred to it as the "schematic" or "axis of uses", representing the mind's qualities or attitudes, which "contains" the elements in the vertical axis and might, or might not, allow their progression. The contents along this axis do not change; they are always the same as they move from left to right.

The first column corresponds to the "definitory hypothesis", a series of facts held together by "constant conjunctions" such as a myth or the content of a session, something said by the patient or in the interpretation. An important aspect is the continuous synchronicity or actuality of the hypothesis, which excludes previous ones, implying that only the present is meaningful. For instance, we will never say to a patient that what he is saying now contradicts what he has stated during the previous session. The same could be said about an interpretation, because the actual interpretation of a moment excludes all preceding ones. A definitory hypothesis can be represented just by a word, for instance "cat", a substantive representing a constant conjunction that collects hair colour, size, species, the cat that we once had, a cat from our memory, etc. It will always presuppose a negative element, because if I say that something "is" I am also implying that something else "is not"; if I say this is a cat, I am also implying that it is not a dog. When frustration tolerance is high, it is then easier to assume that *something* "is", and allow the movement, from preconception to concept, but if tolerance is low then the person could react against that *something* and destroy it enviously and deny its existence. A model could be seen in the baby's incapacity to tolerate weaning because he is dominated by the loss of the breast and cannot accept what remains of the lost. If a definitory hypothesis is not tolerated, it will be impossible to reach a preconception, corresponding to square D4 of the Grid; in other words, a preconception will be able to go beyond the level of attention. For instance, the manifest enunciation of the patient in a session is equivalent to a definitory hypothesis, which will be listened to by the analyst in a state of "waiting in renunciation", capable of tolerating the frustration of "listening without expectation, memory, and desire". This situation Bion named "psychological turbulence", equivalent to Category 1 of the Grid.

Column 2 corresponds to what we know as "defence" or "resistance" in classical theory, and will act as a barrier against ideas and feelings implicit in the definitory hypotheses, obstructing their appearance in order to avoid what Bion refers to as "catastrophic change". It is represented by the Greek letter Psi (Ψ) possibly associated with "lies" from the expression "*proton pseudos*" (προτον ψευδοσ), meaning *proton* = first, and *pseudos* = false. It was used originally by Aristotle in *Prior Analytics* (Book II, Chapter 18, 66a), and by Freud (1950a) in the "Project for a scientific psychology" to portray the hysterical patient's lies.

Columns that follow, Nos 3, 4 and 5, do not have a defensive character like the previous one. On the contrary, they act as assistance to the analytical work, representing concepts Bion borrowed from Freud's 1911 article "Formulations on the two principles of mental functioning", in which he considers the relationship of sense organs with consciousness, on the one side, and the external world on the other. Freud identifies "notation" that tracks the background, discriminating between the new from the known, and Bion uses it as Column 3, representing memory or notation of statements that might unite or relate different constant conjunctions. Column 4, or "attention", is related to how the analyst listens, presence or absence of memory, desire, or understanding, floating attention, and the search for a meaning. Column 5 corresponds to "inquiry", curiosity or exploration of facts related to moral connotations. In the first Grid Bion called this column "Oedipus", depicting the stubbornness and determination implemented by the latter in finding the truth. Column 6 is related to action, acting out, or "motor discharge", employed to ease the mind from accumulation of stimuli. Projective identification as well as the interpretation related to this process, falls into this category.

The vertical axis

The vertical axis includes eight categories registered with letters ranging from A to H, which run from top to bottom. All these categories represent unsaturated elements in search of realizations. Categories increase in degrees of sophistication as they move downwards following a progressive thought scale. This axis represents a "content" that grows and evolves within the "continent" represented by the horizontal axis that symbolizes the mind. From an emotional point of view, the vertical axis might resemble the integration–disintegration movements present in the paranoid–schizoid position. Increments in sophistication in the vertical movement of this axis is facilitated by proper frustration tolerance, the product of a good maternal reverie, as well as by the existence of positive links such as: +H, +L, and +K. On the other hand, low frustration tolerance, the product of a bad maternal reverie, hinders the progressive movement of the axis due to the existence of negative links such as: −H, −L, and −K.

The first category corresponds to the letter A and contains *beta elements*, considered as concrete thoughts, indistinguishable from things. They represent ideation confusion, incapacity to differentiate phantasy from reality, animate from inanimate,[2] subject from object or moral from scientific. Beta elements make up the substance present in pathological projective identifications that imprison subject and object and usually induce acting out. These elements represent "definitory hypotheses" used either as resistances that belong to Column 2, or as actions that correspond to Column 6. For Bion, beta elements correspond to an early matrix, within which thoughts are originated. Such early thoughts contain qualities of inanimate things as well as psychic objects that are indistinguishable from each other (Bion, 1963, p. 22).

The second category corresponds to the letter B and contains *alpha elements*, which are the product of the alpha function. We might speculate that since this function is so meaningful for the evolution of the whole vertical axis towards attaining complexity of thoughts, it should have been placed outside of the Grid next to the vertical axis. Something of this sort could be read in Bion when he said that all categories in the Grid, with the possible exception of File B, could play a role, sometimes more, sometimes less, in any psychoanalytic material (*ibid.*, pp. 29–30).

The third category or file corresponds to the letter C and represents thoughts that can be expressed in sensuous terms, usually in visual images as they appear in dreams, myths, narratives, or hallucinations. The fourth category, File D, represents preconceptions, conceived similarly to Kant's notion of "empty thoughts". These thoughts represent a mental state of expectation towards some realization, like the anticipation of the breast by the baby immediately after birth, or the expectation of the analyst while deciphering the manifest content of the patient's discourse, which will allow him to create interpretations. Bion represents it as $\Psi\xi$ where Ψ corresponds to the unknown, while ξ stands for an unsaturated element which, when temporarily saturated by knowledge, changes into a conception which then would belong in File E. File E contains conceptions which are a product of the union of a preconception with a realization. The rest of the files will function in a similar fashion, where the mating with a realization will upgrade them to the next immediate level of sophistication.

The sixth category, or File F, corresponds to theory formulations, psychoanalytic or not, which attempt to demonstrate scientific observations. "Conceptions" change into "concepts" with the help of abstractions that free these otherwise useless elements, because they represent only an instrument in the elucidation or expression of truth. File G has little use and, according to Bion, we must wait until a deductive, scientific psychoanalytic system develops; something similar could be said about File H, of no use either, with the exception of investigations or publications of certain problems, which will also need to wait until the development of algebraic systems.

The analyst's relaxed listening in floating unsaturated attention to the patient's manifest discourse, will correspond to D4; and the analyst's whole attitude would correspond to an attentive preconception. Understanding the meaning of the patient's material signifies a movement from D4 (a preconception) to a conception or E4. The search of a confirmation comparing the patient's material so far gathered with another one will mean a movement towards E3 or E5. The analyst has reached the F5 level when conceptualizations of sensuous impressions start to take place, the patient's material so far collected begins to become integrated and an interpretation begins to be shaped. When the interpretation is finally uttered with the purpose of affecting the patient, the level will correspond to G6. A similar process will take place in the patient's mind as he or she listens to the interpretation.

The intimate mechanisms that take place in order to induce a descending movement in the vertical axis of the Grid, Bion summarizes as: (a) changes in the nature of Ps $\Rightarrow \Leftarrow$ D; (b) an organizing factor similar to Poincaré's "selected factor"; (c) other mechanisms Bion had referred to as "Psycho-mechanics".[3]

A clinical case

I will attempt now to use the Grid by placing in it the content of a session. Tony is twenty-two years old, the elder of two brothers, whose parents became divorced when he was eight years of age. Two years ago, he was brought for consultation by his mother, a dominating, attractive, and sensuous woman who, at the first meeting, stated that she wanted Tony to see a therapist because she did not want him to "become a poor devil like his father and his father's family", adding that Tony had "low self-esteem, little ambition, does not have a girlfriend and only likes to go out with low-class women".

At the beginning, the transference was determined by constant self-criticism, as if he, attempting to imitate his mother's accusations, was trying to placate indictments coming from a superego object projected into the analyst, a situation capable of eliciting countertransference feelings of commiseration, and the danger of a perverse collusion. He avoided acting out incestuous desires by refusing loving relationships with women of similar social background. At the same time he debased the internal representation of his controlling mother by searching for lower-class women. All women considered by him as "decent" were his mother, as if all of them belonged to one species only. This situation trapped and paralysed him, because it created an inner dissociation that induced powerful sexual desires towards these women, and yet, at the same time, terrified him to think that he was capable of accomplishing those desires. The absence of his father as an essential object that could have rescued him from the oedipal ambush played a determining role in his life.

After a while, we managed to identify a "child element" characterized by feelings of loneliness, isolation, exclusion, and at the same time, intense envy. This condition strongly determined the transference, which usually manifested itself by his not paying attention to interpretations, by making subtle accusations about not making progress and by a significant delay of his payments. In the countertransference, I had the impression of a sadistic element attempting to starve an object, in spite of significant abundance, perhaps as an effort to invert what he might have experienced when prematurely weaned, because of the birth of his younger brother, a feeling reinforced seven years later when his parents separated.

The session started when he excused himself for not bringing the payment for the last two months, explaining that his mother, due to other expenses, did not have the cheque ready: "Imagine, she had to pay five hundred dollars for my brother's school". I recalled, without saying anything, previous excuses like "remodelling the kitchen", "a trip to Europe", and so on. [This part of the session could correspond to an element used to deceive, and could be placed in A2. My thoughts could belong to B3 or D3, or could be used as material for the interpretation, D6]. But now he was announcing his new "explanation" with a certain perplexity, not because it could have been the best of his excuses, but because it seemed as if he was searching for complicity against his mother, based on the delayed payments; something I experienced with a certain degree of suspiciousness. [There is on the side of the analyst, a situation that is not clear; it could correspond to a definitory hypothesis, possibly B1 or B2.]

Maybe, I thought, Tony was attempting to hide something from himself as well as from me, that he, identifying with his mother, was acting as her accomplice in the process of castrating an object projected into the analyst, perhaps similar to what happened to his father. [This hypothesis that takes place as an attempt to understand what might be happening, could represent a notation about the material, corresponding to B4.] In an effort to understand the nature of the projection and to introduce also the feelings of impotence and anger I was experimenting with in the countertransference [which could correspond to B4], I said: "It seems that your needs are not always considered important. Repairing the kitchen, a trip to Europe, or paying your brother's school fees are more relevant than your need to solve your problems. I wonder why?" [This interpretation represents a preconception (D1), a form of action corresponding to B6, as well as an inquiry or B5.] He agreed with me, and added that he has never seen it from this perspective, that he found it difficult to demand or protest, because disapproval from other people about what he did made him feel awful [From Tony's vertex, what he has said could correspond to a conception: E3 or E4; although it could also represent an "as if" sort of response, in order to please the analyst, as a form of defence equivalent to B6, or an inquiry comparable to B5.]

"The other day", continued Tony, "one of my classmates started to complain to the teacher about something he thought was unfair, and I felt very guilty and ashamed as if it was me who was complaining." [This aspect could represent an hypothesis belonging to B1 or perhaps an evocation comparable to D3.] He continued: "Or when somebody says something suggestive to a girl in the street, I also feel ashamed. It is like feeling someone else's shame." Then he speaks about his brother, about how different he is, about how daring and direct he is when he addresses women. He remembers something I had said the day before, about being afraid not so much of saying something but of feeling something; about fearing his own emotions, of not knowing how to control himself. [His evocation of past experiences, as a notation or reminiscence of past events, could be located in D3 or E3.] He continued remembering my words that if he would only let go he could end up seducing his own mother. [Could equally be placed on D3, D4, or E4.] I reminded him that I had also stated that it seemed as if he had difficulties differentiating between his mother and all other women. [This last remark could correspond to D1 and D4; but because there is also an Oedipus element present, it could correspond to C1 and C4.] Then he remembers a dream. [Definitely C3.]

He was at a party with many attractive women. One of them, the most beautiful, approached him and invited him to dance, and while they were dancing they were also kissing, and everybody was looking at them. After some time he left her, but another woman, even prettier, came close to ask him to dance also, and the same scene was again repeated. At the end, both women were looking at each other filled with anger, jealousy, and ready to fight for his attention.

He gave no associations [C2?] and I said that it seemed as if there was a great contrast between what he usually experienced in reality, and the dream content [possibly C4 and F4]. He agreed, and added that in the dream he felt himself just the way he wanted to be, but was not, stating that his brother, who was completely different, was more like the person in the dream [C4]. At this moment, as I was listening with my eyes closed to what he was saying, I was suddenly invaded by a particular blue colour, and I think it might have represented a dream-like phenomenon, or C1, although I later thought it was a representation of O. I became aware of it later on when I associated this kind of blue colour with the one in a water fountain I had built and painted many years previously with my son, when he was around eight or ten years old. [This was like a transformation of $O \Rightarrow K$ and could be placed in C3 or C4.] I remembered that the experience of building this fountain was very rewarding for both of us [C3].

Using this memory, I then said to my patient that perhaps he was feeling that his father had taught things to his brother that he did not teach to him, and that this made him very angry, inducing complicity with his mother against his father. This was similar to the complicity he could have developed with her against me, for example, not paying me on time, because he also feels that I, just like his father had not done in the past, was not teaching him anything either. I thought that he wanted me to teach him how to seduce or make love to a woman without being so frightened [D1 and D6]. He laughed very loudly and added that his father was very good with women, a real Don Juan, who had many lovers always looking for him, "well-to-do women, sometimes from other countries, like Puerto Rico" [D3]. There was a long pause, and then he said in a softly sad voice that he would be very frightened to be like his father, because he would not know how to control his feelings and that he felt he was capable of feeling about his mother in a way that was not proper. [This could represent a form of complying, as some kind of "as if" defence, and be placed in D2, although it could also represent a true insight and then would correspond to D4.] "Perhaps you are right", he said, "but I wouldn't know how to be like that, I would love to, but I don't know how. You are right, my father never taught me how" [similar to the previous: D2 or D4].

Negative Grid

Bion introduced the possibility of adding to the standard layout of the Grid a negative extension, a mirror image, that would expand the horizontal axis from "–n" to −5, −4, −3, −2 and −1. In this way, he concluded, the negative uses could be utilized as a barrier against the unknown or known that is not well liked. Following the theory of "transformations", this form of grid presents the possibility of a non-static movement, opposite to the direction of those in the ordinary Grid: from H to A, in the vertical, and from . . .–n to 1 in the horizontal. Geometrically, according to Bion, it could be represented by arrows showing the direction of the movement: ↑←, signifying the location of an object Bion defined as "violent, greedy, envious, ruthless, murderous and predatory, without respect for the truth, persons or thing" (1965, p. 102). It could refer to the relationship between an object and its absence, like the absence of the breast, or to what Bion refers to as "the place where the breast (or the penis) was".

> I would like now to refer to the case of L, a forty-six-year-old patient, the second of three sisters, twice divorced and in analysis five times weekly for the past four years. We were investigating her relationship with the youngest of her siblings, towards whom she always experienced a disproportional amount of envy because of her achievements. She also feels that her older sister does not seem to hold these kinds of feelings against her. Two days before we finished work for the summer holidays, she brought a dream:

>> She was in a field party at Dr P's house, a friend of her family, and everything was nice and peaceful, and the food was magnificent. There was only herself, Dr P's wife and her older sister; her younger sister was not there. They decided to walk away from where the party was and they found an immense crater like those left by a meteorite. Her sister told her that she was going to jump over, but she thought that she better go around. Suddenly, her former husband appeared, very aggressive, looking for trouble.

She wondered why her younger sisters were not there. Dr P and his wife she described as a wonderful couple, good people, and good hosts; he is around sixty years old. And then after a pause she said, "He is a radiologist, and you are like a mind radiologist also, perhaps he was you, perhaps here in your house you are like my host." She provided no further associations and then, after a short silence, I asked what she thought about the crater. Then, almost immediately, she exclaimed loudly, "Oh, Mother earth!" I did not fully understand, but had the feeling she was referring to the absence of a breast. I asked: "Could that represent the absence of a breast?" Perhaps what she experienced when her younger sisters were born, like losing her mother's breast. She argued that maybe that was why they did not appear in the dream, there is only herself and her older sister: "My sisters spoiled the party", she concludes. She remembers that her mother, on one occasion, commented that she was weaned early after her younger sister was born, because her mother had an inverted nipple that made breast feeding rather painful. I added that perhaps a "weaned part of her" was reacting to the immediacy of our separation because of the holidays, as if this was changing into an absent breast that "spoiled her party", and was making her feel angry like the abandoning husband at the end of her dream. There is also a part of her that, similar to her older sister, is trying perhaps "to jump over" the "absence", with the help of the analysis.

I gather that what Bion attempted to illustrate with the notion of a negative grid was the importance of the absence of the object. Such an absence becomes a powerful presence determining the outcome of symptoms and psychopathology. This is something he also associated with "being aware", with the alertness of a predator in search of its prey, like hunger looking for food, like a lack of existence looking for existence, or a contained looking for a container, or a definitory hypothesis in search of a realization. Bion said it could be personified by a non-existing "person", like the envy of the dead:

> . . . whose hatred and envy is such that "it" is determined to remove and destroy every scrap of "existence" from any object which might be considered to "have" any existence to remove. Such a non-existent object can be so terrifying that its "existence" is denied, leaving only the "place where it was". [1965, p. 111]

I have observed pathology of this kind in cases that portray history of early traumatic losses, like some of those patients I have described in Chapter Three related to "the deaf-mute object".

Notes

1. See "Normal projective identification" in Chapter Seven.
2. See Chapter One.
3. Further information about these mechanisms can be found in Lopez-Corvo, 2003.

CHAPTER FIFTEEN

Dreams: stray thoughts in search of a thinker

"A propos de sommeil, aventure sinistre
de tout le soir"

(Baudelaire)

"Dreams and visions are induced in men for their advantage
and instruction, and their rules are not general, and this is
why they cannot satisfy everybody, although very often, and
depending on the moment and the individual, they allow a
great variety of interpretations"

(Artemidorus of Daldis, 140 AD)

"You meaner beauties of the night,
That poorly satisfy our eyes
More by your number than your light
You common people of the skies,
What are you when the sun shall rise?"

(Sir Henry Wotton, from "Elizabeth of Bohemia",
www.englishverse.com)

Introduction

As a warning to anybody undertaking an evaluation of Freud's monumental contribution to the meaning and significance of dreams, Meltzer (1983), in his book *Dream-Life*, points out with justice that unless such evaluation starts "on firm ground", it faces the risk of not going "any considerable distance" (p. 11). Facing the possibility of such a downfall and ending saying little, I will attempt to discuss some issues I feel deserve some consideration.

In footnotes added in 1914 and later in 1923 Freud (1900a, pp. 579–580; 1923, pp. 111–112), argues about the danger of providing the unconscious with a certain quality he described as a "mysterious unconscious", which he relates in the 1914 note, with Adler insisting ". . . that dreams possessed a function of *thinking ahead*" (my italics). Since I do not have access to Adler's publication, I do not know in which context he made such a statement. However, Freud is obviously referring to "thinking ahead" as a kind of future divination, similar to a warning he also previously made about associating dream's manifest content with irrelevant meanings based on supernatural beliefs. Looking from another perspective," thinking ahead" might also represent the unconscious capacity ("dream-thought") to think "ahead" of the conscious, like those intuitive unconscious revelations mentioned by scientists such as Friedrich August von Kekule, who confessed discovering the structure of benzene after dreaming about the Uroboros, the snake that bites its own tail.[1]

Freud remained faithful to the end of his days to his remark that dreams, similar to unconscious repressed instincts, were specifically driven by wish fulfilment, even after anxiety dreams and traumatic neurosis proved differently and he felt forced to introduce further theoretical validations. Meltzer (1983) considered that Freud was ". . . so deeply rooted in a neurophysiological model of the mind, with its mind–brain equation, that it will not bear the weight of investigation into the meaning of the meaning of dreams".

If the unconscious represents a simple instrument that provides hallucinatory satisfaction to unfulfilled wishes, how is this function different from day-dreaming? What would be the value of repeating an attribute consciousness already exercises?

From another perspective, it could be considered the conscious and the unconscious constitute a sort of ecosystem[2] that maintains an hegemony by turning each other on and off——sleeping and awakening—while the brain remains always turned on.[3] This mechanism, following Bion, is possible thanks to the presence of a construct he refers to as the "alpha function" which manufactures "alpha elements". These elements, by gathering around the preconscious, create an active "screen" capable of discriminating between states of wakefulness and sleeping. A borderline patient whom I saw first thing in the morning, often came extremely anxious about dreams she sometimes did not recall, but to which she emotionally responded to as if the tragedy she was dealing with in her dreams, continued to be present after she was awake. It usually took a short while before she realized the difference. On one occasion she arrived in great distress and described a dream where there was a party, during which her mother and sister, who were present, ignored her completely. She continued crying for a while, immersed in a sort of delirious state moving around her "dream stuff", until I said that she was having great difficulty waking up.

The sense of dreams Bion explains as follows:

> One of the reasons why sleep is essential is to make possible, by a suspension of consciousness, the emotional experiences that the personality would not permit itself to have during conscious waking life, and so to bring them into reach of dream-work-α[4] for conversion into α-elements and a narrative form, consecutive and dominated by a causation–theoretical outlook, suitable for being worked on by conscious rational processes of thought. [1992, p. 150]

Although Bion agrees with Freud about dreams preserving sleep by discriminating between this state and wakefulness, he disagrees about the role of the "dream work":

> But Freud meant by dream-work that unconscious material which would otherwise be perfectly comprehensible, was transformed into a dream, and that the dream-work needed to be undone to make the now incomprehensible dream comprehensible. [*ibid.*, p. 43]

It is the conscious and not the unconscious material that is the subject of dream work, which will make this material suitable to be stored in memory from where it can be withdrawn in order to be used in the configuration of dreams and alpha elements, as well as in changes from schizoid–paranoid to depressive positions. Bion argues about Freud using Aristotle's statement that dreams are the way in which the mind works in sleep, while he thought it is the other way round, meaning that it is the way it works when awake. The alpha function will produce alpha elements from the transformation of raw, undigested or undreamed material that has already been perceived by the sense organs, and to which Bion has referred to as "beta elements" or the "thing-in-itself". These "unthought" elements stored in the memory, triggered by the day's residues, become organized as a narrative through the work of "dream-thought α". The dream would then represent a discharge of undigested elements that remain in expectation of a mind or, better, of an alpha function (conscious) that would decipher its cryptic sense and provide it with a meaning. Freud had already considered dreams as expressions of pathological disturbances:

> You realized that the dream is a pathological product, the first member of the class which includes hysterical symptoms, obsessions and delusions, but that it is distinguished from the others by its transitoriness and by its occurrence under conditions which are part of normal life. [1933a, pp. 15–16]

In the organization of this chapter I have used a very interesting paper published by James Grotstein (1981) who considers two instances: "the dreamer who dreams the dream and the dreamer who understands the dream"; however, we could also consider four possibilities, structured following a temporal sequence, as well as a contained–container association:

1.   The ineffable, the thing-in-itself, "O", the ultimate truth where dream-thought is sustained.
2.   The dreamer awake
3.   The dreamer sleeping
4.   The thinker–translator of the unconscious.

The difference between the "dreamer awake" and the "dreamer sleeping" hinges on the dynamic of the "alpha screen"; while the difference between the "dreamer awake" and the "thinker" is generally related to frustration tolerance, depending on whether or not the reality principle overrides the pleasure principle. Grotstein (1981) suggests, in a similar fashion, that the capacity of the "thinker" to translate "O", present in the dream narrative, will pivot on his "reverie" potential. From a social perspective, we could think about how alpha function is influenced by humanity's degree of cultural sophistication, in the sense that sometimes, interpretation of dreams as it is now performed by a psychoanalyst, could become a matter of public knowledge.

"O" represents the ultimate truth, unknown in itself, but able to be known as a post mortem, inside the mind of a thinker that can contain it

I have already referred to "O" in Chapters Twelve and Thirteen. I would like to add now that all dreams represent a very close vision of what the "becoming of O" means, a "royal road" to the unconscious, as Freud once said. Dreams represent a cryptic, pictographic, and private message that portrays unconscious truth denouncing conscious repudiations,[5] which might or might not be understood by the individual. Meltzer (1983) has defined the dream process "as one way of thinking about emotional experiences" (p. 51), that tries to "solve a problem" (p. 67) and does not maintain the dreamer sleeping, as Freud originally stated.

Where and how is the intention of the unconscious message precisely manufactured? Where and how can all of this have been decided without the awareness of our conscious self? What exactly is this concealed intelligence, capable of conceiving, so speedily, beautiful condensations and displacements in order to produce a dream? These are mysterious questions that still lack an answer. It seems that once the dream has been produced, the emotional conflict-seeking solution has already been established, as if we, or better, the conscious self, had no access to the source of the dream, to the place in the unconscious where images are arranged and placed together to form the message. In 1900 Freud referred to the profundity of these issues when he referred to the "dream's navel", as

the spot where it reaches down into the unknown. The dream-thoughts to which we are led by interpretation cannot, from the nature of things, have any definite endings; they are bound to branch out in every direction into the intricate network of our world of thought. [p. 525]

The dreamer awake

The dreamer can dream for different purposes: (a) in order not to dream or to remember, as a lack of awareness of being alive, of being a person and not an inanimate being; (b) as a defence to please or attack superego part-objects projected into the outside object; (c) to evacuate internal threatening objects; (d) as a magic and omnipotent instrument to deal with anxieties due to feelings of helplessness and hopelessness, making of the future a past; (e) as a revelation of unconscious truth and to assist investigation as observed in psychoanalytic treatment.

We could wonder how sensory experiences, already stored in the memory, are chosen afterwards in order to manufacture a dream; how could they be selected for a purpose without conscious participation? Dreams represent a mental space that resembles the experience of "post-hypnotic suggestion", a command given to someone during an hypnotic state that is later acted out, but without the person being consciously aware of the action. Where is such a command stored? I remember reading about an army psychiatrist suggesting to a soldier under hypnosis, that he would say something every time he heard a specific word, like for instance saying "I am strong" after he heard the word "green", without being aware of saying it. The psychiatrist referred that twenty years later he met the same soldier on the street and, after repeating the same word, the soldier once again gave the same answer without being at all conscious of it.

The dreamer sleeping

The dreamer can use dreaming for different purposes: (a) to keep himself asleep; (b) to denounce conscious lies coming from the dreamer awake; (c) to satisfy a desire that superego's objects in the dreamer awake would not allow; (d) to repeat in the transference early object relations in search of a solution, or to make sure that the solution is not found; (e) to terrorize or destroy the dreamer with the use of anxiety dreams; (f) to create "dreams for evacuation", used like faeces or urine in an attempt to free the dreamer from toxic objects; (g) to give away "gift dreams" created in order to please a castrating object usually projected outside.

Let us examine a dream: Lucien is a sixty-four-year-old patient, the eldest of four siblings, who, at the time of the dream, was dealing with his ambivalence about his recently dead sister, who died suddenly from a heart attack. During this session he states that he fell asleep while working on his computer and had the following dream:

> It was more like an image, somebody was showing, or perhaps was writing, about being concerned with the surrounding of Major Werner's grave.

He wakes up immediately after and decides to look up "Major Werner" on the internet. He was able to find a German soldier with that name, who was considered a hero during the Second World War and who was killed in action in 1945. To his surprise, there was even a picture of his tomb. He stated that he did not remember knowing anything about any Major Werner, and was tempted by the uncanny side of his dream to think that what happened was due to telepathy, or perhaps he was communicating with the dead. I felt that at the same time that he was making these remarks there was also some attempt to establish some kind of transference complicity with me. When asked about associations, he linked "major" with being "the older", and Werner with a friend—he suddenly remembered at that moment—whose name was Warent, whom he had not seen for quite a long time, although three or four weeks previously he had received an e-mail from a mutual friend who provided him with Warent's address. At one point Warent had commented about one of Lucien's letters in which he was complaining about financial and political difficulties in his country, that their communication resembled something Beckett once said, "that it looks like an inventory of pain and miseries". I then said to him that perhaps he was not dreaming about "Major Werner", nor about his friend Warent, but about the fear of his own death, with the fear of feeling "major", meaning older or the oldest of his siblings, older than his dead sister. Then he remembered thinking about the premature death of his sister, and about his own death, and of how his wife and children, who were financially dependent on him, would be left abandoned to deal with "inventories of pain and miseries" and just "looking around" his tomb.

Grotstein (1981) states that:

> ... the dream represents the product of an intelligent Dreamer who has trusted access to memory and hidden emotions in such a way as to construct a narrative for the Dreamer and his/her analyst which is capable of meaningful decipherment. For this to be presumed, an "intelligence" must have conceived the dream from the raw, chaotic elements of experience—but with unified purpose and with a unified hand. [p. 370]

If Lucien had not been in analysis at that moment, it is quite possible that the weight of a magic omnipotent point of view might have dominated his process of thinking, as a kind of "scientific deductive system": Lucien did acknowledge consulting a world atlas and finding out the precise place where Major Werner's tomb was located. He said: "My wife was very excited about travelling to Germany and even wanted to buy a lottery ticket using Werner's date of birth and death." If Lucien had persisted in this course, it is quite possible that he would have continued dreaming using similar symbols and fabricating other metaphors in order to maintain his preoccupation with his own death, with the mourning of his deceased sister, and with his concern about his family.

Let us look at another dream. A patient who says he feels oppressed by the economical and political situation of the country, relates the following dream:

> I was running away from a threatening cloud produced by a volcano's explosion that I felt was not very threatening. I was running parallel to the volcano and thought that if it were really dangerous I would have been running in the opposite direction. Then I saw a long column of smoke simulating a train.

> He associated the volcano with "Le Soufriere" from Saint Lucia, because the name is similar to "suffering",[6] and also with a sign from Brazil that reads "stop suffering". The train reminded him of a film he saw the night before in which a man who suffered from sleepwalking and thought he was responsible for some horrible crime discovered that everything was the product of his imagination because it was just a dream. The dream appears to say, "Stop suffering, the terrible internal anger and resentment you have induced is not so great and it is mostly a product of your imagination".

"Dream-thoughts" represent "wild thoughts" or memories of the future that when comprehended by the dreamer might help him evolve into a translator, for by *containing* the message registered in the dream-thought, instead of being *contained* by it, he would be able to translate it and grasp its meaning. By "containing" I mean the capacity of consciousness to allow the unconscious message to be revealed, instead of—out of fear—repudiating (repressing) its content. When the message is important for the dreamer it could either repeat itself as derivatives disguised with new symbols, or it could be disregarded by consciousness and completely forgotten. What Freud referred to as the "day's residues" represent, following Bion, a sort of external stimuli or "selected fact" that excites and awakes "wild" or forgotten impressions that remain latent in the memory. Such an incentive will prompt an endless number of latent memories that remain interconnected as "constant conjunctions", which will then weave a dream, which will in turn reveal some form of truth as an instant representation of O. The dream is assembled as a kind of narrative, written in metaphorical pictograms that could be causative and perhaps epigenetic.[7] Bion states (1992), "The impression must be ideogrammaticized, that is to say, if the experience is pain, the psyche must have a visual image of rubbing an elbow, or a tearful face . . ." (p. 64). Ferro (2002), on the other hand, has investigated this process of transformation during the analytic session, presumably implemented by the alpha function, where some stimulant, acting upon certain associations or beta elements, changes them into alpha elements and eventually into concepts. For instance, "feelings" that act as incentives, such as pain/anger/irritation, could induce dreams related to "an arrow that injures, a lion's roar, or a broken arm" (*ibid.*, p. 597), respectively. These images could also produce narratives of memories during free associations in a session, linking them, for instance, to a tonsil operation, to an angry reaction from parents against the driver who hit their son, or to references to a girlfriend who has been raped.

What appears to be amazing about the process of dream formation is how such complex selection and transformation of memories, sensations, and metaphorical visual ideograms take place without any conscious intervention, behind our back, so to speak, where the whole process is generated outside of our selfness as if the unconscious was always several steps ahead. Obviously, the unconscious performs with a level of autonomy very similar to how involuntary organs act. The difference hinges on the fact that, while the unconscious particular physiology is familiar and closely related to the conscious mind, autonomous organs like the liver, for instance, use a "biochemical language" based on remote codes completely alien to the conscious mind. Communication between conscious self and the liver is not direct but mediated by the brain, while communication with the unconscious has no intermediaries because the symbolical language used is consciously recognizable. The unconscious represents a kind of hybrid organ implementing two faces like Janus, one aimed at the preconscious, using symbols and metaphors to form a language similar to conscious syntactic; another directed to the soma, reflecting an autonomous and independent physiology associated to involuntary biology.

The thinker–translator of the unconscious

Eusebius (possibly from Cesarea) has preserved some fragments of a philosopher called Oenomaus (possibly from Gadara) who, out of resentment for having been so often fooled by the oracles, wrote an ample confutation of all their impertinences. *I think that if consciousness were to write a letter to the unconscious, it would for sure make similar demands.* "When we come to consult thee," says Oenomaus to Apollo, "if thou seest what is in futurity, why dost thou use expressions that will not be understood? If thou dost, thou takest pleasure in abusing us, if thou dost not, be informed of us, and learn to speak more clearly. I tell thee, that if thou intendest an equivoque, the Greek word whereby thou affirmedst that Croesus should overthrow a great empire, was ill chosen; and that it could signify nothing but Croesus's conquering Cyrus. If things must necessarily come to pass, why dost thou amuse us with thy ambiguities? What dost thou, wretch as thou art, at Delphi; employed in muttering idle prophecies." Oenomaus is referring to Croesus consulting the Oracle at Delphi before engaging in a war against the Persian king, Cyrus, and proceeding to fight once the oracle had said that he "was going to be responsible for the downfall of an Empire". After being defeated, Croesus complained to the Oracle, which then answered that she had only said "an Empire", and never specified which one.

Almost at the end of his analysis, a man I will refer to as Ronald brings the following dream:

> He is with C, an old time student of his, looking down from an over-pass. C invites him to jump, and then jumps landing on the ground below, very elegantly. He looks down again and feels that it is too high, but decides to jump and lands, not as well as C, but feels fine. C is wearing a suit of the exact same colour as the one Ronald used to have.

Ronald remembers that the last time he knew anything about C was around ten years ago, because he moved to another city. However, about five years ago C got in touch with him to tell him that he had a picture of a woman that belonged to Ronald and he was going to mail it to him. Ronald felt very pleased, receiving the sketch that he remembered drawing many years ago and thought lost for ever. It was a rather peculiar story. Twenty-five years before, D, a dear university friend, came to his house for dinner and immediately got interested in this drawing and requested that Ronald give it to him, which he did. A year later, during a serious earthquake, D and all of his family perished when their building collapsed, and Ronald was convinced that, together with his friend, the drawing had disappeared. However, apparently C, who was also D's friend, went to visit him and also liked the picture and managed to steal it from D, keeping it with him until he decided to send it to Ronald. As for the suit, Ronald remembers buying it just when he returned from abroad after finishing postgraduate studies; at that time he felt it was too expensive and that he should have used that money for other purposes, because it was a time of great uncertainty. He stated that he was experiencing similar feelings of uncertainty about ending the analysis, although he was aware that in the dream he jumps from the overpass and lands safely, although he cannot work out why there is a difference on landing between him and C, who does it so gracefully.

Notes

1. For more examples see the end of Chapter Eleven.
2. See Chapter Nine "The unconscious".
3. Bion recalls Sir Henry Wotton's poem, reproduced above.
4. Afterwards Bion changes "dream work-α" to "α-function".
5. See Chapter Nine.

6. In Spanish, *sufrir*.
7. Meaning that the end of the dream might not be implicit in its beginning.

REFERENCES

Aristotle, Book II, Chapter 18, 66a.

Artemidorus of Daldis. (140 AD). *Interpretation of Dreams: Oneirocritica.* (Ονειροκριτικων).

Benveniste, E. (1971). *Problems in General Linguistics.* Miami University Press.

Beres, D., & Arlow, J. A. (1974). Fantasy and identification in empathy. *Psychoanalytic Quarterly, 43*: 26–50.

Binswanger, L. A. (1947). Ausgewählte vorträge und aufsätze, Berne: Franke.

Bion, F. (1995). The days of our years. *Melanie Klein and Object Relations, 13*(1): 1–25.

Bion, W. R. (1948). Psychiatry at a time of crisis. *British Journal of Medical Psychology, 21.*

Bion, W. R. (1962). *Learning from Experience.* In: *Seven Servants.* New York: Jason Aronson, 1977.

Bion, W. R. (1963). *Elements of Psycho-Analysis.* In: *Seven Servants.* Reprinted New York: Jason Aronson, 1977.

Bion, W. R. (1965). *Transformations.* In: *Seven Servants,* New York: Jason Aronson, 1977.

Bion, W. R. (1967). *Second Thoughts: Selected Papers on Psycho-Analysis.* New York: Jason Aronson.

Bion, W. R. (1970). *Attention and Interpretation*. In: *Seven Servants*. New York: Jason Aronson, 1977.

Bion, W. R. (1974). *Brazilian Lectures*, São Paulo No 1. Río de Janeiro: Imago Editora.

Bion, W. R. (1975). *A Memoir of the Future, Book One: The Dream*. London: Karnac, 1990.

Bion, W. R. (1980). *Bion in New York and São Paulo*. Strathtay, Perthshire: Clunie Press.

Bion, W. R. (1987). *Clinical Seminars and Four Papers*. Oxford: Fleetwood.

Bion, W. R. (1990). *A Memoir of the Future*. London: Karnac.

Bion, W. R. (1992). *Cogitations*. London: Karnac.

Bohr, N. (1913). In: A. P. French & P. J. Kennedy (Eds.), *Niels Bohr: A Centenary Volume*. Cambridge: 1985.

Broks, P. (2003). *The Silent Land: Travels in Neuropsychology*. London: Atlantic.

Callimachus (1995). In: N. Loraux (Ed.), *The Experiences of Tiresias. The Feminine and the Greek Man*. Princeton.

Descartes, R. (1641). Meditations. In: E. S. Haldane & G. R. T. Ross (Eds.), *The Philosophical Works of Descartes* (pp. 133–199). Reprinted Boston: Cambridge University Press, 1973.

Diogenes Laertius (1972). *Lives of Eminent Philosophers*. Cambridge: Harvard University Press.

Fairbairn, W. R. D. (1952). *Psychoanalytic Studies of the Personality*. London: Tavistock.

Ferro, A. (2002). Some implications of Bion's through waking dream and narrative derivatives. *International Journal of Psycho-Analysis, 83*: 597–607.

Frank, A. (1969). The unrememberable and the unforgettable—passive primal repression. *Psychoanalytic Study of the Child, 24*: 48–77.

Freud, S. (1900a). *The Interpretation of Dreams. S.E.,* 4–5: 277–508. London: Hogarth.

Freud, S. (1910d). The future prospect of psycho-analytic therapy. *S.E., 11*: 139–151. London: Hogarth.

Freud, S. (1911b). Formulations on the two principles of mental functioning. *S.E., 12*: 213–238. London: Hogarth.

Freud, S. (1911e). The handling of dream-interpretation in psychoanalysis. *S.E., 12*: 89–96. London: Hogarth.

Freud, S. (1912e). Recommendations to physicians practising psychoanalysis. *S.E., 12*: 111–112. London: Hogarth.

Freud, S. (1913b). Introduction to Pfister's *The Psycho-Analytic Method*. *S.E., 12*: 330–331. London: Hogarth.

Freud, S. (1913j). The claims of psycho-analysis to scientific interest. *S.E., 13*: 165–190. London: Hogarth.

Freud, S. (1915e). The unconscious. *S.E., 14*: 159, 216. London: Hogarth.

Freud, S. (1916). Letter to Lou Andreas-Salomé, 25 May. In: P. Pfeiffer (Ed.). *Sigmund Freud and Lou Andreas-Salomé. Letters* (p. 45). London: Hogarth.

Freud, S. (1926d). Inhibitions, symptoms and anxiety. *S.E., 20*: 77–174. London: Hogarth.

Freud, S. (1933a). *New Introductory Lectures. S.E., 2*. London: Hogarth.

Freud, S. (1940e). Splitting of the ego in the process of defence. *S.E., 13*: 275–278. London: Hogarth.

Freud, S. (1950a). Project for a scientific psychology, *S.E., 1*: 283–397. London: Hogarth.

Fromm, E., & Suzuki, D. T. (1963). *Zen Buddhism and Psychoanalysis.* New York: Grove.

Gabbard, G. (1982). The exit line: Heightened transference–countertransference manifestations at the end of the hour. *Journal of the American Association, 30*: 579–598.

Gay, P. (1988). *Freud: A Life for Our Time.* New York: Norton.

Gitelson, M. (1952). The emotional position of the analyst in the psychoanalytic situation. *International Journal of Psycho-Analysis, 33*: 1–10.

Green, A. (1993). Two discussions of "The inner experiences of the analyst" and a response from Theodore Jacobs. *International Journal of Psycho-Analysis, 74*:1131–1136.

Grinberg, L. (1979). Countertransference and projective counteridentification. *Contemporary Psychoanalysis, 15*: 226–247.

Grotstein, J. (1981). Who is the dreamer who dreams the dream and who is the dreamer who understands it? In: J. Grotstein (Ed.), *Do I Dare Disturb the Universe?* (pp. 357–416). London: Karnac.

Grotstein, J. (1996). Bion's transformation in O, the "thing-in-itself" and the "real": towards the concept of "transcendent position". *Journal of Melanie Klein and Object Relations, 14*(2): 109–151.

Grotstein, J. (2004). The seventh servant: The implications of a truth drive in Bion's theory of "O". *International Journal of Psycho-Analysis, 85*: 1081–1101.

Heiman, P. (1950). On counter-transference. *International Journal of Psycho-Analysis, 31*: 81–84.

Heiman, P. (1952). Preliminary notes on some defense mechanisms in paranoid states. *International Journal of Psycho-Analysis, 33*: 208–213.

Heraclitus (n.d.). *Fragments: The Collected Wisdom of Heraclitus.* B. Haxton (Trans.). Reprinted New York: Viking, 2001.

Herrigel, E. (1953). *Zen in the Art of Archery*. New York: Vintage Spiritual Classics.

Huxley, H. A. (1907) *Aphorisms and Reflections*. London: Macmillan.

Jacobs, T. J. (1993). The inner experiences of the analyst: their contribution to the analytic process. *International Journal of Psychoanalysis, 74*: 7–14.

Jones, E. (1953). *Life and Work of Sigmund Freud, Volume 3*. London: Hogarth.

Joseph, B. (1975). The patient who is difficult to reach. In: P. L. Giovacchini, A. Flarsheim, & L. B. Boyer (Eds.), *Tactics and Techniques in Psychoanalytic Therapy. Vol. II: Countertransference* (pp. 205–216). New York: Aronson,.

Kant, E. (1781). *Critique of Pure Reason*. Reprinted Boston: Cambridge University Press, 1999.

Kerenyi, K. (1997). *Los Dioses de los Griegos*. Caracas: Monte Avila Editores.

Kernberg. O. (1975). *Borderline Conditions and Pathological Narcissism*. New York: Jason Aronson.

Kirsen, D. (2000). *Unfree Associations*. London: Process Press.

Klein, M. (1930). The importance of symbol-formation in the development of the ego. *International Journal of Psycho-Analysis, 11*: 24–39.

Klein, M. (1946). Notes on some schizoid mechanisms. In: *Envy and Gratitude*. Reprinted London: Virago, 1990.

Kohut, H. (1982). Introspection, empathy, and the semi-circle of mental health. *International Journal of Psycho-Analysis, 63*: 395–407.

Kuhn, T. S. (1962). *The Structure of Scientific Revolution*. Chicago, ILL: University of Chicago Press.

Lacan, J. (1966). *Écrits*. Paris: Seuil.

Laplanche, J. (1992). Seduction, translation and the drives. Psychoanalytic Forum, Institute of Contemporary Arts, London.

Laplanche, J., & Leclaire, S. (1960). *The Unconscious: A Psychoanalytic Study*. P. Coleman (Trans.). *Yale French Studies No. 48*, 1972.

LaSalle, E. H. (1975). *The Practice of Zen Meditation*. Wellingborough: Crucible–The Aquarian Press/Thorsons.

Lindon, J. (1966). On Freud's concept of dream action. *Psa. Forum, 1*: 32–43.

Loewi, O. (1921). In: W. H. Calvin (Ed.), *Cerebral Symphony: Seashore Reflections on the Structure of Consciousness*. Reprinted New York: Bantam, 1990.

López-Corvo, R. E. (1992). About interpretation of self-envy. *International Journal of Psychoanalysis, 73*: 719–728.

López-Corvo, R. E. (1995). *Self-Envy, Therapy and the Divided Inner World*. New York: Jason Aronson.

López-Corvo, R. E. (1996a). Creatividad, reparación y auto-envidia. *Rev. Asoc. Colombiana de Psicoanal., 21*(2): 139–151.

López-Corvo, R. E. (1996a). Falsehood and aggression. Paper presented to the Toronto Psychoanalytic Society, June.

López-Corvo, R. E. (1996b). Creatividad, reparación y auto-envidia. *Rev. Asoc. Colombiana de Psicoanal., 21*(2): 139–151.

López-Corvo, R. E. (1999). Self-envy and intrapsychic interpretation. *Psychoanalytic Quarterly, 68*: 209–219.

López-Corvo, R. E. (2003). *The Dictionary of the Work of W. R. Bion*. London: Karnac.

McGuire, W., & Hull, R. F. C. (Eds.) (1978). *C. G. Jung Speaking: Interviews and Encounters*. New York: Princeton University Press.

Mahoney, P. (1980). Toward the understanding of translation in psychoanalysis. *Journal of the American Psychoanalytic Association, 28*: 461–475.

Matte-Blanco, I. (1998). *The Unconscious as Infinite Sets*. London: Karnac.

Meltzer, D. (1966). The relation of anal masturbation to projective identification. *International Journal of Psycho-Analysis, 47*: 335–342.

Meltzer, D. (1973). *Sexual States of the Mind*. Strathtay, Perthshire: Clunie Press.

Meltzer, D. (1983). *Dream-Life*. Strathtay, Perthshire: Clunie Press.

Nietzsche, F. (2001). *Beyond Good and Evil*. Boston: Cambridge University Press.

Nunberg, H., (1965). *Practice and Theory of Psychoanalysis, Vol. II*. New York: International Universities Press.

Obendorf, C. (1953). *A History of Psychoanalysis in America*. New York: Harper & Row.

Pfeiffer, E. (1972). *Sigmund Freud and Lou Andreas-Salomé*. London: Hogarth.*

Pines, D. (1980). Skin communication: early skin disorders and their effect on transference and countertransference. *International Journal of Psycho-Analysis, 61*: 315–323.

Pines, D. (1982). The relevance of early development to pregnancy and abortion. *International Journal of Psycho-Analysis, 63*: 311–319.

Poincaré, H. (1908). *Science et Méthode*. Paris: Flamarion.

Racker, H. (1969). Estudios Sobre Ténica Psicoanalítica, Buenos Aires: Editorial Paidós.

Reik, T. (1948). *Listening With the Third Ear*. New York: Grove Press.

Ricoeur, P. (1970). *Freud and Philosophy, an Essay on Interpretation*. New Haven: Yale University Press.

Rosenfeld, H. (1971). A clinical approach to the psychoanalytic theory of life and death instincts. *International Journal of Psychoanalysis, 52*: 169–178.

Sandler, J. (1993). On communication from patient to analyst: not everything is projective identification. *International Journal of Psycho-Analysis, 74*: 1097–1107.

Saussure, F. (1916). *Course in General Linguistics*. C. Bally & A. Sechehaye (Eds.), W. Basking (Trans.). Glasgow: Collins Fontana.

Scott, W. C. M. (1975). Self-envy and envy of dreams and dreaming. *International Review of Psycho-Analysis, 2*: 253–354.

Segal, A. (1957). Notes on symbol formation. *International Journal of Psychoanalysis, 38*: 39.

Segal, H. (1983). Some clinical implications of M. Klein's work. *International Journal of Psychoanalysis, 64*: 269.

Steiner, J. (1982). Perverse relationships between parts of the self. *International Journal of Psycho-Analysis, 62*: 253–354.

Suzuki, D. T. (1949). *Ensayo Sobre Budismo*. Buenos Aires: Editorial Kier.

Suzuki, D. T. (1981). *El Ámbito of Zen*. Editorial Kairós: Madrid.

Symington, J., & Symington, N. (1996). *The Clinical Thinking of Wilfred Bion*. London: Routledge.

Thigpen, C. H., & Cleckley, H. M. (1958). *The Three Faces of Eve*. New York: McGraw-Hill.

Valliet, F. A. (1971). *Zen, l' autre versant*. Paris: Casterman.

Virgil (1992). *The Aeneid, Book XII*. New York: Everyman's Library, Alfred A. Knopf.

Wallerstein, R. (1988). One psychoanalysis or many? *International Journal of Psycho-Analysis, 69*: 5–21.

Watts, A. (1957). *The Way of Zen*. New York: Pantheon.

Weiss, E. (1950). *Principles of Psychodynamics*. New York: Grune & Stratton.

Winnicott, D. (1960). Ego distortion in terms of true and false self. In: *The Maturational Processes and the Facilitating Environment*. Reprinted London: Hogarth, 1965.